16

Praise for *How to Get a Meeting with Anyone*

"In a super-connected world, we're actually anything but. Stu reminds us that in business, you actually have to connect on a human level to really succeed, and he is the Master Guide on how to do that."
—BOB GUCCIONE, JR., **media entrepreneur and founder of *SPIN* Magazine**

"With this book, Stu gives you everything you could possibly need to get all of the meetings you could possibly want."
—BOB MANKOFF, **cartoon editor at *The New Yorker***

"Stu says, When you hear 'Executive Assistant,' think instead, 'Vice President of Access.' This is so true—our role is to ensure that you speak to the right person at the right time during the decision-making process. I highly recommend that all salespeople read Chapter 15 at least three times!"
—BONNIE WOODING, **president of HyWood Services and executive assistant to top business leaders for more than 30 years**

"Stu is a master innovator and creative virtuoso. What he has put together in this book is a true gift to the reader. If opening important doors is important to your success, you can't afford NOT to read this book!"
—DAN MONAGHAN, **cofounder of WSI Digital**

"Building trust and adding value are critical to cultivating profitable business relationships. Stu Heinecke and his Contact Marketing Strategies have greatly contributed to our success."
—DAVID ROSUCK, **vice president of marketing and innovations at Pacific Life**

"Go ahead and list a dozen or two impossible-to-reach, off-limits people that could change your life or career. Read and follow Stu's guidance. Then change your life forever."
—DEAN BATSON, **assistant director of the Arizona State University Alumni Association**

"Stu is one creative dude. Who else can run a campaign that catches the attention of a US president? Almost as crazy as using an AI to schedule a meeting :)."
—DENNIS MORTENSEN, **CEO and founder of x.ai, producers of the world's first artificial intelligence assistant who schedules meetings for you**

"Stu's ideas helped me get a meeting with Amblin Entertainment and Steven Spielberg, and continue to produce results for my company. Thanks to *How to Get a Meeting with Anyone*, now the entire world can get in on Stu's precious secrets!"

—**Jay Silverman, creator and executive producer of**
***The Cleaner* on A+E Networks, director of *Girl on the Edge*,**
and president of Jay Silverman Productions

"Stu's secrets truly will show you—or your entire sales organization—*How to Get a Meeting with Anyone*."

—**Mark Cira, CEO and founder of PrintSF for Salesforce.com**

"I get several hundred unsolicited emails a day and at least several dozen calls from people hoping to develop a business relationship with Williams-Sonoma, Inc. Stu's mailer was one of the very few that got right through to me. My assistant brought it in and said, Look at this. I called him. Very creative—and effective."

—**Pat Connolly, EVP and CMO of Williams-Sonoma, Inc.**

"It's true that many a truth is said in jest but not all are guaranteed to make you laugh out loud or provide attention for your message from a high-level decision maker. Stu Heinecke can show you how in *How to Get a Meeting with Anyone*."

—**Pete Wilson, former Governor of California**

"Stu Heinecke's ability to make contact through unique methods is phenomenal. He's a creative genius."

—**Rick Dees, legendary radio personality**

"In a time of great need, it's too late to start a relationship. Stu has bridged that ominous chasm between lack of access and the beginning of an important relationship using clever approaches to discharge the everyday tensions we all experience in business."

—**Russ Klein, CEO of the American Marketing Association**

"In *How to Get a Meeting with Anyone*, Stu Heinecke opens your eyes to new creative and proven techniques that are a prescription for success for any sales force that wants to open doors and build lasting relationships—and have fun doing it!"

—**Sandy Athenson, vice president and general manager at**
Immucor Transfusion Diagnostics

"Success in sales—or any career for that matter—is heavily dependent upon reaching the right people, in the right way, at the right time. By following Stu's methodology, you are likely to form strong and lasting relationships, which will ultimately be critical to your success."

—**Sid Kumar, global head of inside sales at CA Technologies**

HOW TO GET A MEETING WITH ANYONE

HOW TO GET A MEETING WITH ANYONE

The Untapped Selling Power of Contact Marketing

Stu Heinecke

BENBELLA

BenBella Books, Inc.
Dallas, Texas

BenBella

BenBella Books, Inc.
10300 N. Central Expressway, Suite #530
Dallas, TX 75231
www.benbellabooks.com
Send feedback to feedback@benbellabooks.com

Printed in the United States of America
10 9 8 7 6 5 4 3 2 1

Library of Congress Cataloging-in-Publication Data
Heinecke, Stu, author.
  How to get a meeting with anyone : the untapped selling power of contact marketing / Stu Heinecke.
     pages cm
  Includes bibliographical references and index.
  ISBN 978-1-941631-78-2 (trade cloth : alk. paper) 1. Sales management. 2.
Direct marketing. 3. Direct selling. 4. Customer relations. I. Title.
  HF5438.4.H45 2015
  658.8'72–dc23
                            2015029363

Copyediting by James Fraleigh
Proofreading by Kim Broderick and Sarah Vostok
Indexing by Clive Pyne, Book Indexing Services
Text design and composition by Silver Feather Design
Cover design by Sarah Dombrowsky
Cover illustration by Stu Heineke
Author photo by Amy Helmuth Photography
Printed by Lake Book Manufacturing

Distributed by Perseus Distribution | www.perseusdistribution.com
To place orders through Perseus Distribution:
Tel: (800) 343-4499 | Fax: (800) 351-5073
E-mail: orderentry@perseusbooks.com

Significant discounts for bulk sales are available. Please contact Aida Herrera at aida@benbellabooks.com.

This book is dedicated to the beautiful, powerful, inspirational women in my life. To my mother, Norma, who has always been my biggest supporter and fan. To my wife, Charlotte, my dream girl from Copenhagen who continues to make my dreams come true every time I wake next to her. To my sister Kristin, whom we nearly lost to a terrible injury in a horse-riding accident, but who continues to inspire with her remarkable recovery, kindness, and love of life. To my other sister, Karin, who quietly yet heroically devotes her life to raising her two girls, giving them the best possible launch in life. And to my daughter, Rikke, whose budding artistic accomplishments as a filmmaker will someday come full circle to make the film I never did about meeting, marrying, and making a family with my Danish dream girl. Thank you, each of you, for your kindness, inspiration, love, and support.

Contents

SECTION III: YOUR CONTACT CAMPAIGN IN ACTION

SECTION IV: TOOLS & RESOURCES

Foreword

I've known the author for a long time, and as the founder of the Guerrilla Marketing movement, I've always liked how his work fits so neatly into my message of doing more with less, of finding ways to fight an asymmetrical war with mega-dollar marketers—and winning.

Stu quickly discovered how cartoons engage readers wholly and immediately, and how they can be used as powerful marketing tools. He then went on to create a long line of record-breaking campaigns for some of the biggest names in corporate America. What I find gratifying is that he did all that in the face of a great headwind from the advertising establishment against the use of humor. They didn't believe it could work, and Stu proved them wrong.

But that was the fodder for his first book, *Drawing Attention*. In this one, I'm delighted to see an even more brilliant illustration of the principles of Guerrilla Marketing at work.

As Stu tells it, he discovered Contact Marketing—as he calls it—quite by accident. His creative business was starting to take off and he was looking to bring it to the next level. He already knew his use of cartoons was working extremely well in the campaigns he'd created for *Rolling Stone* and *Bon Appétit*. Now he wanted to break through to the rest.

And therein lies the rub. How on Earth do you get in touch with impossible-to-reach VIP prospects? Like any good Guerrilla Marketer, Stu had a plan. And it worked brilliantly. He experimented with various forms of cartoons, each personalized with the names of the prospects. These ranged from framed and unframed prints,

1

coffee mugs, stretched canvas prints, and more, all packaged with a well-crafted contact letter. And he started seeing immediate results.

Not only did he break down the barriers to entry throughout the publishing industry, but he also started generating similar results for clients. Before long, Stu was creating contact with heads of state, celebrities, top-level executives, and key decision makers with ease.

That alone is a big story for marketers, but that's not what makes this a great Guerrilla Marketing story. Here's what does: Stu's Contact Campaigns have generated response rates and return on investment that have been considered impossible, and it can all be done on a shoestring budget. That means anyone can use Stu's Contact Marketing strategies to create explosive growth in their businesses, regardless of their size.

Stu is not alone in the endeavor to reach important, top people. It's been done for years. But here's what I really like about Stu's Contact Marketing approach: Anyone can do this. Anyone can use a Contact Campaign to grow their business rapidly.

One of the important lessons I teach Guerrilla Marketers is to convert your competition into allies. I strongly advocate setting up strategic partnerships, as does Stu. Only he goes about it in an utterly unique way using—you guessed it—Contact Marketing.

This book not only can enable anybody to rise to the level of reaching CEOs and other VIPs, but also to belong in their midst. Sending a contact piece and getting a CEO's ear is meaningless unless you know exactly what you're there to accomplish, and how you can help that CEO achieve his or her goals in the process. You need to know how to deal with executive assistants, whose job is in part to keep people like you and me out, and also to spot the golden opportunities the executive assistants might have otherwise missed.

So as the reader of this book, you get to put your hands on a set of tools and techniques that have been largely hidden. You'll learn how to turn the executive assistant into your ally nearly every time. And you'll approach CEOs with a firm understanding of how you can help them achieve their goals, while approaching them on equal business footing.

Too often, I see marketing and sales teams regarding each other with great suspicion. If you're part of either camp, you need to find ways to work together. After all, you're on the same team, right? Stu's Contact Campaign concept is one of the best examples I've ever seen of how to make that happen. Marketers, you get to use Contact Campaigns to produce response rates approaching 100 percent and ROI figures in the tens of thousands of percent—how else can you do that? And sales professionals, you get to be a part of a campaign that will lift your sales figures to far greater heights. Even better, you're not a spectator in this event, you're an integral part of the campaign.

Read this book, learn from it, and go forth and prosper. It is one of the best forms of Guerrilla Marketing I've ever seen. And coming from me of all people, that's saying an awful lot.

—JAY CONRAD LEVINSON
author of *Guerrilla Marketing*,
the best-selling marketing book of all time,
and father of the Guerrilla Marketing movement

From *The Wall Street Journal*, permission Cartoon Features Syndicate
f ⚑ in @byStuHeinecke ©CartoonLink, Inc.

"That would look really good in my office."

Introduction

I've been asked more than once, "What's a cartoonist doing writing a book about sales?" And it turns out, there's an interesting story behind it all. The truth is, I am a business owner and a marketer—a hall of fame–nominated marketer—in addition to being a cartoonist. And I, like you, spend much of my day selling. But I have an enormous advantage in that I'm one of *The Wall Street Journal*'s cartoonists, and as a cartoonist, I possess a secret weapon for reaching important people: I use the magic of cartoons to create an unfair advantage for myself and my clients.

When I started my marketing agency years ago, I set out to use cartoons in direct-mail campaigns. Personalization had just become a force, so I combined it with the power of cartoons to create both unique and memorable pitches in those early campaigns. The industry's top experts advised against the use of humor, but I found it worked extremely well.

My first two marketing clients were *Rolling Stone* and *Bon Appétit* magazines. They were prestigious clients and sophisticated marketers. So when my first two campaigns set new response records, I knew I'd struck upon something truly special, something I needed to introduce to the rest of the magazine industry. But how would I reach those decision makers? I needed to connect with the top circulation marketing executives at some of the biggest media companies in the world. These were sharp, busy people with pressure-cooker New York careers. They would not be easy to reach.

That's when the marketer in me responded to the challenge, which was this: How would I break through to two dozen critically important prospects with a near 100 percent success rate? My plan was to use the same personalized cartoons that had driven record response in the direct-mail campaigns, but in a different form. There wasn't even a term for what I'd planned to do, so I called my outreach effort a "Contact Campaign."

Since the audience was so small, I could afford to budget *more per person* while *spending far less* than what a marketer typically does on a campaign. So I produced a set of twenty-four prints, each suitable for framing and featuring a cartoon personalized with the recipient's name, and sent it with a letter.

My total spend was less than $100, but I reached and sold to all of my targets. Suddenly, my small freelance business had a roster of clients that included Time, Inc., *Forbes*, *Harvard Business Review*, *The Wall Street Journal*, Condé Nast, and Hearst Magazines, all paying up to $25,000 per assignment. I've never calculated the cost/return ratio on that early Contact Campaign, but it is surely in the *millions of percent*.

Think about that for a moment. A campaign that generated a 100 percent response and millions of percent return on investment (ROI). Tell that to any marketer and it's like saying you've just seen a

UFO. It's just not supposed to happen. In fact, 100 percent response rates have always been considered impossible, let alone ROI figures in the thousands or millions of percent.

But it did happen. In fact, it has happened many times.

Once I'd broken through to the publishers, I wondered how much further this could go. So I reached out to people I should never have been able to contact, sometimes on behalf of clients, sometimes just out of curiosity. For the NHL, I produced an invitation to the All-Star Game that caught President Reagan's attention in particular. He liked the personalized cartoon so much that he requested additional copies to be framed for his personal study.

On another occasion, I sent a print of a cartoon showing an executive practice-putting in his office, with his secretary leaning in the doorway asking, "Would you mind if President Bush plays through?" That prompted a personal response from the forty-first president. The stories go on, but the point is, I was discovering that I was able to reach virtually anyone using my Contact Campaign techniques. It didn't matter if they were heads of state, celebrities, CEOs, or just top corporate decision makers. I was breaking through in more ways than one.

For many years, I was content to use my "private secret weapon" to create powerful connections, strike up strategic partnerships, and of course, to sell to many of the *Fortune* 500 companies and small business owners alike. Then I started wondering, "What is everybody else doing to break through to their VIP prospects?"

What I discovered was an unnamed shadow practice among sellers and marketers. And the people producing the campaigns were coming up with some spectacularly clever solutions, ranging in cost from zero dollars to $10,000 per effort. The desire to learn about more of these creative approaches led to the writing of this book.

To provide the broadest possible view, I have meticulously researched the phenomenon. I have interviewed sales thought leaders, C-level executives, and top executive assistants. What I have collected for this book is an utterly new, utterly unique crowdsourced knowledge base that can propel you and your career to new heights.

In a nutshell, *How to Get a Meeting with Anyone* is about breaking through to VIP prospects to create breakthrough results in your business and life.

It's fitting that Jay Conrad Levinson wrote the foreword to this book. The essence of Contact Marketing, of accomplishing so much with so little, of shooting for enormous gains against nearly impossible odds, is very much in the spirit of his iconic, best-selling *Guerrilla Marketing* books. When Jay wrote his first *Guerrilla Marketing* book, he had no idea how much his concept would resonate across the business spectrum. As a result, small business owners and *Fortune* 500 companies alike adopted his revolutionary thinking.

Sadly, Jay passed away just thirty days after contributing his foreword to this book. He was a good friend, a mentor, and a true inspiration. He was one of my heroes. I feel a great sense of honor that he gave his final stamp of approval to the thinking, strategies, and tactics behind the Contact Marketing form illustrated in this book.

In the same way *Guerrilla Marketing* was useful to so many throughout the business world, I believe the ability to reach out and connect with someone important, and to do it consistently and to great effect, will be equally appreciated across the business spectrum.

Who Should Read This Book?

In a broad sense, this book is for everybody, because, after all, everybody sells. It doesn't matter if your title has the word "sales" in it or not, we all sell. And if you're going to sell, you need the ability to break through to the people who can do you the most good.

But it is especially for a few particular groups who will benefit tremendously from being able to get a meeting with anyone.

Are you a sales professional looking for a way to penetrate big accounts to create more cash flow for yourself? The ability to break through to the C-suite at will can easily make you the superstar of your sales team. And the disciplines and solutions contained within these pages will certainly help.

Do you have responsibility for a sales team? Equipping your staff with the means and training to break through to their dream prospects and named accounts greatly empowers you and your company. This book should be required reading for your entire team.

Does your job description include the words "business development"? Then you already know how critical it is to break through to the companies you want to develop strategic relationships with, and at the highest levels, starting with the CEO. Yes, this book is for you, too.

Now let's think more strategically. Do you own a business, or are you a member of your company's C-suite? Surely you know how important it is to develop strategic alliances to expand the scale of your business and share important resources, intelligence, best practices, and so much more. You, especially, need the ability to break through to members of your "Strategic 100" list at will. This book was written for you as well, because the fortunes of your company depend on your ability to network and deal.

How to Approach the Book

This book is organized into four sections. Section II is the one you'll be tempted to jump to first. That's where I describe twenty categories of Contact Campaigns, ranging in cost from $0 to $10,000 per effort. They include remote-control helicopters, social media, email, mail and phone tactics, swords, egg cartons, newspaper ads, videos on iPads, disposable phones, homing pigeons, and yes, cartoons. These are the chapters with the candy. But resist the temptation to simply skip ahead, for there is much to do before you plan your first Contact Campaign strategy.

In the first two chapters, I delve into the nature of Contact Marketing. This is a view of marketing that will flip tradition on its head. Marketing campaigns are not supposed to generate 100 percent response rates or returns on investment in the hundreds of thousands of percent. But that is precisely what the wonderfully strange world of Contact Marketing is all about, and I want you to fully understand the rationale behind it before putting it to use.

Then, in Chapter 3, we're going to take a peek into the lives of the CEOs you'll be trying to reach. CEOs don't live in the same world you or I do. While many of us think in terms of the next month or two, their vision is focused six months, a year, two years, and five years out. Their time is extremely valuable and they're driven by the need to outperform their own goals. To succeed with them, you'll need to understand how to add value to their lives.

If you're going to fit in with CEOs and C-suite executives, you'll need to become a peer. So in Chapter 4, you'll discover how to give yourself a VIP makeover. And then it's time to compile your Top 100 prospects and get to know who they are as people. That's what Chapters 5 and 6 are about: finding your targets and taking purposeful aim to ensure maximum results.

You'll learn lots of useful Contact Campaign tactics and methods in Section II, but you can't start one unless you understand how they work. Chapter 12 is devoted to helping you plan out and navigate through your campaign to maximize your results.

Next, what will your contact letter say? How will you script your calls and other contacts to ensure maximum impact? How will you create leverage to get your target contacts to engage with you? These questions and more are addressed in Chapters 13 and 14.

Chapter 15 could almost be a book unto itself. This is the chapter in which I reintroduce you to the dreaded executive assistant. Once you have read the chapter, you will no longer regard assistants as gatekeepers but, instead, as talent scouts and potential allies; you will appreciate the myriad ways they can help you. Adjusting your view of these all-important players will make a tremendous difference in the outcome of your Contact Campaigns.

In Chapters 16 through 18, we address the critical stage of making contact, negotiating the call with the CEO, and following through to ensure complete and utter dominance of the challenge at hand: to achieve near 100 percent penetration and enormously profitable ROI figures. Beyond response rates and ROI, there are other factors to consider as you fully define your success and strategize the next round of campaigns, all of which are examined in Chapter 19.

As I made my way through the interviews for this book, I was often reminded of two things. First, we are now in the era of "Sales 2.0," where much of selling is based on buyer empowerment, referrals, and inbound inquiries, and reaching out to prospects is considered passé. I see this as an imbalance; selling has always been based on knowing who you want to do business with and how to break through.

> *Selling has always been based on knowing who you want to do business with and how to break through.*

Second, we are also in the era of social media and "Social Selling," which is revolutionizing every aspect of selling, including Contact Campaigns. So in Chapter 20, you will find critical information about putting your social media presence to work in your selling and in your Contact Marketing.

In Chapter 21, I explore next steps for you as a newly-minted Contact Marketer and for Contact Marketing in general. For that latter perspective, I interviewed the CEOs and presidents of several professional sales and marketing organizations, as well as Jay Conrad Levinson's successor and daughter, Amy Levinson, now the co-owner and CEO of the Guerrilla Marketing International organization. You won't want to miss what they have to say. I've also included a helpful resource section that will make you a Contact Marketing force and your selling a lot more informed, easy, and fun.

I have also included a bonus chapter, dedicated to a technique I have used for years to channel my "inner coach." You have one, too, and I'll help you find and activate it.

Let's get started, shall we?

SECTION I

WHAT IS CONTACT MARKETING?

"Here, try these."   "Perfect!"

CHAPTER 1

The Wonderfully Strange World of Contact Marketing

Imagine for a moment what it would be like if you suddenly had the ability to connect with virtually anyone. How would that change your life? How would you put it to use?

If you sell for a living, which I do as a business owner, you'd probably use it to break through to your top prospects to sell more. If you manage a sales team, you'd use it to multiply the profitability of their efforts. If you own a business or are a member of your company's executive team, you'd use it to make strategic connections that could change the scale of your enterprise.

That is what Contact Marketing is all about, but this is no ordinary form of marketing. It is a fusion of selling and marketing.

From a seller's perspective, it is a form of marketing that directly supports individual sales efforts at the highest level with your most strategic prospects. From a marketer's perspective, it is a form of marketing that produces extreme results with minimal expense, and directly involves sales reps as the response channel.

Either way, Contact Marketing is a means to greatly increase your effectiveness as a sales professional, sales manager, executive, or business owner.

I didn't invent Contact Marketing. It has been in use for a long time, but oddly, has never been recognized as a form of marketing or selling. Instead, it has been quietly used on an as-needed basis to solve specific, contact-based objectives. I developed my first Contact Campaign to break through to two dozen key contacts in the magazine industry. I used it to launch my business, spending less than $100 on a campaign that brought millions in return.

I didn't invent it, but it deserves a name and a definition.

> **Contact Marketing** is the discipline of using micro-focused campaigns to break through to specific people of strategic importance, often against impossible odds, to produce a critical sale, partnership, or connection. A Contact Campaign is an instance of usage of Contact Marketing.

This is not simply a book about marketing or sales. It's about both. It's about using Contact Campaigns to directly support key sales and quickly expand the scale of an enterprise. It's about giving you an unfair advantage in your marketplace. It's rocket fuel for your business. And anyone can afford to do it.

Every Metric Is Wonderfully Bizarre

Marketing campaigns have three critical metrics: cost, response, and return on investment or ROI. And in the world of Contact Marketing, every one of these is truly wonderful and bizarre.

Marketing campaigns typically involve a lot of money and often produce fairly low response and ROI. Most marketers would disagree with that assessment, but they're simply not used to the kinds of numbers associated with Contact Marketing.

Let's start with cost. Contact Campaigns can cost anywhere from $0 to $10,000 per effort. That's certainly bizarre, and well outside the range of typical marketing. But because the campaigns focus on a small number of target contacts, and because some Contact Marketing techniques have no cost, this is one form of marketing that is easily within everyone's reach.

And then there is the response metric. In the campaigns I've been associated with for large direct marketers, there was often talk of 1 percent response equaling success. While there is no typical response rate for direct marketing, 1 percent is too low of a standard for Contact Campaigns. In my own Contact Campaigns, I typically see at least 80 percent and have gone as high as 100 percent several times—a truly phenomenal result compared with traditional marketing response rates. Among the campaigns shared with me for this book, the range seems to be 20 percent to 100 percent. Even at the low end, Contact Marketing easily outperforms essentially any other form of marketing.

As extraordinary as 100 percent response rates are, the ROI figures for Contact Campaigns are nearly beyond comprehension. Looking back on those direct response campaigns that I did for large direct marketers, we often saw response rates at or below 1 percent, and the mailings rarely broke even. So the ROI was always less than 100 percent. Compare that to the results I saw in the "Sandler" Contact Campaign (explained in the next section)—it produced a

100 percent response and *8,000 percent* ROI, just from the sales occurring during the initial meetings. Or the "Local Builders" Contact Campaign (also explained in the next section)—it generated a 60 percent response and nearly *630,000 percent* ROI.

The Sandler Test and Local Builders Campaign

The metrics may be wonderfully bizarre, but they need context. So let's take a look at the two examples I mentioned.

Some years ago, I wanted to make contact with Bruce Seidman, who was president at the time, of Sandler Training. Sandler is one of the world's leading sales training companies, with more than 200 franchised offices worldwide, training thousands of companies on the "Sandler Sales Method" of its founder, David Sandler. With several hundred trainers serving thousands of clients, they easily qualified for my Top 100 list for strategic contact.

To reach Bruce, I used one of my own Contact Campaign devices, something I call a "BigBoard." Essentially, it's a giant, 18" × 24" foam core postcard delivered by courier to the target executive. The piece features one of my cartoons personalized with the recipient's name on one side and a personal message from the sender to the recipient on the other, explaining why they should meet. As soon as Bruce received the piece, he was hooked. More importantly, he wanted to test it with one of his franchisees, which was exactly what I'd hoped would happen.

For the next few months, we spoke nearly every day, further refining the creative concept we would test. So far, I'd been relying solely on the power of the personalized cartoon to draw response, which had already been working superbly. But Bruce challenged me to go further, which led to the introduction of what became a critical element of Contact Campaigns—the "hold-back device." Bruce's idea was brilliant. We rewrapped copies of David Sandler's book *You Can't Teach A Kid to Ride a Bike at a Seminar* in a new, personalized dust jacket and offered it as a reward for taking a meeting. The new cover transformed it into a book about how each CEO who met with the franchisee had changed the sales culture of their company, making it look like the CEO had written it. The book still sold the Sandler Method, but it now became a prize the recipient couldn't resist. Of course, it also became added insurance that the campaign would yield results.

And it sure did. The Sandler franchisee targeted five *Fortune* 1000 CEOs, we had the BigBoards produced and delivered, and one by one, each of the targets called in. "I have this big card in my lap, now what do I do?" they'd ask, to which the franchisee responded, "We meet." All five agreed, and during just the initial meetings, two bought starter programs on the spot, worth an estimated $50,000 each.

Let's get our bearings for a moment. What I have just described is a campaign that generated a 100 percent response and an 8,000 percent ROI, just from the initial meetings. That's supposed to be impossible.

Then there was sales trainer, *Creating a Million-Dollar-a-Year Sales Income* author, and *Sales and Sales Management* blog author Paul McCord's campaign to recruit the local home builders in his area to become mortgage referral sources. Prior to working for the mortgage brokerage, McCord worked for a time in the building industry, so he knew his targets well. He knew, for example, they were used to receiving architectural plans in cardboard tubes, so they were likely to pay attention to his mailing if it also arrived in a tube. He also knew builders used flow charts to follow the progress of their projects, so he produced an ingenious adaptation to express the bank's unique value proposition.

Of the seventy builders on his list, McCord received response from 60 percent; twenty-five became referral sources, and the campaign produced roughly $1.1 million in fees. All that from a campaign that cost just $175, including postage. Divide it out and you get another supposedly impossible result, a 628,571 percent return on investment.

No Gimmicks, Total Authenticity

As I interviewed people for this book, I encountered some surprising reactions I need to address. The first came from some of the sales experts, who warned against the use of gimmicks. "You can't base a sales career on gimmicks," they would say. And they're right.

But Contact Campaigns are no more a gimmick than any other form of marketing. They are a tool that can greatly increase penetration rates among a strategic list of VIP prospects, and they have the power to change the scale of a business almost overnight. They achieve all of this with no requirement of a large budget, and in some cases, with no budget at all. Calling Contact Marketing a gimmick would be like calling sales a gimmick. But it's an understandable reaction based on conventional expectations of marketing and sales performance.

> *Calling Contact Marketing a gimmick would be like calling sales a gimmick.*

Similarly, people on the receiving end of sales outreach said it was absolutely necessary that the caller be scrupulously authentic and honest. And again, I totally agree.

If we, as sales professionals and business owners alike, are to be taken seriously, our outreach to CEOs, C-level executives, and other VIPs must be completely honest and transparent. How else would you approach the start of a relationship that could mean millions of dollars to you or your company?

Contact Marketing should be an accepted, recognized form of marketing. If it is to get there, gimmicks and deception have no place in it.

Anyone Can Afford to Do This

The Contact Campaign techniques included in this book range in cost from zero to thousands of dollars per contact. Even if you have *nothing* in your budget for marketing, there are techniques you can put to use to start breaking through to your toughest, most important prospects.

Most of the zero-cost techniques are rooted in social media, phones, and email, which are, of course, free or nearly free. Some of the cleverest techniques involve a few simple steps that can create contact with some of the most important people on the planet, which certainly includes any of your most desired contacts.

The best Contact Marketing techniques are infused with audacity. These are the most memorable campaigns, the ones with the greatest sticking power. I once landed a deal for *The Wall Street Journal* that resulted in thousands of new subscriptions, all from a five-dollar cartoon print sent to the CEO of American Express. A carrier pigeon delivered to the office of one of the most famous CEOs in the world once resulted in a lunch appointment and a $250,000 contract. The cost of employing the pigeon for a half-day's work? Chicken feed, quite literally. The $10,000 per contact technique used to reach Siebel Systems CEO Tom Siebel resulted in the acquisition of a company for millions of dollars. Another of the techniques cost $1,000 per contact, but produced a 100 percent contact rate with targeted CEOs and a string of assignments, each worth as much as a million dollars. Every one of these Contact Campaigns exhibited audacity in great abundance. It makes life fun, makes business fun, and can make its users wealthy.

Contact Marketing is something every salesperson, sales manager, vice president of sales, C-level executive, and business owner can afford. In fact, if you truly value your success and care about how quickly you reach your goals, you know what I'm about to say: You can't afford *not* to do this.

Why Reach Out to a CEO?

I want to be clear that when I talk about reaching CEOs, I mean it as a descriptor for anyone who has final decision authority—as *The Sales Blog* author Anthony Iannarino terms it, "the CEO of the problem you want to solve." It may be the actual CEO you'll need to reach, but it is also easy to waste time and expense when shooting too high. The "CEO" you need to reach is always the "Center of Enterprise Opportunity."

There are a number of authors who have become quite successful advising salespeople to call only on CEOs. I'm not in complete alignment with their thinking, but I'm not too far off, either. Contact Marketing can certainly get you in touch with them, but if you're selling something nonstrategic, like window washing services, the CEO should not spend time with you.

Selling to VITO author Anthony Parinello says selling to CEOs is the only way you'll rocket to the top of the sales profession. He's right, as long as you can present your offering in a way that makes it strategic. *SNAP Selling*, *Agile Selling*, and *Selling to Big Companies* author Jill Konrath espouses a similar message, in that she sees selling to large companies as the quickest way to change your fortunes. After all, the big companies are the ones with the big budgets.

Either way, you need an enormous competitive advantage to break through. It's certainly not easy connecting with top decision makers, whether at the big companies or small- to medium-size businesses. Important people are always busy and always exceedingly challenging to reach. Low-level buyers, tire kickers, and time wasters are easy to reach, but their lack of decision-making or buying authority will lead you nowhere.

If you are already successful, or if you see yourself as becoming successful, you belong among other highly placed, successful people. Immediately. And Contact Marketing can certainly help you get there.

So what's it like, having that extraordinary ability to contact virtually anyone? I've been doing this for a long time and have enjoyed immensely rewarding and surprising successes throughout my life. This book is the result of connecting with some of the toughest-to-reach people in the world, including many of today's hottest sales and marketing authors, and the agents and publishers who made this book possible (and throughout the book I've included many of their comments from my interviews with them). I've reached presidents, prime ministers, celebrities, and countless CEOs and top decision makers. I have high-level strategic partnerships playing out in some of the biggest marketing channels in the world, always with more on the way. I regularly speak with, sell to, and partner with people at the very top of the business world and beyond. I am even married to a beautiful Danish *Penthouse* cover model, whom I contacted from halfway around the world, met, and married.

> *If you are already successful, or if you see yourself as becoming successful, you belong among other highly placed, successful people. Immediately.*

The mischief I have enjoyed has been amazing. I've been reaching people I should never be able to reach for so long, I've become accustomed to breaking through whenever I want, to whomever I choose.

And now it's your turn.

POINTS TO REMEMBER

- ✔ Contact Marketing is not a gimmick; it is a legitimate form of marketing in direct support of the sales function.
- ✔ Contact Marketing is a powerful fusion of marketing and selling.

✔ Contact Marketing is the discipline of using micro-focused campaigns to break through to specific people of great strategic importance.

✔ The purpose of Contact Marketing is to create immediate, explosive growth in sales and the scale of your enterprise.

✔ Contact Marketing is not new, but has never been recognized as a form of marketing until now.

✔ Contact Marketing can produce bizarrely high response rates and returns on investment (ROI).

✔ Contact Marketing techniques range in cost from $0 to $10,000 per contact, so anyone can afford to use it.

✔ Contact Marketing helps you break through to the "CEO," or the "Center of Enterprise Opportunity," of the problem you're trying to solve.

✔ Being able to connect with virtually anyone can create surprising results in your career, business, and life.

"Business is fun, isn't it?"

CHAPTER 2

What Is a Contact Campaign?

When I first started using Contact Campaigns, I used to think of them as direct mail on steroids. After all, I was sending a giant postcard, a blown-up version of what I often created for mail campaigns. Still, these "mail-ings" measured 18" × 24", were produced on quarter-inch foam core, and instead of using a wad of postage stamps, delivery was accomplished in person via courier.

Clearly this was not direct mail.

The method for generating a response was entirely different as well. I wasn't asking the recipient to return a business reply card, make a phone call, or visit a web landing page. *I was the response device.* My call or face-to-face meeting was the means for cultivating a response to the campaign.

I thought of it as direct mail on steroids, but the list of recipients was minuscule. It could be focused on as few as a single individual, designed to advance a singular goal. Or it could be pointed at a group of a dozen or so at a time, but never more than 100.

Since I was constantly reaching for highly important people, I was often dealing with their executive assistants to complete the contact. The Contact Campaigns evolved to include assistants as an integral part of that outreach. That's not the way a direct mail campaign works, either.

> *The campaigns exist to support the sales process, and to help reps and others break through to their toughest, most important prospects. They're designed to create leverage to get a critical meeting or conversation to take place.*

But Contact Campaigns aren't simply a form of marketing—they're really more about selling. The campaigns exist to support the sales process, and to help reps and others break through to their toughest, most important prospects. They're designed to create leverage to get a critical meeting or conversation to take place.

People don't enter the sales profession because they're shy. And they don't last long if they're not resourceful. So there are many fascinating stories of what I would consider "sales stunts" used to break through. Two of those involve colorful parking violations.

Partners in EXCELLENCE blog author Dave Brock tells the story of a rep who'd been trying to reach a C-level executive at a large consumer goods company, one of the *Fortune* 50. No matter what she tried, the executive remained inaccessible. One day, she tried stopping by in person to request a meeting. Still nothing. But on the way in, she noticed a reserved parking spot with her target's name on it.

So the next morning, she parked her car in the spot and waited. Sure enough, the fellow found his spot occupied and fumed as he entered the lobby, telling the receptionist to call a tow truck. The rep stood up, introduced herself, and said she'd move her car if he would walk with her. She explained that she'd tried numerous times to connect, and this was the only way she could think of to get his attention. He agreed and they continued on to have a meeting.

Guerrilla Selling coauthor and Guerrilla Marketing trainer Orvel Ray Wilson tells another story of a rep who'd been trying for months to reach the CEO of, as Forrest Gump would say, a certain "fruit company." In similar fashion, she reasoned that the way to gain access would be to camp out in the CEO's parking space in a lawn chair, armed with doughnuts and coffee. When he pulled up, she explained her purpose, and he gave her ninety seconds to speak as they walked to the lobby. When they reached that destination, he waved security personnel aside and took the meeting to his office.

Entertaining as they are, these aren't Contact Campaigns. They're stunts that are just as likely to get their perpetrators arrested as they are to precipitate a valuable meeting. Moreover, they carry the risk of souring your brand to the target executives, which is obviously not desirable. Sales trainers all seem to warn against basing your efforts on stunts, because they're not sustainable. I would add they're manipulative, and some are deceptive and dishonest.

So then, what exactly is a Contact Campaign? To start, they share these elements:

- **Micro-focused:** Truly a one-to-one campaign targeting just a single, high-value individual or all the members of your "Top 100" list.
- **Operates in direct support of specific sales or alliance-building actions:** Revolves around putting the sender in direct contact with the target executive.
- **Sender is always the "response device":** No business reply cards to pop in the mail, micro-sites to visit, forms

to fill out, or toll-free numbers to call; the purpose of the campaign is always to get the target exec to take the call or meeting with the sender.

- **Flexible, inclusive, and involving:** Flexible strategy that evolves and responds to factors as they happen, and involves all stakeholders, especially executive assistants and, at times, fellow executives.

- **Audacity, fascination, and intrigue:** The best Contact Campaign techniques exhibit some measure of audacity, sometimes a lot of it. At the very least, a proper Contact Campaign should elicit fascination and intrigue in the mind of the target executive, within the parameters of the mission and recipient's interests.

- **Highly personal:** Contact Campaigns are the truest form of one-to-one marketing; each is a campaign of one, targeted to the specific interests, needs, fascinations, or pain points for each recipient.

But sometimes it's easier to explain what something is by examining what it is not. So let's take a look.

How Contact Campaigns Differ from Traditional Marketing

Contact Campaigns obviously have elements in common with direct marketing. It goes to a targeted audience, so it's a lot like direct response. It operates in support of sales, so it's also closely related to lead generation. It can involve print, email, websites, and social media, so these are touch points as well. All forms of marketing have common elements, because they're all part of the same thing: moving the enterprise forward in the marketplace.

But if all forms of marketing simply were alike, if they all accomplished the same thing with the same efficiency, there would be no reason to use one versus the other or in any combination. We all know that just isn't true. If you need to reach a broad consumer audience, you use traditional, social, and digital media. If you're selling to a broad business audience, trade media, direct response, social media, and lead-gen make the most sense. For younger audiences, digital, mobile, and certain social media are your best bet.

If all that's true, then where does Contact Marketing fit? And why should you consider diverting your energies and budget to this form of marketing? Let's take a look at what differentiates Contact Marketing from these other forms of marketing and how it defines an entirely new role for your marketing spend.

Contact Marketing vs. Sales Promotion

Sales promotion is considered part of the traditional promotional mix, which also includes advertising, personal selling, direct marketing, and publicity. Its mission is to stimulate market demand using methods that include contests, coupons, rebates, sweepstakes, and the like. In some sense, Contact Marketing could be considered part of the sales promotion mission, because the goals for both are to increase sales volume. But while sales promotion is broadly applied, Contact Marketing focuses only on the most important prospects, and only on producing direct contact, for sales or alliance building.

Contact Marketing vs. Demand Generation

The demand-generation mission is closely related to that of Contact Marketing. It uses targeted marketing programs to generate awareness of and interest in a company's offerings, leading to easier sales penetration, shorter cycles, and greater presale market acceptance. Contact

Marketing easily supports this mission, with a pure focus on getting reps in the doors of the company's most important prospects. If the "80/20 rule" says the top 20 percent of your prospects account for 80 percent of your sales potential, Demand Generation would address those top 20 percent to precipitate sales. In contrast, Contact Marketing would address the top 1 percent to precipitate the biggest possible deals as quickly as possible.

Contact Marketing vs. Lead-gen

Lead generation uses various marketing forms to accomplish its goal, which is to get interested parties to identify themselves as qualified sales prospects. That can take place through the mail; web search; and digital, traditional, or social media. Lead-gen campaigns can often look like Contact Campaigns, especially when dimensional mailings are used, and when there is a built-in incentive to agree to a sales meeting. A dimensional mailing containing a remote-control model Ferrari with a letter explaining that the rep will bring the missing control unit to the proposed meeting actually is one of the Contact Campaign forms described later in this book. But the two approaches diverge in the method of generating a response. If the campaign relies on a response device, it's not a Contact Campaign. If the campaign goes out to a mass audience, it's not a Contact Campaign. Contact Marketing is based on reaching out to as few as a single strategically chosen target contact, about which at least some specific information is known. And the method of response is always to speak or meet with the sender. Mass lists and business reply cards aren't part of the Contact Marketing mission.

Contact Marketing vs. Direct Response

The advantage of direct marketing has always been the ability to target a specific audience and get a precise read on response. That's also true of Contact Marketing, but the focus is much tighter. It's a laser beam to direct marketing's searchlight. In direct marketing, the prime directive is to find combinations of lists, offers, and creative to produce the highest result and best ROI. And this may be the biggest point of departure between the two: Direct response typically produces low response rates and ROI, while Contact Marketing produces just the opposite. In fact, most direct marketers will find it impossible to believe that Contact Marketing is capable of producing 100 percent response rates and ROI figures in the hundreds of thousands of percent. That's because in direct marketing, those numbers really are impossible. The final difference is that direct response uses "response devices"—business reply cards, forms, micro-sites, landing pages, and more—to harvest orders and leads, while Contact Campaigns operate in direct support of actual sales activity. So the rep is the response device, always superior in that role to a business reply card.

> "Contact Marketing is capable of producing 100 percent response rates and ROI figures in the hundreds of thousands of percent."

How Contact Marketing Functions, and Its Components

Okay, so Contact Marketing differs from other forms of marketing that are often tied directly to sales. But what exactly is a Contact Campaign?

Let's start with the mission of Contact Marketing. There is always a relative handful of key people who, if you're able to break through to them, can change the course of your career and the fortunes of your enterprise. These may be large potential buyers of your product or service, mega-potential referral sources, or potential alliance partners who can change the scale of your company by giving you access to vast new sales channels.

You should know who these people are at all times. And you should keep a list. If you're in sales, call it your "Top 100" list of prospects. If you are a business owner, entrepreneur, or C-level executive, call the list your "Strategic 100." Either way, you need to have a firm sense of who these people are at all times—and a firm commitment to enlist them as part of your success network.

Armed with your list, you'll need to create a profile for each person or group of people you will be contacting. It is critical that you take the time to research these people, to understand what they're experiencing, what their goals are, what they're doing to get there, who their competitors are, and the framework of their situation. You need to involve yourself in their social media messaging, to understand what has their attention, what they admire or dislike, what they do in their free time. The purpose of all of this is to have a full understanding of how you can help them, where you fit in. This is what will enable you to turn a quick start of a conversation into a dialogue, a dialogue into a relationship, and a relationship into deals and referrals. You must be able to express your value proposition in just a few seconds, with the aim of cultivating a critically important relationship. Wasting someone's time with an unclear purpose is a terrible way to start that off.

Then it's time to create your campaign. In Section II, I have listed twenty Contact Campaign categories, but you must resist the temptation to simply pick out a technique someone else has used and jam it into your purpose. If this was a book about advertising and I listed the top twenty campaigns of all time, you wouldn't simply say, "I like the 'That's a Spicy Meatball' Alka-Seltzer ad, let's do that." Neither should you react the same way to the campaigns you will read about shortly. They're there to give you inspiration, to help you formulate your own specific campaign, something that addresses your goals and the information you've gathered on your Top 100 or Strategic 100 lists.

Contact Marketing is like having an advertising agency create a specific campaign to support a single, critical sales or business development approach to each VIP contact. Like any form of marketing, you'll need to test, then sharpen your approach. I tend to test in rounds of ten contacts, then evaluate and adjust the approach as needed.

Most VIPs have executive assistants, and your Contact Campaign strategy needs to include them. It's surprising to me that most salespeople think of assistants as gatekeeping obstacles. They're actually some of the sharpest people in the organizations, and their job is as much about letting certain people in as it is keeping others out. Your campaign needs to reflect that view by including the assistants in your strategy. You need to treat them as allies and address them in your campaign.

Most of my contact calls start by seeking out the target executive's assistant. When I call, I immediately ask if my target has an executive assistant I can speak to. When I make contact, I have a script in mind, and start by explaining that I'm one of *The Wall Street Journal* cartoonists and I have a print of a cartoon I want to send to the executive. I tell them that, while it's meant to be a surprise for their boss, I don't want it to be a surprise to the assistant. I ask if I can send an email to confirm the details, which gives me direct access to the assistant, provides a written explanation of my reason for contact, and gives them something they can easily pass along. Writing my story means I get to control its telling; there are no lost details or mistranslated points.

Once the assistant has rendered his or her help, I include them further by sending a handwritten card with a personalized cartoon. Likewise, you should plan to send something of modest value but great personal significance to thank them for their help in your campaign. It will keep the door open and influence your target. As I interviewed CEOs for this book, it became quite clear that their assistants are considered key members of their team, and the executives notice how they're treated by outsiders. It could be a thank-you card, a gift certificate, or something else that says in the kindest, most appreciative terms, "Thank you for your help."

While I tell stories of Contact Campaigns that have produced 100 percent response rates, don't expect that to happen in your campaign. At least not initially. It's more likely you will see lower response rates as you adjust your approach, but that doesn't mean you should give up on the contacts that didn't connect. So your campaign should include at least a second effort, to address those who haven't responded. In my campaigns, that usually takes the form of another card, this time with a rather pushy cartoon. Picture a guy on a pay phone at a broken-down gas station in the desert, saying, *"Hi ((insert name)), it's me again. Listen, I don't know if you've been checking your voice mail all last week, but I'm still here at the same number, waiting for your call."* That usually breaks the cycle of not answering or returning a call.

Not every Contact Campaign will include these elements. Some can be as simple as a phone call or social media contact. But this will serve as a basic template. A Contact Campaign should include a list of critically important target contacts, pre-contact research, and a strategy-driven creative package that addresses the executive, assistant, and anyone who doesn't respond to the first effort. Contact Campaigns can embody much more as well. Some strategies call for simultaneous contact with multiple contacts in an organization. Others deploy to target contacts based on triggering events. Just like an examination of advertising campaigns, Contact Campaigns can take many forms, as long as they remain focused on establishing specific, critically important contacts for sales and alliance building.

How Do Contact Campaigns Fit with Modern Marketing?

The pace of change in our lives is amazing, and it's always accelerating. Do you find that to be true?

I would agree to a point. There is a rush of innovation, especially in technology. The same is true for marketing. Remember, Google only started in 1998. Back then, print and broadcast were dominant, and direct response was the only direct route to identified groups of prospective customers. Today, broadcast media is still powerful but fragmented, while digital, mobile, and social media rule. And print and direct marketing are on their way out—or are they?

Progression is not linear. As the fashion industry demonstrates, many things cycle in and out of favor. Sending something through the mail has become novel again. It's now become interesting to have something you can hold in your hands rather than view on a screen. Perhaps magazines and newspapers will see a revival, not so much as a physical product, but as the preferred format for receiving and consuming information. I still find it satisfying to hold something printed, to flip through the pages and take in the sensations of something physical in my hands.

I see the same situation in selling. It's no longer sales, it's "Sales 2.0." and "Social Selling." Mobile media is the new *de rigueur* frontier. But I still return to the same truth, that selling most often occurs as a result of human-to-human contact, and trust and value-based relationships. I also believe in the 80/20 rule, that 80 percent of your business comes from 20 percent of your clients, and enjoy the fact that Contact Marketing takes it to the extreme.

Does Contact Marketing have a place among the current landscape of digital, social, and mobile marketing? Absolutely. There will always be a need to identify and address the people in positions of great power who can help your enterprise thrive. And there will always be a place for a form of marketing that produces 100 percent response rates and ROI potentially in the tens or hundreds of thousands of percent. To ignore that kind of potential gain, regardless of what the current fashions are in selling and marketing, would be foolhardy.

Points to Remember

 Contact Campaigns aren't just a form of marketing; they're a unique fusion of marketing and selling.

✔ Contact Campaigns are not sales gimmicks or tricks; they are a viable and legitimate form of one-to-one marketing.

✔ Contact Campaigns are micro-focused on as few as a single, high-value contact.

✔ Contact Marketing operates in direct support of sales or building alliances.

✔ The sender or sales rep is always the "response device."

✔ Contact Campaigns are flexible, inclusive, and involving.

✔ Contact Campaigns are highly personal and often involve a great dose of audacity.

✔ Contact Marketing is related to, but not the same as or part of, sales promotion, lead generation, or direct marketing.

✔ Contact Marketing does integrate with the demand-generation mission, but concentrates on the highest-value potential clients or alliance partners.

✔ Contact Campaigns typically include a Top 100 or Strategic 100 list, pre-contact research, and a strategy-driven creative approach that addresses the needs, wants, and concerns of the target contact and executive assistant.

✔ Contact Marketing fits perfectly with other forms of modern marketing.

✔ To ignore the enormous potential for response and ROI from Contact Marketing in favor of marketing and sales trends of the hour would be foolhardy.

"Check your phone and see if it's light outside, would you?"

CHAPTER 3

The Nature of CEOs and VIPs

Calling on CEOs is not easy. They're hard to reach, impatient, judgmental, and intense, and they don't want to take your call. Their assistants fiercely protect their time and routinely prevent access. So why bother at all?

It's pretty simple. This is where the money is. It's where the power to transform your business is. It's where the greatest rewards of your career are.

This is about making quantum leaps as a way of life.

If you are a sales professional, selling to the C-suite may be daunting, but once you're used to it, once you're prepared for it, you'll be able to sell to anyone. Think for a moment what that can do for your career. You become known as a rainmaker, someone with abundant connections who is able to penetrate nearly any account, starting at the top. Does that sound like someone you'd want to hire if you were a sales manager or vice president of sales? Does it sound like a future CEO? Many CEOs started their careers in sales, and this is how they got there, by being exceptionally effective.

The higher up the ladder we go, the more obvious this is. Sales managers, vice presidents of sales, and chief sales officers dream of finding someone who can easily break through to any company of any size, at any level, especially the top. They know CEOs have the ultimate discretion to make decisions for the company, and when the CEO wants something done, it gets done. There may be discussion about where the funds may come from, but the CEO is not asking anyone if he or she can spend the money. If you convince the CEO, chances are you've got a deal. And you have visibility and power throughout the organization to generate even more business. After all, you've been vetted by the CEO. Having an army of sales reps capable of breaking through and speaking thoughtfully, relevantly, and quickly, who also deliver value to C-suite executives, is a sales manager's dream.

> *Selling to the C-suite may be daunting, but once you're used to it, once you're prepared for it, you'll be able to sell to anyone.*

Now think of this from the vantage point of the C-suite executive, owner, or entrepreneur. Yes, they want the kind of sales and deal-making power I've just described, but they also know how important it is to build their own direct network of VIP contacts. Relationships at the top levels, between top people in various fields, are critical to their mission. And Contact Marketing is an exceptionally effective tool to make *that* happen.

I don't know about you, but I tend to be motivated by more than business or financial success. I'm also motivated by mischief, by achieving things I should never be able to pull off. It makes business fun. When I send one of my cartoons to a CEO or someone of great importance in some other respect, I can't wait to hear their reaction. I love hearing how one of my BigBoard contact pieces was carried throughout the office by the company president, as he showed it off to anyone who would listen (and they all have to listen to the president). Or how a CEO still keeps the cartoon piece in her office, tilted slightly to the side on the credenza because it doesn't quite fit. I like hearing about the constant comments the BigBoards prompt among the visitors to the CEO's office. I love the fact that it continues to produce awareness of the sender and their company for years.

When I describe reaching CEOs, it's important to remind you that I don't always mean just the actual CEO. As I explained in Chapter 2, we're engaging the "CEO of the problem you want to solve." So when I say "CEO," from this point forward, I'm talking about the person with the ultimate authority for whatever you're trying to achieve with the target company, the "Center of Enterprise Opportunity." It could be the CEO, or it might be someone else in the C-suite. It could also be someone further down, who has been tasked with achieving a particular goal for the company.

The "CEO" might also be several stakeholders simultaneously. Sometimes, an approach to the CEO is made to secure their top-down referral to the real decision maker. And sometimes, it is simply the actual CEO.

So as you read further, think of the "CEO" in this discourse as the person with the ultimate authority and interest in what you want to accomplish with a given company—the Center of Enterprise Opportunity. And be prepared to touch virtually anyone. Fortunately, you're about to equip yourself to do just that.

The Time-Compressed World of a CEO

CEOs can seem gruff, even mean-spirited, when you first get them on the phone. Can you blame them?

CEOs receive hundreds of emails a day. They receive just as many phone calls. They're tasked with running the company while plotting a course that achieves stellar growth. They don't quite see the world the way the rest of us might. The typical person focuses on what's immediately ahead in the next few months. A CEO inhabits the world as it will be five years from now. They're trying to see around corners, looking for what's ahead and how they can turn that into a strategic advantage for their company. And they're pushing to exceed the goals they've set for the company every day.

Can you see why, if you can't quickly establish your value, something of great importance to whatever has the CEO's focus that very moment, your call is no more than an annoying distraction? It's even worse if they perceive you're not on an equal level of importance to their own. If that is the case, they can't wait to get rid of you and they won't be shy about it, either.

Let's think of this another way. We constantly hear how obscenely well paid CEOs are. If you're calling on a CEO of a *Fortune* 500 company, and if his or her annual compensation is a relatively modest (in CEO terms) $30 million, each minute of their time is worth $240. Actually, that's just what the company pays the CEO. Their actual worth may be a hundred times that number, because they're responsible for making the enterprise climb to new levels, open new markets, and achieve new levels of valuation.

This means, when you ask our hypothetical CEO above to spend twenty minutes with you on the phone, you're asking them to invest $4,800 of their time and perhaps half a million dollars of the company's potential on your call. It had better be worth it, and it had better be quick.

Their Focus = Your Focus

To do an effective job as a CEO requires extraordinary vision and an extreme ability to tolerate uncertainty and risk. These people live pressure-filled lives and thrive in it. Their job is to set, achieve, and exceed goals as they plot the course for the company.

That means your focus needs to shift if you're going to work with CEOs. If you're a sales rep, you need to start thinking in terms of providing value, not selling. Make that your focus—not *pitching*. That alone is a tough transition for many to make. Some might say, "If I get the CEO's attention I'm going to make the most of it. I'm going for the sale right away." But that will only lead to closed doors and sparse sales, if any.

> *If you're someone who provides exceptional value and intelligence, you've got the CEO's ear and you will sell. A lot.*

If Sales 2.0 is inbound-based selling, make this "Sales 3.0"—selling by providing value and becoming an indispensable member of the target executive's inner circle. Can you see how selling from that position becomes a lot easier, once you have the respect and trust of the person at the top?

Beyond setting, achieving, and exceeding goals, CEOs are locked in a constant battle to best their competition. They do that by studying what their competitors are doing and looking for weaknesses. They're also reading the marketplace and society at large, looking for new ways to exploit trends before they happen. Your job is to help them do that. From the CEO's perspective, if you are someone trying to invade their space to make a pitch, you're not helping. If you're someone who provides exceptional value and intelligence, you've got the CEO's ear and you will sell. A lot.

To accomplish exceptional goals, the CEO must also build an exceptional team. The C-suite executives are his or her "A-team," but effective CEOs consider all of their players critical. Your focus should be figuring out how to become part of that team. It doesn't matter that you're not on the payroll. If you're a trusted source of critical insight, information, and creative thinking, you may also become a trusted source—perhaps the only source—of whatever it is you sell.

Author Anthony Parinello says CEOs have five critical missions: increasing revenue, improving efficiency, cutting expense, increasing stock value, and regulatory compliance.[1] He's right, but I think it can be boiled down even further to one vital mission: winning.

Helping the CEOs you're about to contact to win is how *you* will win. That needs to be your new focus.

Determining How You Fit in Their World

There is only one way to figure out how you fit in a particular CEO's world: Do your homework. Become an expert in who the CEO is, what their unique challenges and successes are, where their company is heading. Understand who their competitors are and where they're vulnerable. Survey the same weak points for your target's company. Most of all, understand who the CEO is as a person.

The Internet and social media make this task exceptionally easy. A quick search will produce volumes of information, starting with the target's social media pages. Take a look at their LinkedIn page, for example, to see how they describe their mission in their current post. Take a look at whom they've connected with already. Could you see yourself being one of them?

Then check out their Twitter page and get a quick sense of what has their attention. What articles are they favoriting or retweeting? What are they interested in personally? What are their favorite causes and passions? Do they reveal anything about their work as CEO?

Search newsfeeds to find recent articles featuring the CEO. Use tools like Hoover's, Data.com, Connect (formerly Jigsaw), and

DiscoverOrg to get all of the correct contact information and learn who the key players are in their organizations. These will be critical later when you're formulating your contact strategy, starting simply with where to deliver your campaign.

With that information in hand, take a realistic look at how what you sell or do can make a difference to the company, or perhaps to the CEO personally.

When I approached Constant Contact to form an alliance with my CartoonLink service, I had several key pieces of intelligence in hand. I knew the CEO, Gail Goodman, had just written her first book, *Engagement Marketing*. And I knew the test results from my "cartoon device"—a personalized cartoon within the email—would fit her mission perfectly. I knew that because our "cartoon devices" had been routinely doubling open rates, and her mission is to make sure her 700,000 users remained engaged in the Constant Contact platform.

My Contact Campaign included outreach first to the CEO, then to the person she referred me to. As a result, I gained access to a vast sales channel I never could have duplicated on my own. That success came from understanding how what I sell fits the CEO's mission, then reducing it to as few words as possible: "My cartoon device doubles open rates. Are you interested?"

Your job is to understand the CEO's world well enough to know how you can create an unfair advantage for their company. Unless you can do that, you should not be calling. But let's put it another way. Your job isn't about selling your product or service. It's about giving the CEO an overwhelming advantage through what you know or do.

Just as I approached Constant Contact, you will need to strike a nimble stance to determine who ultimately needs contact with you. It could be the CEO or someone else in the C-suite. It could be someone you'll be referred to by the CEO, or it could be several people simultaneously, to create maximum impact among all stakeholders.

Determining in whose world your offering fits is what will determine your Contact Campaign strategy. And it all starts with doing your homework and knowing the people thoroughly before you ever make a call.

How to Talk to a CEO

In the preceding example, I described my approach to the CEO of Constant Contact. My expression of value was made using just nine words. In those two brief sentences, I told her how I could support her mission while bringing something uniquely intriguing and beneficial to her platform. I paid great respect to the value of her time by keeping it short and absolutely on target. That's what you need to do.

SHiFT coauthor and *Shift Selling* blog author Craig Elias goes even further. He says you must express your value proposition in seven or fewer words, and in a way that leaves the CEO asking, "How would you do that?" I suppose I could have shortened my message to, "I can double your members' open rates." Still, I broke through and have a valuable alliance to show for it.

I really like Craig's advice, though. Keep your first spoken words to seven or fewer and leave the CEO asking how you can accomplish what you're describing. And make sure that whatever you're promising helps solve a problem the CEO is facing.

It's also important to know that some conversations with the CEO will actually take place entirely through their executive assistant. You may end up speaking directly with the CEO, or you may not. If the CEO likes what you're bringing to the company, they can always direct a course of action through their assistants. I have the greatest respect for executive assistants, and we'll cover these amazing players more in Chapter 15. For now, keep in mind that assistants will always be a critical part of your success in your contact mission, and that they actually do speak for the CEO.

Regardless of how it takes form, contact with the CEO is critical to your new mission. You're about to make great new bounds in your career. And you're about to become a VIP yourself, deserving of contact with any CEO you choose.

Points to Remember

✔ While CEOs are not easy to reach, they're worth every effort to make the connection happen.

✔ CEOs hold the promise of quantum leaps in your career and for your business.

✔ The more able you are to routinely reach CEOs, the more valuable you are to your company.

✔ By "CEO," I mean the "CEO of the problem you want to solve," who may or may not be the actual CEO.

✔ In this book, "CEO" is a euphemism for anyone with the ultimate authority and interest in what you are offering— the "Center of Enterprise Opportunity"—including the actual CEO.

✔ "CEO" can also be several stakeholders simultaneously, each of whom you must address in your contact campaign.

✔ CEOs live in a time-compressed world and you must find a way to fit in, offering unique value to their mission.

✔ To sell to a CEO, you must first understand their mission and make it your own.

✔ If you add value and provide unique intelligence, you will be accepted as part of the CEO's team.

✔ Being part of the CEO's inner circle will allow you to sell a lot more than if you were to simply pitch your product or service.

✔ If possible, limit your value proposition to seven words or less, structured in a way that causes the CEO to ask, "How would you do that?"

✔ When you speak to a CEO's executive assistant, you are also speaking to the CEO.

"I'm terrible with name tags. Who are you again?"

CHAPTER 4

Your VIP Makeover

If the world of Contact Marketing weren't foreign enough already, we're about to depart in an even less familiar direction. I don't recall ever encountering a chapter on transforming yourself into a VIP in any other book about sales, marketing, or business.

But this is not simply an unusual feature of this book; it's something you should have been doing all along. A life and career well lived should result in some measure of importance and notoriety, but now it's time to turn up the heat.

If you're going to adopt Contact Marketing as part of your strategy, you'll be rubbing shoulders with important people, and the more you build your network, the more connected and important you will become. Can you see how becoming important yourself makes it easier to open the doors most critical to your success?

So sit down, relax, and get comfortable. We're going to give you a VIP makeover.

When we're finished, you will have a unique VIP statement, something you can use to quickly establish your importance so your calls are not only taken, but taken seriously. Here's my own VIP statement: *I'm one of* The Wall Street Journal *cartoonists, a hall of fame–nominated marketer, and an author*. That's it. It's short, to the point, and in just a few words delivers a convincing argument that I am someone to be taken seriously. Not only that, as one of *The Wall Street Journal* cartoonists, I plop something wonderful in their laps. I become someone the VIP can brag about that evening to their spouse: "You'll never guess who I talked to today..." That's the effect I want you to generate.

Establish Equal Business Status

The moment you reach out to a VIP, two questions flash in their minds. *Who are you? And what do you want?* They are the most basic questions any person asks when approached by a stranger. We're programmed to continually evaluate people based on those two questions.

But as we have seen, in a CEO's case, those questions become all the more critical because of the demands and value placed on their time. They don't have a moment to waste, so they are constantly protecting their time from unnecessary distractions, especially from people they don't know.

The question of what you want is obvious. You want to sell to their company or form an alliance. You'll make them aware of that fact when you express your value proposition in a single sentence containing no more than a dozen words. Still, they don't know who you are. More to the point, they don't know your worth. They don't know if they can invest their trust in you, your company, or what you're selling. They don't know if they should even invest the next few seconds with you on the phone.

Imagine how that all changes if you were Harrison Ford, the actor, on the line. Let's forget for the moment that it would be odd if Harrison Ford actually were on the phone, looking to complete a sale. The fact that a movie star is on the phone greatly increases the value of the call, and the target will grant a bit more time to understand its purpose. If Harrison were to ask the CEO to join an alliance for a charitable cause, Mr. *Star Wars* would likely get what he wanted.

Can you see how the perception of importance becomes a critical factor in whether or not a contact is made?

We don't have to be movie actors, cartoonists, or famous at all to create the perception of a greater or equal status. Our importance in the business world is not only a critical element of our success; it is already under our direct control. You can change yours anytime you want.

Fortunately, we live in the age of the Internet and social media. Both are designed to give exposure to anyone who cares to contribute, tweet, or share. I address social media separately in Chapter 20. So let's look instead at some of the steps you can take immediately to start building your status and importance, apart from social media. The aim is to build a brand around your name by greatly boosting your exposure.

Start a Blog

One of the surest ways to elevate your status is to find something you're good at and passionate about, then create a blog. Ideally, for purposes of your career, it should relate to the business you're in to attract the sort of audience you want to influence. *A Sales Guy* blog author Jim Keenan advises finding your passion and writing about it a bit every day. "Eventually, people will catch on to what you're saying, they'll start connecting with you, and before you know it, you have your own following," he advises. Keenan says the exposure you create is the most valuable asset you can build in your life. He adds that it's "even more valuable than your house."

> *Blogs have the added benefit of giving you a legitimate platform to use to interview some of your top contact targets.*

Starting a blog is easy enough, either from your company's website or on one of several excellent platforms, WordPress, Blogger, Tumblr, and Google+ among them. Blogs have the added benefit of giving you a legitimate platform to use to interview some of your top contact targets.

Guest Blog

Starting your own blog is nice because you control access to your audience, but it takes time to build. The solution may be also to write as a guest expert on other well-circulated blogs. I write monthly articles for the Salesforce and Constant Contact blogs, which give me instant access to roughly 750,000 readers. And they're not just readers—they're marketers, sales reps, and managers, even C-level executives with sales and marketing responsibilities. It's a perfect fit, and a good example of the quick access you can create in your own industry. Before long, you'll achieve useful name recognition, with the added benefit of having articles you can send directly to your contact targets, branded with the credibility of a big-name blog and the hosting company or organization.

Start an Association

This is a big undertaking, and you must do it with the clearest intentions of building something bigger than yourself and your company. It needs to be a service you make available to an entire industry or profession, including companies in competition with your own. You also must do it in response to an unmet need that such an association of like-minded professionals can fill. If you meet all of those conditions, starting an association can bring a new abundance to your career, because you become a central figure in your industry. Contacting a CEO on your campaign list as the founder and president of an association gives you newfound credibility and status, something you can easily leverage in your Contact Marketing strategy.

Join the Board of a Charity

Many charities are in constant need of capable volunteers to move their missions forward. Doing charitable work in your free time not only does good in the world, it also transforms you into a more important person. The mission of many charities is critical and serious, and I am not suggesting that your involvement be made in any sort of calculating way to gain personal importance. That's not the spirit of it. But you will notice that it allows you new access to VIPs, and that may be helpful if blended with your Contact Marketing strategy.

Become an Author

Being an author carries great status and is particularly useful in Contact Marketing. Authors are recognized as celebrated experts, and as you will see in Section II, having a book of your own can form the basis of a powerful Contact Campaign strategy. Even as you're writing the book, you can gain special access to VIPs for interviews. It gives you the power to include anyone you want in the book. The world of publishing has changed drastically in the past few years, opening the possibility of becoming an author to anyone with the time and discipline to share their unique expertise. It can be as easy as pouring a thoughtfully written and edited Word document into a converter to create a paginated book. Entering the world of big-time publishing and best-selling books is still quite challenging. If you do write a book, be sure to have it produced in print as well as e-book formats. Printed books allow you to send autographed copies, along with a note directing the recipient to a particular page. Being an author produces instant respect among CEOs, because they understand the level of expertise and amount of effort involved, and many harbor fantasies themselves of writing a best-seller someday.

Start an Internet Radio Show

As the host of your own interview show, you get instant credibility, because you're not selling anything—you're giving CEOs a chance to speak about their company, their goals, their lives. It's an honor to be asked to be an interview guest, and it gives you several touch points. The first comes when you're making initial contact. You get through because this is the sort of surprise opportunity executive assistants love to bring to their executives. Posting the recording of the show gives you another reason to get in touch and simply offer value, but it also gives you an opportunity to talk about direct business together, if the CEO doesn't ask first. Internet radio shows are also an excellent way to generate and accumulate valuable content that, as *Life after the Death of Selling* author and *Whale Hunting: How to Land Big Sales and Transform Your Company* coauthor Tom Searcy suggests, can easily be transcribed and turned into a book.

Start an Industry Recognition Award

Consider the example of Richard Blackwell. Although he had moderate success as an actor and fashion designer, he achieved worldwide fame for his annual "Worst Dressed List," which became one of the most-quoted "awards" in history. You don't have to push it that far, but starting your own industry recognition, positive or negative, can give your name a big injection of importance. For some reason, I always gravitate toward the positive, but Mr. Blackwell's Worst Dressed List and the Razzies (the Golden Raspberry Award for terrible cinema) demonstrate that negative can also be enormously powerful. Whether the award is positive or negative, imagine the impact of calling to ask a CEO for input or for an interview to evaluate them as an honoree. If you start such an award, be prepared to keep it up indefinitely and consistently. And be sure to promote it relentlessly to the news media and through social media. You might even become legitimately famous, which will certainly help your chances of breaking through to most VIPs.

Become a Trusted Source of Insight

Changing the Sales Conversation author Linda Richardson advises sales professionals to recognize the shift in buying behaviors brought on by the ubiquitous feeds of information on the Internet, and realize they must evolve to become trusted sources of insight rather than product information. Just as in social media, you can benefit by scouring the Internet for news items and articles your CEO contacts will find useful. Over time, you will become someone they will see as a trusted source of information, intelligence, and insight.

What It Looks Like

When I set out to write this book, I wanted it to be inclusive, to involve many of the top thought leaders in sales and marketing. It turned out these people are also excellent examples of self-made success and importance.

The New Rules of Selling & PR author and *WebInkNow* blog author David Meerman Scott restarted his career after being cut loose in 2002 from his position as vice president of marketing for NewsEdge. His makeover is still underway, I suspect, but all of the descriptors one would use to describe who he is—best-selling author, top sales blogger, keynote speaker—are things that happened *after he lost his job.*

The same can be said for many of the people included in this book as sources. Matt Heinz, Anthony Iannarino, Tibor Shanto, Linda Richardson, Dan Waldschmidt, and many others certainly have made their marks through their work, but also through their widely read blogs. When a CEO receives a call from any of these people, they connect because they know the call will be worthwhile and may even lead to some new strategic advantage.

Live the Intrepid Life author Todd Schnick takes a slightly different path, by interviewing CEOs at will for his family of podcasts. His approach is simple: a quick call to say, "I'm interested in what your company does and I'd like to give you a chance to tell your story to our audience." When he calls, executive assistants make sure he gets through to their bosses, and by the time they're finished with the interview, they have shared a full hour of bonding. From that point on, they're connected. Tom Searcy takes that a step further, by recording and transcribing his VIP interviews, so they become content for books and gifts to the CEOs he has interviewed.

All of these people have something very important in common. They all have put enormous effort into adding new dimensions to what they do, and in the process, they have thoroughly burnished their own status as VIPs.

Being a VIP Causes Business and Opportunities to Flow to You

The more important you become, the more people seek you out. And that makes your contact mission a lot easier.

Your VIP makeover becomes a Contact Campaign in itself. The more important you are, the more people are drawn to you, along with opportunities you may have otherwise never known about.

Still, you shouldn't abandon your outreach efforts. You must be free to steer your own course and connect with whomever you want. Having a VIP statement that has the CEO saying, "Wow, I'm honored you called," will carry you a long way toward your goals, and help produce rapid growth in your career or business. Putting effort into your VIP makeover will be well spent. It will be something you will hone the rest of your career to great effect.

POINTS TO REMEMBER

✔ Having a short, twelve-words-or-less VIP statement can make an enormous difference in the success of your Contact Marketing efforts.

✔ A VIP statement is a quick way to establish equal business status with CEOs and VIPs.

✔ You will want your VIP statement to be so powerful, the CEO will brag to their spouse about your call that evening.

✔ Without establishing equal business status, the probability of connecting with your target VIP drops sharply, as will the quality of any resulting call or meeting, if it happens at all.

✔ Fortunately, the ability to change your VIP status is already well within your grasp.

✔ Some of the most effective methods of raising your
    status, such as blogging and Internet radio shows, are
    ways to offer the target CEO an opportunity to tell their
    story to your audience.

✔ Involvement with charities is a powerful way to enhance
    your standing, while offering a real benefit to your
    community.

✔ Becoming a trusted source of information, intelligence,
    and insight is an invaluable way of connecting deeply
    with your Top 100 list members.

✔ Becoming a VIP is often a process of reinventing and
    strengthening your reputation and career.

"The idea, ladies and gentlemen, is to find a niche and market the hell out of it. I happen to like this one."

CHAPTER 5

Identifying Your Top 100 Prospects

Our mission should be getting clearer and clearer by now. A well-executed Contact Marketing plan can change the scale of your career or business. You're on your way to becoming a connected, powerful person, a VIP yourself. You're about to make thrilling breakthroughs in your life, as you achieve things you thought were impossible.

But first, you must give careful thought to who holds the keys to that new level of success. If you're a sales rep, you may already have a list of named accounts. If so, your job of defining your Top 100 list is already done. Or is it? Are there still high-value prospects in your territory who haven't yet been identified and included on your list? Do you have the autonomy to dig further and mine more opportunities from your area? Are you free to develop relationships that lead to referrals?

If you don't have an assigned group of VIP prospects, it's time to figure out who should be receiving your powerful outreach efforts. I tend to have a mixture of direct sales, strategic alliance, and wildcard contacts on my list. It's a blend of Top 100 and Strategic 100 lists, with a bit of mischief thrown in.

NoWait, a tech startup, recently launched their restaurant app with a stellar Contact Campaign. It involved sending an iPad preloaded with a video addressed specifically to each recipient. The total investment was $35,000, a lot for a new business. It's a lot for any business, really, so it needed to pay off. Can you see how the choice of recipients is critical to a successful outcome?

Remember, the philosophy of Contact Marketing is simple. There is a small group of people who, if they become your clients or strategic partners, will transform the scale of your business. NoWait set their sights on the CEOs, CFOs, and COOs of twenty of the top restaurant chains and franchises. Part of their list strategy was to determine which person in the organization would be most receptive to their approach. They discovered that COOs were their best targets, and as a result, the business is already booming, with several roll-outs already underway with national chains. It's a great start, and it is happening as a result of contact with just thirty-five people—thirty-five carefully considered people.

> There is a small group of people who, if they become your clients or strategic partners, will transform the scale of your business.

My own list continues to evolve over time. Some people fall off because there wasn't a fit after all. Some graduate off the list because they have become clients or partners. Others come off the list as my priorities change.

You will find that formulating your Top 100 or Strategic 100 list is an inspiring, exciting, and ever-evolving exercise. You may struggle at first, but you'll soon see this for what it is: your opportunity to reach virtually anyone you choose. You can put anyone on the list you want. It doesn't matter if they seem completely out of reach. You're about to start achieving the impossible anyway.

Dream Clients and Dream Partners

The tech startup in my example is off to a great start, but it's still just the beginning of the process. As a result of their outreach to just thirty-five key people, they now know their efforts should be directed to COOs in large chains. But they also learned their penetration of restaurant franchises will be most effective if they target the franchisor rather than individual franchisees.

Now it's time for their list to evolve and expand. They will need to identify which restaurant chains and franchises hold the most promise for quick growth of their revenue base. But they shouldn't simply jump at the fifty biggest chains, because clearly some of them, such as McDonald's, Burger King, and Wendy's, don't need an app to help their guests make reservations and manage table availabilities.

The list must be carefully composed to represent the deepest core of the company's market opportunity. Their list of target contacts will grow as they repeat what has worked in the initial round of their Contact Campaign. Still, the process is just getting started.

Once the COOs of the top chains and franchises have been addressed, it's time to look for new sources of gain. Did all of the COOs respond to the campaign? Those who didn't should be addressed again, this time emphasizing they're falling behind their competitors who have already adopted the app. Perhaps the CEOs of those companies should be added to the list, while the COOs who have become clients come off the contact list and go onto an engagement list.

And what happened with the franchise contact efforts? Did they all become adopters of the app? Probably not, so the company must evolve their Contact Marketing strategy to address those opportunities. They should be addressed at the franchisee level, but it doesn't make sense to mount a Contact Campaign to several thousand franchisees. So wouldn't it make sense to cultivate relationships with thought leaders among the franchisees? Absolutely. A few strategically placed supporters among the group will give the company a big advantage as they push into the network. And what about the franchisors who didn't respond? They should be approached again, to tell them they're in danger of falling behind, and the whole process repeats.

Contact Marketing isn't about contacting everyone. It's about reaching out to just the handful of people who can make the biggest difference to your efforts. *They are the multipliers of your success.* The COOs and franchisors represent hundreds, possibly thousands, of sales of the company's app system. Once the company reaches the point of addressing single-point sales, Contact Marketing no longer fits and other forms of marketing and direct sales should ensue.

> " *Contact Marketing isn't about contacting everyone. It's about reaching out to just the handful of people who can make the biggest difference to your efforts.* "

Still, they're not finished with their Contact Marketing mission. While pursuing direct sales opportunities, they should also be looking for strategic partners who can open new sales channels to the company. Who are the major restaurant supply chains, and how can they create a partnership? Are there noncompetitive software providers who have already a broad penetration in the market? How can the company create a win-win partnership that increases its own penetration nearly overnight? Roll out the Contact Campaigns there, too, to establish relationships at the tops of those organizations.

Are we done yet? Not even close. Since we're talking about an app, consumer uptake is critical to the company's success as well. And as in so many other areas in life, there is always a small group of people who can greatly expand the company's efforts. They may be influential food bloggers, news media figures, cooking show hosts and producers, and tech-trend thought leaders, all of whom can give the company a critical boost in consumer acceptance and participation with the app. Think about what that does to their market position among the chains and franchises who have resisted the company's app system. Now they'll resist at their own peril, so it's time to address them again in the company's Contact Campaign strategy. And what happens when the company develops a new app for another market?

The point is, there is always a core group of people who can offer a critical boost to your success, who can multiply your efforts with large sales and quick access to even more of them. They are, as *The Ultimate Sales Machine* author Chet Holmes used to say, your "Dream Clients." You should always know who they are and keep your list of them current. New clients exit the list while new prospects and opportunities take their place. Others come on to the list as priorities shift.

Each company's list will be composed differently as well. The strategy for the restaurant app company is driven by the potential value of each sale, which in their case, is about a $10,000 lifetime value per restaurant location. In other cases, the lifetime value of a sale may be millions of dollars, warranting a direct Contact Marketing approach to each qualifying prospect.

The point is to know at all times who qualifies as your own unique set of Top 100 and Strategic 100 list members. Even if you never use Contact Marketing as part of your strategy, it is critical to know who these people are and find ways to address them.

Your Top 100, Strategic 100, and Engagement 100 Lists

The process of defining the group of people who can most effectively multiply your efforts will reflect your mission. If you are a sales rep, your focus should always be establishing new high-value client relationships. If your employer had ten people doing this job, they'd be producing the results of a hundred typical reps, because the focus is always on addressing the people who can compound their efforts. If you become the kind of rep who regularly engages big-value companies at the highest levels, able to connect with anyone you need to, your value to your company also multiplies.

As a sales rep, you need to have a clearly defined Top 100 list. The list may not contain 100 people; it may be fewer. But it should never exceed that number. Keeping it at or less than 100 members allows you to focus on the greatest multipliers on the list. It also keeps the process affordable.

C-level executives and company owners should also engage in a contact strategy, but their mission is a bit more complex. Part of a CEO's job is to be plugged in. Their connections have a lot to do with their value to the enterprise. They should know enough of the right people to pick up the phone and quickly solve a problem or capture an opportunity. They should have allies, supporters, and followers everywhere. This speeds progress by making strategic movement easier. It connects them with the people who can open doors or help them in their critical mission of seeing where markets, tastes, trends, and other controlling factors are headed and how they can capitalize on them. And all C-suite members and business owners should never forget their duty to sell for their companies.

So they must construct a carefully composed Strategic 100 list. Their Contact Campaigns should also reflect their elevated mission. Whatever they do to connect should feel *presidential*. Careful attention should be paid to every detail, to communicate how special it is to be on the sender's Strategic 100 list. Notes should be written by hand on bespoke engraved cards or letterhead. Branding should be conspicuously tasteful or even absent. At this level, it's not about branding; it's about connecting, human to human, peer to peer. And the enterprise will be all the stronger for it.

In addition to addressing your Top 100 and Strategic 100 lists, there should be an Engagement 100 list. Who are the people who are already contributing to the company's sales and market standing? Who are the nonpaid champions of your brand who promote you and convince others to flock to your offerings? Who are the top 100 people already multiplying your efforts out there in the marketplace? Who are your top clients who are always telling others about you and your company? They should all be addressed in your Contact Marketing strategy, too.

At the sales rep level, it makes sense to continue to thank your best clients, but you should also be serving as a trusted source of intelligence. Include gift baskets in your engagement strategy if you must, but your efforts would be better spent helping the client "see." The more you help them succeed, the more successful you will be.

On the strategic level, C-level execs and company owners should be constantly engaged with their top clients and influencers. Similarly, their engagement strategy should be built around providing value, but that value can also come in many forms. Send articles that provide helpful information, but keep in mind, people at the top levels already have access to a lot of information. The real worth of your engagement strategy should stem from providing specific value to the members of your list. Are you writing articles for your blog? Find ways to feature your important contacts in your articles. Interview them, get to know them. Include them at events as fellow speakers. Watch for ways to pass along value. Better yet, engage a Contact Marketing agency to constantly percolate fresh ideas, approaches, and opportunities. It'll be well worth the effort and investment.

Get to Know This List

It's clear that even if you don't intend to use Contact Marketing in your company's growth strategy, it's critical to have a clear sense of who the people, companies, and organizations are that can transform your business or career. Whether it's a Top 100 or Strategic 100 list, these are the people who represent the quickest path to your ultimate success.

But how do you get to know them better, before you know them at all? We'll examine that in the next chapter, where we'll look at techniques for finding all sorts of useful information to discover the right people and assemble their dossiers. Many of the people on your list will become some of the most important people in your life. So take the time to get to know them, and more importantly, get to know how you can provide value to their lives, businesses, and organizations.

At the start of this chapter, I mentioned mixing a bit of mischief into the list of people you'll contact. I'd like to share my own most vivid example. Some years ago, I decided I wanted to make a movie based on my high school fantasy of meeting one of those beautiful Scandinavian women I'd seen in movies, magazines, and commercials. Never having made a movie, I figured my first steps would be to hire a screenwriter and take a video camera to one of those countries, get footage of the people and the place, and maybe interview a few models and actresses. The footage would serve as the basis of a pitch video for the film, and it would give me a sense of whether I had imagined it all correctly.

So I hired Maurice Richlin, the Oscar-winning writer who wrote the original *Pink Panther* screenplay, to do a story treatment, then booked tickets to Stockholm. But as I prepared to take my trip, I happened to spot a model in a magazine, and I was transfixed. "If I was going on this fantasy for real, this is the woman I would bring home," I thought. So I raced to find out who she was and how to contact her. Are you starting to see the relevance of my story?

Through the magazine, I connected with the photographer, who put me in touch with her. She lived in Copenhagen, so I changed my booking and, as it turned out, ended up meeting my future wife. Having a legitimate reason for getting in touch, and a request to interview my target contact, is what made this happen. And I discovered that interviewing important people is a powerful form of Contact Campaigns.

I've always been mischievous, which has been a critical part of how I build a Top 100 list that, along with direct sales and business development opportunities, always contains a few sparkles of intrigue and "impossibility." Assembling your list in that same spirit will make this a life-transforming change in how you work. After all, you're about to have the ability to reach virtually anyone. It's very powerful, but only if you aim it carefully to take you where you want to go.

Points to Remember

- ✔ Contact Marketing is a powerful tool, but only if directed to the right people.

- ✔ You must give careful consideration to who goes on your Top 100 and Strategic 100 lists.

- ✔ Members of your lists are the people who can multiply your efforts, either with bigger sales or access to bigger opportunities.

- ✔ Your Top 100 list should address your highest-value sales prospects.

- ✔ Your Strategic 100 list should cover the people who can help your enterprise and market stature grow.

- ✔ Your Contact Marketing strategy should also include an Engagement 100 list of your top 100 current clients and brand champions.

✔   The lists can contain fewer members, but never more than 100 at a time.

✔   Your lists will constantly change as you connect with new contacts and as your priorities shift.

✔   Contact Marketing is not just for sales reps; it's also critical for CEOs, C-level executives, and company owners.

✔   It is vitally important to get to know the members of your lists and find ways to constantly provide them with extraordinary value.

"So far, our search for intelligent life has turned up a couple of false alarms and someone named Bob from New Jersey . . ."

CHAPTER 6

Getting to Know Your Targets

We're on a mission to change your life through your new ability to reach virtually anyone. In the previous chapter, we started the process by identifying which VIPs belong on your list. Please devote a lot of thought to whom those lucky 100 will be, but move confidently, knowing your list can and will constantly change as you move through the process, pick up new clients, strike new deals, and establish your most critical new relationships. Do an artful job of assembling the best possible team of target contacts.

Fortunately, we live in the Information Age, a time when all sorts of intelligence sources are literally at our fingertips. Most of these sources are free, some require a fee, and some, while intending to charge for their service, leave the door open to distributing critical information at no cost.

This is important for many reasons. Practitioners of Sales 2.0 and Social Selling have pronounced utterly and completely dead the days of walking blindly into a prospect's office, knowing nothing of what they do, what their challenges are, what their passions and hobbies are, and how those all fit together to form a composite. There is no excuse for not knowing who you're calling on, what currently has their attention, and how you fit in terms of the value you can deliver. If you don't know those things, you don't belong in your target prospect's life; you haven't earned a few minutes of their time.

Fortunately, the solution is an easy one. Do your homework. Prepare a dossier on each of your contact targets. Engage them on social media. Get to know them before you get to know them.

Research before Reaching Out

When I add new people to my list, I start by setting up a spreadsheet. I need all of their contact information at hand when I start campaigning, so it starts with the basics. What is the correct spelling of their first and last names? What are their actual titles? What is the proper spelling and full name of their company? What are the delivery and mailing addresses for their companies? Phone numbers? Email address? What are their social media account names? Get it all and get it absolutely right, because it will be the foundation of your Contact Campaign.

Next, I want know everything I can about each contact target as a person. I use two primary tools for this: Web search and the Charlie app. A quick search usually yields an amazing amount of information about the prospect's company and career. Their LinkedIn profile often shows up at the top of search results. Visit their page, take notes about where they attended college and grad school, where they worked before, and how they got to where they are now. If they have a profile picture, download it and label it with their name, and file it for future use.

Search for news about each target. This is where you start to get a sense of what their current challenges and successes are, and where their focus is. *Edgy Conversations* author and *Dan Waldschmidt Blog* author Dan Waldschmidt does this with the precision of a warrior, scouring the daily news for stories of missed earnings projections and business leaders in trouble. In addition to writing his blog, Waldschmidt is a top-ranked turnaround specialist, and this is his process for finding new members of his Top 100 list on a daily basis.

Connect with each target on social media. LinkedIn is wonderful for gaining a résumé-based look at the person, and for seeing who their connections are. Twitter is where you'll see what the target is talking about, what has their attention, what they care about, and how you can craft your approach. Facebook, Google+, and Pinterest tend to show in pictures what they're passionate about, what their hobbies are, and more.

> "
> *The depth of information you will need is also determined by your Contact Campaign approach. Some require highly detailed and personalized information for each individual, whereas others may not....It's worth the effort to know each of these people before making the approach, because they're people, and this is about creating human-to-human connections.*
> "

The depth of information you will need is also determined by your Contact Campaign approach. Some require highly detailed and personalized information for each individual, whereas others may not.

I'm working with a client who provides Internet security services at a time when it seems like the entire country is under a hack attack.

When data breaches occur, they are devastating to the brand. Target, Home Depot, big banks, and more—it seems there is a new story every day about yet another data breach. When Target suffered its breach, the company's profits diminished by 46 percent almost overnight.[2]

It doesn't take a lot of research to know that chief information officers and chief information security officers are all looking nervously over their shoulders, lest they find their company in the news next, the subject of a new data-breach exposé.

So our approach to these prospects can be standardized, in that we're going to be talking about the same risk of data breach to all of them. We know they don't want to be in the news, at least not that kind of news, and we know my client has the solution. When my client's reps come knocking on their doors, we already know what the CIO's focus is, and it has nothing to do with their hobbies or favorite causes. It's their survival.

Still, it's worth the effort to know each of these people before making the approach, because they're people, and this is about creating human-to-human connections.

Sometimes, you will find that a given target has a common name or doesn't participate in social media. That complicates your mission, but there are still ways to get what you need. Even doing simple things like bundling the person's name with their company name, or company name and title, in a web search can produce useful results.

This may be the most tedious part of the Contact Marketing mission, but it is crucial to get it right. Just like the foundation of a house, nothing is right if its footing isn't sturdy and level.

Helpful Intel Sources

Gathering your intelligence is generally not hard. You'll bounce around a bit from resource to resource at times, but you'll find this has been made easy by the tools listed next.

Google

By "Google," I mean any Internet search tool; Google and Bing are my favorites. Everyone knows what this is by now, but as I just described, sometimes it's a bit challenging to locate the right person. From your search, you should be able to get all the basic contact information: the correct spelling of their name, their title, the company name, its mailing and physical addresses, and more. You may even find a good, clean headshot you can use in your Contact Campaign. Grab what you can and keep it in an organized file system for easy retrieval. Use your Google search to find the other resources mentioned next.

LinkedIn

You should be able to locate virtually anyone's LinkedIn profile among the initial results of your Google search, or by visiting LinkedIn directly. When you locate the target's profile, it's okay to visit, but I wouldn't say it's a good idea to get in touch just yet, unless you have been referred by someone the target executive knows. You should take a look at who you may know in common, which LinkedIn displays to the right of the person's profile page. Make note of the things they have included in their profile; this gives you a quick, general snapshot of their current and past titles, responsibilities, and work history. Because of the rather static nature of profiles on this platform, you may or may not find entirely up-to-date information, but it's a good place to start and a useful tool as you reach out in your Contact Campaign.

Twitter

If you use Twitter already, you know this will yield a wide mix of factors, from personal peeves to favorite causes to retweeted articles the VIP prospects found useful. Pay close attention to those; they're a gateway into the mind-set of the target executive. Connecting via Twitter is a much less formal action than it is with LinkedIn, so it's a good idea to follow them right away. That puts you in their network with a constant feed of their tweets and gives you a chance to start showing up in a nonthreatening way, by retweeting and favoriting their tweets. More on this later; just know this should be one of your primary tools for getting to know and connect with your targets, starting in the pre-contact phase.

Hoover's

This is an old-guard corporate data service, and it's very useful for gathering basic and correct contact information. The free part of their site shows a company's full name and headquarters address with great reliability. If you're inclined, you can go much further behind their paywall, where you can pick up names of key executives and employees, email addresses, and titles. If I'm looking for their help, I'll Google the company's name along with the words, "corporate headquarters hoovers." That always returns the result I'm looking for, which is the company's main profile page on Hoover's.

Data.com, Jigsaw.com, and Others

These are paid information services, also excellent, and also worth mentioning if you have the budget for their use. But they tend not to have the kind of basic information in front of their paywalls that Hoover's does.

Charlie

This is an interesting intel source, because it does the work for you, but only for the people already on your calendar. If you have a call set up in your Google or other calendars, the Charlie app scours the Web and reports to you the day of the meeting with an entire dossier on your contact target. The information includes a description of the person in their own words, pulled from one of their profiles, and continues with relevant mentions in the media. It's a wonderful tool that makes getting to know your target simple and easy.

WHOIS

There is a trend among some businesses to obscure their contact information on their websites. If you find yourself unable to locate an address or even the name of a company owner, this information is sometimes available in a WHOIS search. You won't do this if you're targeting a *Fortune* 500 or even an *Inc.* 5000 company, because you won't find relevant information on C-level executives, but you might find contact info for the owners of private companies. Netsol.com, GoDaddy.com, and other domain registrars all have a WHOIS link on their main pages and it's easy to use. Sometimes the registration information for the domain holder is obscured by a privacy service. In that case, I've sometimes had luck using Geektools.com's WHOIS search, which seems to be a bit more robust than the others.

The Target Executive's Website

Websites are not uniform, so you will find some are helpful, while others are a waste of time. The best examples will feature an "Executive Team" section, which often includes a profile picture, bio, and description of their responsibilities, along with their proper title and the correct spelling of their names. If you're not targeting the actual CEO of the company, it's still a good idea to gather intel on the top executive and other possible stakeholders while in that section. Knowing who the contact's boss, colleagues, and team members are will be useful as you devise your approach.

Who Are They as People?

As you work your way through this roster-building portion of your contact mission, I want you to realize this is not just some dull task you must plow through to get to the good stuff. This is the part where you build the vision for your future. Choosing the people you will focus your campaign upon is much like choosing the ingredients of a spectacular new recipe for the next version of your life.

So as you place VIPs on your list, do it with great care. Add the top officers of some of the companies you could only dream of working with before. Build a stellar roster of clients and strategic partners. But then add a few people who bring something completely unexpected to the mix, people who will add exciting new dimensions to your life.

When I started my company, I realized I needed to broaden my offer to include cartoons by multiple sources, so I built a stable of some of the most famous cartoonists in the world. Gahan Wilson, Leo Cullum, Eldon Dedini, Bob Mankoff, and Arnold Levin weren't just business associates; they were (and are) some of my greatest heroes. Getting to work with them, getting to call them my friends, greatly added to my enjoyment of my career through the years. And Contact Marketing helped me connect with each of them.

If you choose your Top 100 or Strategic 100 list members carefully, you will find your life expanding in delightfully unexpected ways as well. Along the way, you will make new lifelong friends and assemble deals that would have been impossible without the outreach you'll perform through your Contact Marketing efforts.

This only works if you carefully consider who goes on the list, and who they are as people. Your Contact Marketing efforts won't create the effect you seek if you don't do a thorough job getting to know everything you can about your VIP prospects before reaching out.

These are *your* VIPs. They're your new success team. The more you get to know them prior to contact, the more effective you will be in every respect.

POINTS TO REMEMBER

✔ It is critical to get to know your contact targets before reaching out.

✔ It is no longer viable to show up at a prospect's office with no clear idea of what they do, what's important to them, what has their current focus, or how you can provide value.

✔ Finding information is easy, thanks to the Internet and social media.

✔ It is important to use the tools at your disposal to gather as much information as you can, starting with basic contact details.

✔ Some social media contact should be initiated during your pre-contact research phase; some should not.

✔ Gathering preliminary intel on your contact targets is as fundamental and critical as building a sturdy, true foundation for your home; without it, nothing will be right.

✔ The Internet is your gateway to several crucial intel sources, most of which are free.

✔ The VIPs on your list are *your* VIPs, based on their importance and relevance to *your* goals.

✔ Getting to know your contact targets as people is important, because your goal is to establish real, substantial, and vital relationships with them.

✔ Getting to know them beforehand is also critical because you may only get one quick shot at connecting with them.

SECTION II

CONTACT CAMPAIGN TACTICS & METHODS

"Do you sell remote-control golf balls?"

CHAPTER 7

Contact Campaign Methods and Tactics

In the Introduction, I told you the story of how I became a Contact Marketer, and what eventually inspired me to write this book. Through the use of my cartoons, I discovered I could connect with virtually anyone. But the more I thought about it, the more I realized there had to be many others out there facing the same challenge, producing similar kinds of solutions to break through.

The more I reached out, the more amazed I became. The Contact Marketing solutions I discovered were astounding in their brilliance, audacity, and ingenuity. I discovered I wasn't alone in producing 100 percent response rates and ROI figures in the tens of thousands of percent.

When I decided I had to write a book about Contact Marketing, it was obvious it had to be an inclusive and collaborative effort. So I set out to gather the greatest assemblage of brilliant Contact Marketing ideas I could find. To do that, I interviewed many of today's top thought leaders in sales, who generously shared their brilliant concepts. Sometimes, they'd start the interview by saying, "I don't do anything particularly clever," and then reveal yet another ingenious method for reaching VIPs.

One comment I heard consistently, something I wholeheartedly agree with, is that the use of sales stunts is a losing proposition. To be fair, some of these do create contact with some very difficult-to-reach folks. Some even generated sales.

But I believe whatever you do to reach these people reflects your brand, and I certainly would not want a stunt to define who I am or what I'm capable of delivering. So while I hold some admiration for the tactics involved in sales stunts, I am resolute that they have no place in Contact Marketing.

What follows in this section could be thought of as the core of what Contact Marketing is, but that would be a mistake. I don't want you to approach this chapter as a menu of ideas to quickly deplete. They are presented not to suggest that you copy what these Contact Marketers have done, but to let their creativity inspire you to come up with your own unique solutions. As with any form of marketing, the point is not to copy what someone else has executed, but to allow the best of what's been done to motivate you to tell your own, unique story in your own, extraordinary way.

Ideas for Your Inspiration, Not Imitation

Remember the "Got Milk?" ad campaign from the early nineties? It was obviously a clever campaign, and when it appeared, it caused a sensation; drinking milk became cool, and it significantly increased milk sales. If you were studying advertising for the first time, you might conclude that if you cloned this slogan with your own product substituted for "Milk," you'd have the makings of a winning campaign yourself. But, when you see billboards, T-shirts, and trucks emblazoned with slogans of, "Got Junk?", "Got Oranges?", and "Got Refrigerators?" how clever do these marketers seem to you?

To me, this approach says, "We're unoriginal, this is the best we could come up with." How much room is there in the marketplace for endless takes on "Got [fill in the blank?]"? None. Imitation may be the sincerest form of flattery, but it is no way to build your own unique brand and voice.

I also want to impress upon you that this list is in no way complete. It's just a survey of what has been happening out there, a snapshot, a beginning. At the end of this book, I provide information on how you can reach me to share your own Contact Marketing experiences and solutions. The best way to do that is to tune in to Contact Marketing Radio (Thursdays at 10 A.M. PST/1 P.M. EST on ContactMarketing.Agency [http://ow.ly/QrK8L], archived on iTunes), my weekly Internet radio show and podcast, which continues this process of discovery. I hope you'll join in the discussion and fun.

> " *Imitation may be the sincerest form of flattery, but it is no way to build your own unique brand and voice.* "

Campaign Costs Vary

For all my talk about the ingenuity and audacity of the methods you're about to read, the metrics are what may be most astounding about Contact Campaigns. Simply looking at the cost per effort figures associated with each solution is a testament to how broad the spectrum of thinking behind them is.

It's wonderful that many of these techniques have no associated cost, other than a bit of your time. *It means Contact Marketing is within anyone's grasp.* That, again, is unlike virtually any other form of marketing, because really, none of that is free. It certainly complicates ROI calculations, too, because how do you get a meaningful number from dividing by zero? But all that means is that something extraordinary is taking place if you're using zero-cost tactics to produce lots of income. We'll just have to somehow grapple with ROI figures of "infinity" and wear a Cheshire Cat grin.

> *You're about to gain a significantly unfair advantage in your marketplace. And the good news is, you can spend whatever you want to get there.*

Still, the most memorable campaigns are the ones that involve at least some spending, sometimes what would seem like a scary amount per contact. This should be tempered with an understanding of what each VIP contact is worth. If you're trying to sell your company for millions of dollars, spending $10,000 to engage the right buyer or stimulate a buying frenzy among competitors is worth every penny—which is exactly what happened with one of the techniques you will read about in the pages ahead.

You're about to gain a significantly unfair advantage in your marketplace. And the good news is, you can spend whatever you want to get there.

My Own Personalized Cartoon Method

My personalized cartoons were what got me started as a Contact Marketer, so I want to share my method with you first. Again, when I was starting my career, I wanted to combine the stunning effect of cartoons with direct marketing, and I wanted to work with the biggest, most prestigious clients I could find. That meant the big magazine and newspaper publishers: Time Inc., *The Wall Street Journal*, Condé Nast, *Forbes*, and so forth.

My first Contact Campaign consisted of an 8" × 10" print of a cartoon, with the caption personalized using the names of each recipient. That was accompanied by a letter explaining what I'd just accomplished for my first two clients, and a suggestion that we put it to the test for their titles. The campaign launched my business; I broke through to *all* of the publishers and *all* of them became clients. It was worth millions of dollars to me, and it all started with a campaign I spent less than $100 to produce and mail.

Over the years, that original concept has morphed and evolved. I tried cartoons in lots of formats, including framed prints, suitable-for-framing prints, odd-sized outer envelopes framed in special corrugated cardboard packaging, and more. The format that has emerged as my favorite is what I call BigBoards. These are 18" × 24" × ¼" foam core boards that use digital indoor signage technology to produce what is essentially a giant postcard, which is then delivered by courier.

On the front, the BigBoards feature a cartoon, with the caption personalized using the name of the target executive. The rear panel includes a message from the sender to the recipient, proposing a meeting and explaining why it's worthy of the CEO's consideration. The panel also includes the sender's branding, the recipient's address, and an inset showing the hold-back device. (Hold-back devices are covered further in Chapter 14.) In my case, that device is usually an autographed copy of my cartoon book, *Big Fat Beautiful Head*, offered as an incentive for agreeing to the meeting.

The BigBoards are part of a larger system, which includes a series of cards, also featuring personalized cartoons. These are used to thank and engage executive assistants, and for various follow-up applications as the contacts progress.

I've found that the cartoons allow a very special set of advantages in my Contact Campaigns. If I am the sender, I'm able to call the target executive's assistant and explain that I'm one of *The Wall Street Journal* cartoonists, and I am sending a print of one of my cartoons about their boss. That usually gets them very excited and eager to participate.

When the BigBoard arrives, it often sparks an excited reception by the target contact. I've heard stories of company presidents walking around the office, showing off their cartoon boards, even taking selfies with them, then dispatching the photos to the sender to express their elation and gratitude.

One of the truly unique benefits of this approach is that cartoons are always about something. They're not just some goofy little drawing; they are an expression of deep truth. When the recipient sees it, the effect I'm looking for is a smile and an immediate, "Yes, that is so cool, that is so true." They probably don't even realize that I have already gotten them to agree with my central point for reaching out.

But I need to offer a word of caution. Cartoons are not easy to create and even more difficult to properly target. Without fail, every initial conversation I have with new clients starts with, "Can we change the caption?" Or, "How do we get our brand in there?" Injecting your brand into a cartoon ensures failure, because it disables the gag and strips away any personal value to the recipient. The trick is to steer the choice of cartoon based on the truth it reveals, and how that relates to the issue you want to address with the recipient.

I once created a campaign for *Outdoor Life*, a magazine about hunting and fishing. *The New Yorker* cartoonist and friend Leo Cullum created a brilliant cartoon showing two fishermen on a dock, one holding an enormous fish in his arms, the other remarking, *"That looks like the one ((insert recipient's name)) threw back."* The response was amazing; we nearly doubled the paid orders the earlier control had produced. And we never mentioned anything about *Outdoor Life*, subscribing, or the savings off the newsstand price. If we had, the piece would have failed.

If you'd like to explore the use of cartoons in marketing and other business missions, you will find my earlier book, *Drawing Attention*, quite useful. It contains the collective wisdom of thirty years and millions of dollars' worth of utterly unique test experience, and reveals everything you need to know about using these amazing engagement devices in your own campaigns.

For now, I'll leave you with one final observation about the cartoon BigBoards. Among the many techniques contained in the following sections, I am still amazed at the staying power of the cartoon-based contact pieces. They're too big to file away and too valuable to throw away. They're also too big to easily place somewhere in the office, so they often end up sitting on the executive's credenza, cocked to one side because there just wasn't enough clear space. From there, they remain on display indefinitely, where they'll often spark conversations among the CEO's visitors. "Hey, where'd you get that, what is it?" is enough to have the VIP recount your story over and over again. It amounts to a totally unfair advantage for you as a marketer.

But enough about my own techniques. Let's get to the good stuff, the wonderful Contact Campaign secrets shared by the many experts interviewed for this book. What follows are four chapters and twenty Contact Campaign types. As you read through these, you may notice that Contact Campaigns are not easily confined to one category or another. Many involve elements of several categories. Some cost little to nothing, others a lot. There are gifts and events and full-page ads in *The Wall Street Journal*, even a live carrier pigeon dropped off at a target executive's lobby to arrange a lunch meeting.

Simply keep in mind, as you read through this treasure of ideas, that there are many ways to achieve your goal of breaking through, and that your own solution should be something completely different and unique.

Points to Remember

✔   The methods described in this section are not meant simply to be copied, but to inspire you to create your own, unique Contact Marketing solutions.

✔ They are gathered from interviews with the top sales thought leaders throughout the world.

✔ While some sales stunts may be effective in the short run, they have no place in Contact Marketing and ultimately reflect poorly on your brand.

✔ The techniques described in the following chapters are simply a snapshot of what Contact Marketers have done to break through to VIP contacts; there's much more to be discovered.

✔ The range of costs per contact—$0 to $10,000—reflects the expansive range of thinking behind the Contact Campaign techniques presented here.

✔ My own contact techniques consist of personalized cartoons with unique, oversized formats such as the 18" × 24" × ¼" foam core BigBoards that are delivered to their intended targets via courier.

✔ One of the great aspects of using cartoons and the BigBoard format is that they tend to be kept as career heirlooms in the recipients' offices for years to come, giving this technique exceptional staying power.

✔ Cartoons are not goofy drawings; they're expressions of truth. When the recipient laughs and says, "That's so true," you have already warmed the contact and have them agreeing with your key premise.

✔ It is never a good idea to inject your brand, offer, or any other aspect of your own identity into the cartoon; it needs to focus solely on the identity of the recipient.

"Let's change the way we think."

CHAPTER 8

Gifts and Visual Metaphors

In this first category, we examine several forms of gifts used as the basis of Contact Campaigns. Gifts are a natural solution because they so often make the recipients feel excited. But they must be carefully planned; some VIPs aren't allowed to accept gifts over a certain value. For example, when I furnished a print of one of my cartoons to Ben Bernanke, former chairman of the Federal Reserve, we had to make sure its value did not exceed $20.

Private-sector executives generally have less stringent rules about accepting gifts, but can become suspicious if the offering seems simply like a bribe. You might conclude that cheaper is better, but even that is not a reliable rule to follow. Some gifts can be quite expensive and enormously effective. As with personal gift-giving, it is the thought that counts most, and in your Contact Campaign, you must carefully consider the concept and message behind the offering. Let's take a look.

Category #1: Art, Humor, and Film

Estimated cost per contact: $1 to $500

As I discovered in the interviews for this book, cartoons have played a major role in many of the thought leaders' Contact Campaigns as well. Dave Stein, author of *How Winners Sell* and a columnist for *Sales & Marketing Management* magazine, was lucky enough to have met *The New Yorker* cartoonist Mick Stevens one day, while walking on the beach on Martha's Vineyard. The two hit it off and Stein ended up using a lot of Mick's work in presentations and as Contact Campaigns. As Stein points out, "We want the customer warmed up by the time we get there and humor does that."

Author Orvel Ray Wilson has also employed my personalized cartoon trick, using a cartoon he licensed from The Cartoon Bank. He notes, "Endorphins are released in the brain from laughter." Again, just don't give in to the temptation of changing the caption to highlight your brand. As I've mentioned, injecting brand into a cartoon kills the humor and often removes the meaning of the gag. The best path is to start with a cartoon that already makes a point you can amplify in your accompanying message.

Humor comes in many forms. Blogger Dave Brock says he occasionally uses Dr. Seuss's book *Green Eggs and Ham* to break through to his VIP prospects. "It's one of the best books on selling there is," he explains, "because in the first half, Sam-I-am is unsuccessful, but in the second half he changes his approach and succeeds."

Brock includes a personal letter with the opening, "Hello, I'm Dave-I-am." The letter continues with a brief, Seuss-style poem about why they should meet. When he calls, he identifies himself as "Dave-I-am," which often causes them to laugh. It humanizes Brock to the assistant and target executive, making the call considerably more productive. Dr. Seuss may not be your idea of sophisticated humor, but the message from the book, even though it's intended for children, is undeniable and leads to discussions about how Brock can produce the same kinds of transformations in the VIP contact's sales team.

The category of presented art certainly is not limited to cartoons. *Smart Prospecting That Works Every Time!* author Michael Krause suggests having a professional photographer snap a portrait of something important to the prospect, then present it as framed art. He tells the story of a landscape photographer who made the rounds in his city, presenting beautiful framed portraits to commercial property owners of their buildings as a way to break through for new business.

Personalization is a key element in most uses of art as Contact Campaigns, which *The Wall Street Journal* has used to great effect to support its ad sales operation. The publication is famous for the hand-drawn, engraved-style portraits used in its editorial coverage. Only a handful of artists are employed exclusively by *The Journal* for this purpose, and when they really want

> "
> *Personalization is a key element in most uses of art as Contact Campaigns.*
> "

to get an advertiser's attention, they have used framed, engraved-style portraits of their target executives to great effect.

Not everyone can draw in that style, but I have discovered a simple, inexpensive method for producing *The Wall Street Journal*–like portraits, using a four-dollar Photoshop plug-in. Since most people have profile pictures posted as part of their social media accounts, finding source material is quite easy. Once captured, the "Super Engraver" action set (a Photoshop script of actions within the program to produce the effect) from creativemarket.com will render the photo in a very similar style. These can then be produced as framed portraits, but I prefer a more mischievous approach: They can also be used to produce a dummy story that looks like it came right off the pages of *The Journal*. Frame that, or use it as card art. Either way, it's an undeniable attention-getter.

The most important factor when giving art of any kind, which is true of all gifts used as Contact Campaigns, is to follow a *theme* to support the *value* you plan to bring to your Top 100 VIP list members. Without that focus, the art is meaningless and the campaign will fail.

Movie DVDs can form the basis of powerful Contact Campaigns, in that they usually present compelling stories and engaging characters who are always involved in some sort of transition in their lives. The stories always seem to include an element of conflict, which motivates us as humans to respond in some way that resolves the plot.

These story elements can combine to prompt a target contact to share a deep understanding of what you hope to do for them and why. The challenge is to find the right film that imparts precisely the message you want to convey.

Although you can't change the films, they provide plenty of opportunities for messaging within your campaign. Like cartoons, the stories define obvious themes you can pick up in your letter copy. When I send copies of the movie *Contact*, I include a greeting card with a personalized cartoon and handwritten message inside. The cartoon, which appears at the start of Chapter 6 in this book, shows a group of scientists standing somewhere in the desert among several radio dishes. One of the scientists is telling the others, "So far, our search for intelligent life has turned up a couple of false alarms and someone named Bob from New Jersey," and as you know by now, "Bob" and "New Jersey" are placeholders for any recipients' name and home state.

The card briefly explains why they're receiving the DVD. But the DVD packaging itself is another opportunity to customize the messaging to your campaign. Most come in a shrink-wrapped plastic box, which, when opened, reveals several promotional flyers for other movies and merchandise. Take those out, substitute your own branded elements, and reseal the case to complete the effect of having sent what ends up looking like a customized version of the movie.

CartoonLink BigBoards

These are my Contact Campaign system, based the use of my "CartoonLink" image bank of more than a thousand personalized cartoons on 18" × 24" × ¼" foam core BigBoards delivered via FedEx or UPS. Includes additional elements for executive assistants and other stakeholders, plus creative, training, and coaching.

http://www.cartoonlink.com; **$500 per contact, membership required**

The Cartoon Bank

Repository of all the cartoons published in *The New Yorker*, plus 40,000 or so that weren't. Roughly 120,000 cartoons are available for license or as various gifts.

http://www.cartoonbank.com;
$24.95 and up for a simple license or finished merchandise

CreativeMarket

Super Engraver action set for use with Adobe Photoshop. Use it on any photograph to produce a *Wall Street Journal*–style engraved rendering.

https://creativemarket.com/DesignBeagle/12097-Super-Engraver; **$8**

Office Depot/OfficeMax/Staples Impress

If you have custom art to print, Office Depot/OfficeMax/Staples has a surprisingly easy and inexpensive option. Their Impress desk at the back of most store locations can print digital art on various substrates and products, including mugs, mouse pads, and stretched-canvas prints ready for hanging on your target executives' walls.

http://www.officedepot.com/a/design-print-and-ship;
$15 to $100

Metacritic

Metacritic maintains a database of virtually all movies released on home-view (DVD and Blu-ray) formats, along with a user scoring system to provide viewer ratings of each film. A helpful resource to search for the right film for your campaign.

http://www.metacritic.com; **free**

Redbox, Moviefone, Fandango

Find updated selections of the latest movies released on DVD and Blu-ray on these companies' sites. They index movies by genre, popularity, and release date. If you only want to consider recent popular releases, they're the ideal places to search for that perfect title.

http://www.redbox.com, http://www.moviefone.com,
http://www.fandango.com; **free**

Amazon, Walmart, Movies Unlimited

Purchase most DVD and Blu-ray titles on Amazon or Walmart. Check out Movies Unlimited for hard-to-find, classic films.

http://www.amazon.com, http://www.walmart.com,
http://www.moviesunlimited.com; **$9 and up**

Category #2: Gifts & Re-Gifts

Estimated cost per contact: $50–$1,000

The giving of gifts is a broad subject and there is already a well-established industry based on corporate gift-giving. So why is this claimed as part of Contact Marketing? Because it is a great way to get someone's attention, which is the core of the Contact Marketing mission.

Included in this section are a fascinating range of gifts and "re-gifts," gifts given as something to be given away by the target executive to others. In fact, many of the gift concepts that follow focus not just on the recipient, but on the people around them.

John Ruhlin, founder of the Ruhlin Group, is a master at this, and his Contact Campaign techniques certainly involve a good measure of audacity. One of his favorite methods for reaching VIPs starts with a card delivered through the mail, informing the target that someone has gifted a $150 custom-fit shirt, and they will be contacted shortly by a clothier. His clothier arranges a time for the fitting, then shows up with fabric samples and takes the necessary measurements. Naturally, the target executive is full of questions—who sent this and why? The clothier explains it's being sent by Ruhlin, but she's not here to tell him why—she's just here to fit him for the shirt.

Two weeks later, the shirt arrives with a note from John explaining, "It's not about function, it's about fit, and I think we may be a good fit for you. Let's have a talk about it." As author Tom Searcy explains, "The technique creates an opportunity not only to talk, but to establish a strong personal brand before the contact ever takes place." Ruhlin says, "If I don't get a call, I have an open door to connect, even if it's just to ask how the shirt fits."

Ruhlin believes personalization is the key to success with gifts as Contact Campaign devices. His company is also the largest sales producer for Cutco knives, which he uses as gift campaigns as well. He's able to have the knives laser-engraved with the recipient's logo and often turns them into a serial gift; he starts with the knife block containing a few knives, then sends the missing knives over a few weeks' period. "What's so ingenious about this is that the CEO's spouse becomes part of the campaign," says Searcy, "so the sender creates allies around the target executive."

When Bridget Gleason was Yesware's vice president of sales, she had a different take. She preferred to give gifts that could be shared in the office or with select members of the target executive's team. In an earlier phase of her career as a sales consultant, she often used this technique to break through. "I'd send a half a dozen coffee cups with the words 'Top Producer' silkscreened in big bold letters," she told me, "and they'd always get me through to my targeted executive." The accompanying letter explained they were intended as awards to be given to the contact's top sales performer each month. Meanwhile, she made her pitch to do a whole lot more than the cups could to help push sales performance up, up, up.

Do YOU Mean Business? author and *Sales Aerobics for Engineers* blog author Babette Ten Haken advises giving gifts if a client has done something positive, but warns that some people are embarrassed by receiving gifts. "Gifts tend to embarrass engineers and IT people," she reports. Still, even the smallest gift can make a difference and they certainly don't have to be expensive. They just have to project meaning.

Blogger Dave Brock recalls the story of a top saleswoman who'd been trying to break through to a certain CIO for a long time, but kept coming up with a fistful of excuses instead. After being told repeatedly, "I don't have time to meet with you, even for lunch," she sent a pizza one day with a note saying, "I'm worried about you, would you like to have a pizza sometime with me?" That gift, while obviously inexpensive, was a significant humanizing gesture, which finally helped her break through.

Sales blogger and trainer Tony Cole tells a similar story of less expense equaling big results. The district president of KeyBank in Cincinnati came up with a list of 100 companies he wanted to break through to and devised what he termed the "Flower Power Campaign." The campaign consisted of twenty flower arrangements at a time, sent to target company owners on his list, along with his business card. He followed up with a call asking, "Is there a nice arrangement of flowers on your desk?" The campaign consistently netted a 20 percent or greater penetration.

The Hacker Group founder Bob Hacker reports an almost inconceivable result from one of his agency's Contact Campaigns. Getting key background details was critical for the campaign, as they noticed all of their VIP list members happened to have offices near baseball stadiums. The resulting campaign consisted of a set of 125 invitations to sit in box seats with company officials, which produced not only a 126 percent response rate, but a 6,000 percent ROI. How was that possible? It turned out the invitations were so treasured, many of the targeted executives brought their bosses along—the very people you're ultimately wanting to reach!

While there might be conflicting advice among Contact Marketers regarding cost, it is clear the old adage holds true for gifts used as the basis of a Contact Campaign: It's clearly the thought behind the gift that counts.

Category #3: Half of a Gift

Estimated cost per contact: $40 to $4,000+

An interesting variation on the theme of gift-giving as Contact Campaign is the idea of giving just half of the gift up front, with the promise of the other half when the requested connection takes place. I'm a little wary of this approach, but it certainly has merit. The trouble is, what happens if the incentive outshines the value you hope to present to the target executive?

Author Michael Krause shares a familiar tactic that came up often in my research: sending a remote-control model Ferrari without the control device. The gift is accompanied with a letter explaining that the missing element will be delivered when the proposed meeting takes place. Krause believes this approach may work best around the Christmas holidays, but others say it's valid at any point on the calendar.

The Fundamentals of Business-to-Business Sales and Marketing author John Coe reports that this approach works well, but cautions that it can also backfire. He's heard of more than one instance in which the executive agrees to the meeting, but only with the intention of nabbing the prize, then ushering the sales rep quickly out of the office. "Sometimes, they tell their assistants to interrupt five minutes into the meeting with an 'important phone call,'" he explains, "just so they can end the meeting."

The remote control toy theme extends to flying models as well, and some of these can be pretty interesting. Helicopter and miniature drone models can be had for as little as $50, but I think the concept can be stepped up a notch with full-size drones that are able to shoot video. These are more spendy, but carry a tremendous appeal because of the burgeoning popularity and fascination with the devices. The target executive might not have a real use for a video-capturing drone, but their curiosity is likely to overrule any objections they may have to your meeting.

Author and Guerilla Training keynote speaker Orvel Ray Wilson offers an interesting take on the theme if your quarry happens to be a baseball fan. He advises sending a stand for three signed balls, with the last one omitted; that will be the reward for taking the meeting. He once used this tactic to get VIP prospects to stop by his booth with the offer of having legendary Yankee outfielder Mickey Mantle signing the ball right there in person.

National Association of Sales Professionals CEO and *Are You Up for the Challenge?* author Rod Hairston offers yet another take on the half-of-a-gift theme, sending a set of golf balls, a ticket to play at a top course, and a single shoe. The package arrives with a note explaining, "Oops, I forgot your other shoe. I'll bring it when we meet." Coe offers yet another take on the concept, this time simply sending the left shoe of a fine pair of dress shoes, with a note saying he'd like to get his foot in the door, and will bring the other shoe when the meeting takes place. I have to wonder if a set of remote-control golf balls might make this approach even more interesting, because it would give the VIPs a chance to have a lot of fun during their next few rounds.

The danger in this approach is obvious. If the CEO simply wants to grab the remote-control toy for a grandchild and send you on your way, the gift isn't doing its job. Hairston points out that the gift must reflect that you have done your research, that you will be delivering something of far greater value than the gift itself.

Tower Hobbies

A complete selection of remote-control model cars, planes, boats, and miniature drones—even a remote-control blimp that looks like a shark swimming through the air.

http://www.towerhobbies.com; **$40 and up**

Parrot

This company makes a fascinating set of remote-control drone devices with one huge difference from the rest: All of their drones use an app on any iOS or Android device. Form factors include conventional quadcopters, sci-fi rolling drones, even a ceiling-walking spider drone.

http://ardrone2.parrot.com; **$130 to $500**

DJI Phantom 2 Quadcopter with HD Video Camera

A nearly commercial-grade drone with HD video onboard and a gimbal stabilizing system.

http://www.dji.com/product/phantom-2-vision; **$800 to $1,200**

DJI Spreading Wings S1000

Want to go even bigger? The same company that brings you the Phantom 2 Quadcopter also makes the commercial grade octocopter, an eight-bladed wonder that can produce cinema-quality aerial video. It's quite a toy. Send me one if you want to reach me.

http://www.dji.com/product/spreading-wings-s1000-plus;
$4,230 plus digital SLR camera

Category #4: Visual Metaphors

Estimated cost per contact: $10 to $10,000

Some gifts offer the sender a greater opportunity to brand or express the value of their proposition. These so-called visual metaphors create a chain reaction of thought that can instantly plant a point of agreement in the mind of the target executive, much like the humor in a cartoon does.

To achieve this effect, you must give your concept a lot of thought and search for some pretty unusual gifts, some of which may need to be individually commissioned by an artist or craftsman. Author and turnaround specialist Dan Waldschmidt provides a wonderful example of a unique and effective visual metaphor. In his business, Waldschmidt is tasked with scanning the news for stories of missed earnings reports; that's his cue to reach out to his next VIP prospect.

What Waldschmidt does next is truly audacious. He has a full-size medieval sword made by a famed Hollywood prop maker, complete with the target executive's name engraved on the blade. It's packed in a fine wooden box along with a handwritten note saying, "Look, I understand more than ever that what you're going through is war, and you need the best weapons to lead your people to victory. I'm sure your internal people are capable, but if you ever need additional warriors, I've got your back." He reports that the recipients call 100 percent of the time, though not all of the target VIPs end up as clients.

What's brilliant about the gift is that it delivers a message. Waldschmidt isn't just sending a gift—he's sending a physical representation of the ferocity with which he does battle for his clients. He reports that the typical spend is $1,000 per contact, but that the resulting million-dollar contracts completely justify the cost. But he also warns, "If you don't go big enough, it's a complete bust."

That may be true, but a lot of the thought leaders I interviewed found success at a much lower price point. *High-Profit Selling* author and *The Sales Hunt* blog author Mark Hunter has sent a sack of nails to make his point, visually demonstrating that the target had been hard as nails to reach. Lottery tickets have often brought up to 100 percent response rates when teamed with his message that you can play the lottery and *hope* to hit it big, or hire Hunter as a sure thing to increase sales.

Author and blogger Babette Ten Haken has had success with a range of downmarket visual metaphors: everything from lemons, horseshoes, and roses to worn-out running shoes, to convey messages of turning around adversity, making your own "luck," and asking why you'd intentionally run at a disadvantage, respectively. Since she specializes in selling to engineers and IT professionals, her focus is on using gifts that especially resonate with that group. Two favorite items are abacuses and slide rules—old tools for the jobs these people do. They're novelties, but they also make a strong point about using outdated tools.

If you're a poker player, you'll appreciate Orvel Ray Wilson's approach. He sends a single playing card in an envelope, with no markings, no note. The next day, he sends another. This continues for two more days and on the fifth day, he shows up at the target's office. When he's asked for his card, he pulls out the fifth and final card, the Queen of Hearts, completing a royal flush. Wilson reports, "It works every time. I not only get through, but I'm warmly welcomed." There is an element of sales stunt in his technique, but there is also a strong metaphor about his presence completing a winning hand. The target executive won't be framing the playing cards; it's not that kind of gift. Yet they will surely remember Wilson and think of him when they need to boost their sales game.

While Wilson's visual metaphor positions him as part of a winning poker hand, George Petri, author of the SymVolli blog, tells the story of a Contact Campaign that used the opposite approach. A printer wanted to gain new clients quickly, so they produced a standard letter package that was actually a blooper. The letter was produced upside down, the envelope was addressed upside down as well, the stamp was crooked, and so on. The copy theme in the letter was, "If you work with us, this is the last thing that will get screwed up." Petri insists the Contact Campaign must break the pattern the target executives are in, but how do you break through? Through clever execution that brings your message to the next level. "You need to be the person they can't afford not to listen to," he says, "and they get the message because you're already demonstrating value in your Contact piece."

> " The Contact Campaign must break the pattern the target executives are in, but how do you break through? Through clever execution that brings your message to the next level.
> —blogger GEORGE PETRI "

How to Sell Anything to Anyone Anytime author Dave Kahle talks about the small visual metaphors he uses to highlight aspects of his sales training sessions: sending an egg timer to set a theme around time management, for instance. But his favorite visual-metaphor Contact

Campaign came from an ad agency. They identified 100 high-potential prospects and launched a multi-wave campaign. Each wave was delivered weekly via UPS, in a custom box wrapped in plain brown paper, addressed by hand in female penmanship.

The first box contained a lemon, with a note saying, "Don't let it go sour," but with no identifying features. Next came sugar cubes accompanied by the message, "Keep it sweet." By the time the third box had arrived, the office workers began to gather around to see what was in the box. Tinsel marked that next theme, "Make it sparkle." When the fourth box arrived, it had everyone's attention. Inside was a business card with a Post-it note explaining, "I'll call you on Monday the 4th." The agency reported that 100 percent of the target executives took the calls, but more importantly, the box campaign had already demonstrated their bold marketing prowess; it had served as a vivid visual metaphor for the quality of their thinking.

Top Sales Dog blog author Steve Meyer tells a story of famed iconoclast designer Tibor Kalman. Kalman was not only the founder of M&Co Labs, once the hottest graphic design studio in Manhattan, but he also designed the "10-One-4" watch that was accepted for display in New York's Museum of Modern Art. Kalman mounted an interesting Contact Campaign for his studio, in which he sent a blank book with patterns cut in the pages in the shapes of scissors, rock, and paper. He followed up with a letter stating, "I'm the guy who sent you the rock, paper, scissors book," and connected with his contact targets. His design prowess, rooted in simple yet effective design, was demonstrated by the book.

I think Kalman and Dan Waldschmidt exemplify the best use of visual metaphors as Contact Campaigns, because their contact pieces not only make compelling gifts; they also make a bold statement about their sender. These are still gifts, but at their best, they should be uniquely involving, intriguing, and come with a well-focused purpose. For that reason, my favorite approach to visual metaphors is to find something people can't put down, perhaps even something they've never seen before.

Favorite sources for these are museum and scientific stores, which often feature unusual and fascinating products. Browsing through their catalogs, you're sure to find items that can serve as a thoughtful gift that also imparts a strategic message about you, your brand, or the value you hope to bring to the prospect. At their best, visual metaphors deliver all three.

Here's a great example: The logo for my Contact Marketing agency, "Contact," shows a set of points and concentric circles spanning a globe. It's meant to show how just a few of the right touch points can have a global effect on the scale of your business, referring to the kinds of extraordinary results Contact Campaigns can produce. I explain this in my contact letter, but when I accompany it with a Hoberman Sphere—the popular kid's toy of hinged pieces that form a fascinating expanding ball—I don't need to explain the logic of leveraging just a couple of key points to expand the scale of an enterprise. They pull once on the toy and get the point immediately. It ties perfectly to my brand, too, because it looks so much like my logo.

Even better, when they play with the toy while we speak, it continues to reinforce my value proposition. At their best, visual metaphors should do just that—be a fascinating item people can't put down, while serving as a physical representation of both your brand and what you can accomplish for your prospect.

The MOMA Store

A fascinating collection of museum-quality interpretations of everyday items: staplers, calendars, chairs, lamps, bottle openers, and more. Each piece will have your target executives engaged in your message—and fascinated by your gift.

http://www.momastore.org; **Under $25 to $1,000+**

Guggenheim Store

This museum store also offers a fascinating range of gifts, although the theme is decidedly art-focused.

http://www.guggenheimstore.org; **$10 to $5,000+**

San Francisco Museum of Modern Art Museum Store

Similar to the MOMA Store, this West Coast variant offers a variety of inspiring gift items for the workspace and more, plus an assortment of print-on-demand art reproductions—even 3D-printed jewelry and candy.

http://museumstore.sfmoma.org; **Under $30 to $400+**

Opulent Items

Museum-quality furniture, kitchen decor, computer accessories, electronic gadgets, and more. Also includes sections for men's, women's, and kids' gifts.

http://www.opulentitems.com; **$10 to $10,000+**

UncommonGoods

A bit down-market from the preceding shops, it's still a fascinating collection of novelties that are less likely to break your budget. Most of the items shown in their catalog are under $50, but there are many bits that can serve well as visual metaphors.

http://www.uncommongoods.com; **Under $25 to $200+**

Touch of Modern

An online store of wonders, Touch of Modern hosts a parade of fascinating gadgets, objects, and doodads that are sure to yield a few visual metaphors for your Contact Campaign. There's really no way to describe it, because the product selection is always changing. Best just to visit and see for yourself.

https://www.touchofmodern.com; **Under $10 to $2,000+**

Edmund Scientifics

A quick look reveals gifts addressing alternative energy, anatomy, astronomy, and more. You could spend hours looking through their catalog, and you'd find a multitude of visual metaphor ideas for your Contact Campaign. Be sure to check out their Science Gifts section.

http://www.scientificsonline.com; **Under $10 to $4,000+**

DVICE.com

This is not a store, but they do feature a number of fascinating gift ideas, from a chunk of aerogel to Mars rocks, gallium crystals that melt in your hand, ferrofluid, and more. It's a great source to find the perfect, very unusual, fascinating visual metaphor for your campaign.

http://www.dvice.com/archives/2010/12/11_cheap_gifts.php;
$9 to $150

POINTS TO REMEMBER

 Gifts are a natural solution for Contact Campaigns, but must be considered carefully.

- ✔ Some executives are embarrassed by or suspicious of expensive gifts, especially if they appear to be bribes.

- ✔ Government and many private organizations have strict limits on the value of gifts an executive is allowed to accept.

- ✔ The thought behind the gift is the critical element.

- ✔ As discussed in Chapter 8, cartoons make wonderful gifts that often melt the ice immediately with target executives.

- ✔ Art of all types, especially when combined with personalization, makes an excellent Contact Campaign gift item.

- ✔ Some gifts are calculated to appeal not only to the recipient, but their staff or family members, who influence the executive's thinking.

- ✔ Gifts can be bestowed with the purpose of being given to others by the recipient, with great effect.

- ✔ Giving half of a gift can be effective, but is also risky if its value exceeds the perceived value you bring to the proposed meeting. Some executives agree to meet simply to get the remaining element of the gift, and then usher the Contact Marketer swiftly out the door.

- ✔ Remote-control models and drones can make especially alluring gifts, with the control unit held back until the meeting occurs.

- ✔ Gifts that double as visual metaphors may be the best type of gift to use in your Contact Campaign.

- ✔ An effective visual metaphor subliminally communicates a positive message about your brand and value proposition.

✔   The best visual-metaphor gifts are items that are so
     fascinating the recipient can't put them down, while
     serving as a constant illustration of the value you offer.

✔   Visual metaphors do not need to be expensive to work:
     A bag of nails, lottery tickets, and other low-dollar items
     can be very effective at communicating your point.

"It's an original idea, but someone else had it originally."

CHAPTER 9

Free and
Nearly Free

Now we'll take a 180-degree turn from gift-based Contact Campaigns to look at some of the steps you can take at zero cost, starting with the phone. Sure, it costs money to have phone service, but the assumption is that you'd have that fixed expense no matter what.

Category #5: Phone

Estimated cost per contact: free

In the previous sections, we looked at methods to break through to VIP prospects by sending something of value, something that may even plant a subliminal impression in the target executive's mind about your brand. With costs ranging from $10 to $10,000 per contact, the obvious question is: Why would you spend *anything* if you didn't have to?

The phone has been a longtime staple of sales operations everywhere, so it might also seem presumptuous to claim use of the device as the basis of a Contact Campaign. But Contact Marketing is itself a form of outbound sales, just done at a stratospheric level to reach CEOs and VIPs.

For this section, I'm confining the discussion only to the techniques related to breaking through to the top. Even I, the author of a book on Contact Marketing and prolific sender of cartoons and other items to great effect, will often bypass the more involved route in favor of simply picking up the phone and connecting directly. In fact, it's often quite easy.

One of my favorite techniques is to ask repeatedly to be directed to the right person. I start with the receptionist, asking to be referred to the right person and asking if I can explain the reason for my call. Because I'm asking for help rather than pitching, I find that people are usually quite willing to listen patiently, without putting up their guard.

Once the receptionist has referred me, I run the same procedure with the next person, and so on. Eventually, I end up speaking to the person I need to reach, but I continue to ask for help. The benefit here is that I still get to explain the reason for my call, without pitching, and without the other person locked in a defensive mode. When I've finished with my explanation, I often hear, "Well, I'm the person you need to speak with and this sounds pretty interesting."

That's great if you're not going after the CEO of a *Fortune* 1000 company, but what if they *are* your target? *Predictable Revenue* coauthor Aaron Ross says, "While most people train their sights on the top fifty of that list, I go after the other 950, where I usually find more success." If he doesn't make it through to the CEO, he uses a technique similar to my own, which he calls the "lost lamb" approach. He starts by asking the executive assistant for help to determine who he should contact. "Have a short answer about what you do," he explains, "then pause and let them digest and acknowledge."

Several experts point to the timing of your call as a critical element for breaking through. Blogger George Petri and *Music Scene Magazine* publisher John McDermott both suggest calling early or late in the day, outside of normal working hours, if your goal is to bypass the executive assistant. "You can try calling at 7:30 A.M. or after six, because the assistants usually aren't in the office," Petri explains, "but that may not work due to voice mail." McDermott adds, "If you call after hours, the target is sometimes likely to return the call early the next morning."

But as *Dirty Little Secrets: Why Buyers Can't Buy and Sellers Can't Sell and What You Can Do about It* author Sharon Drew Morgen points out, "The receptionist and executive assistant can be your best friend, because they're there to let the

> Your objective should not be to circumvent the executive assistant, but to turn them into an ally.

right people in." I agree. Your objective should not be to circumvent the executive assistant, but to turn them into an ally. Still, there are always difficult assistants and these are excellent suggestions to counter a surly personality.

Author Mark Hunter has a really interesting take on timing. He recommends calling between five minutes before the hour to three minutes after. Why? As Hunter explains, "That's when the CEO will often pick up the phone directly, because most scheduled calls start on the hour." My suggestion would be to use this tactic especially around 10 A.M. and 2 P.M., two of the most commonly chosen times to start those calls.

Hunter goes on to emphasize that no one guards their time more closely than a CEO, so when you do get them on the phone, ask for a twenty-minute slot for your own arranged call. They'll usually block out thirty minutes and often have the latitude to go longer if the call is important enough.

Beyond the time of day of your calls, *The Truth about Leads* author and *ViewPoint* blog author Dan McDade says you should establish a cadence to your calls and follow-up emails. He suggests four to five phone calls and three to five emails over the course of ten days. Then go back six to eight weeks later to follow up. He says the routine regularly helps him break through to his top prospects.

Blogger Dave Brock agrees with some of the earlier comments about timing, suggesting calling between 6 and 7 A.M. or 6 and 7 P.M., and adds new meaning to the term "ambush call." At one point, he'd read an article in *The Wall Street Journal* about Jerry Johnson, then the number-three person at Kodak, talking about restructuring the way they sell. Brock dispatched a letter, only to find that Johnson had already received seventy other letters on the subject.

"Furthermore," Johnson explained, "I don't take calls from consultants." But he went on to say he remembered Brock's letter and gave him ninety seconds to explain himself. Rather than taking the bait, Brock suggested that he patch in his client at Gillette, knowing Johnson had expressed admiration for what that company had achieved with their sales. They connected with the client, who gave a glowing report on Brock, and the call eventually resulted in $3 to $4 million in business.

If you find yourself having to leave a voicemail, how do you make sure it isn't ignored? Author and blogger Craig Elias recommends that you never leave a voice mail on the first call, while *Sales4Startups* cofounder Bennett Phillips advises mixing in a bit of email with your first message. "Send an email that gets cut in the middle of what you were saying," he advises, "then send another immediately saying you hit the 'Send' button too early." He says this tactic may make you look sloppy, but more importantly, it humanizes you. He even advises mixing in a few typos to reinforce the sense that this is you typing, not you running a campaign.

Elias has another trick up his sleeve, in that he advises watching for triggers before reaching out to anyone. He spends his time looking for people who are in a new job. "That's when they are most open to new ideas," he says, "because they're ramping up their tenure quickly and don't necessarily have established vendor relationships yet." He says if someone in that position is spending $1 million or more on something, they'll likely make the buying decision within three months—and 80 percent of the time, the first person in gets the business.

His method for breaking through involves a weeklong plan aimed at getting the target executive on the phone that Friday morning. It starts with an initial call on Tuesday. If there's no answer, he doesn't leave a voice mail, but calls again on Wednesday, usually before or after the assistant's work hours, to leave a voice mail. He follows that with an email with just two words in the subject line to create curiosity. Inside, the email contains something short, something easy to say "Yes" or "No" to—but he never sells a product, he "sells verbs." His focus is on useful actions, not canned solutions, and he says by the time he makes the call on Friday morning, he generally gets through.

Once you do break through to the target executive, you'd better be ready to have a quick, substantive call, one that grabs the CEO's interest immediately and moves the conversation where you need it to go. That's not easy when you're under pressure, but our experts offered several methods for overcoming the challenge.

If the target contact is an active blogger or an author, that's easy, says blogger Steve Meyer. "Just tell me you read something I wrote," he says, "but tell me you have a question you'd like to ask." He says it is a sure way to get the conversation started. *Amp Up Your Sales* author and *The Sales Fix* blog author Andy Paul puts it another way: "How do I ask the question that he or she wants answered?" He focuses his time on developing what he calls "killer questions" before making the call, giving himself the opportunity to understand what the target executive's problems are and find ways to define them in new terms. "That's the surest way to get their attention," he says.

DiscoverOrg cofounder and CEO Henry Schuck made an interesting discovery while calling IT decision makers. His company sells access to a marketing database of these executives, so it was important to understand how they like to do business with vendors. When asked, "When do you respond to a cold call?" their answer was, "Never." When Schuck pressed further, they explained they only take calls when the vendor happens to be calling about something they're working on at the moment. So timing and pre-call research are critical.

That's an important view, but Avidian vice president of sales David Archer has an even more direct perspective. He says words matter, as does the focus of your call: "It's always about them, never about you." Archer relates an interesting story that may help. There was once an insurance rep who was calling his list, using a script to generate insurance quotes. But he wasn't having any luck, until he dumped the script and tried a more human approach. "Hi, this is Jim from Prudential. We haven't spoken before, but may I tell you how you can stop getting calls from people like me?" That got their attention. He went on to explain, "The reason you're getting these calls is because you're on a list of people who have put their families at risk. May I explain how you can get off the list?" And that lead to an avalanche of new quotes.

Matt on Marketing blog author and Heinz Marketing CEO Matt Heinz says a lot of people are reluctant to use the phone because they don't have certainty about what to do next. But as *Inside Sales Experts* blog author Trish Bertuzzi puts it, "Content is the new spam. We've forgotten how to have a conversation, but using the phone is the new way to be human, to make a real connection."

When making that connection, Scott Plum, president emeritus of the Professional Sales Association, reminds us that persistence is key when using the phone. "The worst thing you can do is not follow up," he says, as "it leaves the CEO thinking, 'See, I was right. It wasn't important.'"

> *We've forgotten how to have a conversation, but using the phone is the new way to be human, to make a real connection.*
> —*blogger* TRISH BERTUZZI

Category #6: Email

Estimated cost per contact: free

The phone is one way to mount a no-cost Contact Campaign. Email is another. In fact, they're often used together to great effect. I frequently use my personalized cartoons here, too, capitalizing on a simple trick to install the cartoon at the top of the message, personalized with the target executive's name.

My favorite tool for this is my trusty Gmail account. Gmail allows me to insert the cartoon graphic, center it at the top of the page, then write out the centered caption immediately below in a nice italicized font. The effect is wonderful and it often grabs attention, especially from the executive assistants who are often the first recipients of my emails. Putting a cartoon about the target executive in the message is a great way to get the email opened and passed along.

This isn't a book just about using cartoons, however, so let's take a look at some of our experts' email tactics for breaking through to VIP prospects. There is a recurring theme throughout this book of getting the timing just right, and our experts' email tactics follow that pattern.

Skaled CEO Jake Dunlap specializes in fast sales growth strategies for mid-stage startups, and his primary goal for each new client is to establish ten to fifteen top-level connections immediately. To do that, he uses a seven-touch format: email the target executive on a Tuesday, call on Friday, then repeat the process for the next two weeks, ending in a call the final week. He reports that each wave tends to produce 5 percent increments of contact, with a cumulative 35 percent or so as the final outcome of each Contact Campaign. That's plenty to get his clients rolling in some serious new business.

Dunlap also advocates making a clear request in the email, stating the time and date the sender will call, and a subject line of "It's time to connect—((insert date))." He also advises using referral-style language and building the email for mobile devices first, meaning it should not go long. He finds that if the copy says, "My CEO asked me to reach out to you," the response rate goes up, but it is critical to find the "X factor," something that differentiates you and your reason for connecting, something that focuses on solutions to their immediate problems.

Authors and bloggers Mark Hunter and Craig Elias get even more specific about timing. Hunter says top executives don't have time to read emails during the week, so he advises sending one either at 5 A.M. Saturday morning or late Sunday afternoon. He says, "Who are the senior-level people you can't reach? You'll reach them on the weekends with an email." But he also cautions, "Don't send a pitch, be informational."

Elias tells about a certain C-level Dell executive who would only respond to emails sent Sunday afternoon, and an 8:30 A.M. Saturday conversation he had with a CFO who'd been unresponsive for weeks, all from a simple, well-timed email that morning. Hunter says CEOs often receive 300 to 400 emails a day and simply can't keep up. During the weekend, however, those same executives receive thirty to forty emails a day, making your chances of breaking through far better than during the week.

Author Aaron Ross advocates prospecting without cold calling, using the referral approach mentioned in Category #5, but his preferred method is to send the request directly to CEOs in email form. In the email, he asks who handles sales, with the goal of obtaining a top-down referral. When calling, he asks for help rather than blurting out a sales pitch.

Blogger Bennett Phillips takes a similar approach. "Aim to be pushed down," he explains. "Aim above the person you want to speak with, so you'll end up with a referral from above." His approach is also similar to Elias', in that he advocates a multistep process. His strategy takes shape with a three-part message, starting with a mention of something the target executive already has in process—perhaps something in their Twitter newsfeed. Part two focuses on the issue he can help the CEO accomplish, and the final effort requests a referral or meeting.

Phillips says subject lines are critical as well. He tries to include something the recipient may not know, with particular focus on what he calls "FUD"—Fear, Uncertainty, and Doubt. He often highlights developing a new skill, uncovering news, or providing a valuable insight, but always with a view toward something the CEO should be afraid of, and with an idea of what they can do about it together.

Phillips also advocates very short copy, and backs it up with the story of how he once connected with Salesforce founder Marc Benioff. "I sent him an email saying just, 'We're doing this, is that something Salesforce should be involved with,'" he says, "and Marc responded within thirty seconds." Phillips also advises using symbols in subject lines, such as, "((the recipient's company name)) + ((your company name)) = ((something desirable))."

The content of the message is also of supreme importance, but some of our experts had some very interesting insights beyond the "never pitch and make sure you provide value" mantra. *Hello, My Name Is Awesome* author Alexandra Watkins likes to keep it entertaining. If she finds herself facing a string of unreturned phone calls, she sends her "Magic 8 Ball" email. The email says, "Dear John, every Monday I ask my 8 Ball, 'Will John return my call this week?' And today, the answer was 'Most Definitely.'" She says it works nearly 100 percent of the time.

Insight Selling coauthor John Doerr says he once saw the chairman of Ford walking by and later wrote an email saying, "I passed you in the hall and didn't get a chance to talk." He continues, "I know what you're trying to do and I think you're going down the wrong road. I think I have something to offer." That email helped him break through, but what is significant is the tone and reference to something very personal: *I saw you today and didn't get a chance to tell you something important.*

Blogger Steve Meyer says the personal touch can also extend to something the CEO has written, tweeted, or posted. But SalesLoft CEO Kyle Porter and author Aaron Ross take an even simpler approach. "We just email them," says Porter, "but with smart information related to something happening in their lives." Ross adds, "I just ask a very direct question." His email campaign to CEOs while serving as vice president of sales for Salesforce has achieved near–urban legend status due to its unusually high response rate, and all it said was, "I'm at Salesforce, can you direct me to the person in charge of CRM?"

Category #7: Social Media

Estimated cost per contact: free

Social media is a broad topic, and I certainly do not consider myself an expert in the field. Still, in my discussions of Contact Campaign types, the subject has come up a lot. Social media is changing so much of our lives, and certainly how we connect with the world. It also makes connecting with VIPs far easier than it has ever been before.

Social media functions like a combination of old-fashioned personal introduction with a 24/7 networking event in hyper mode. If you're a user of LinkedIn (and you should be), the interface includes a diagram showing how you are already connected with people you don't know through people you do know. It even maps out how you can secure introductions from several sources. It's a roadmap for making important connections.

Social media contacts fall into two categories: those who come to you and those you seek out. It is clear that nearly all of the thought leaders interviewed for this book are convinced that the first category, those who *come to you* as a result of your activities in the various channels, are fundamentally changing the way we buy and sell goods and services. But Contact Marketing takes the opposite approach. We're concentrating on those you seek out: the high-level, high-value VIP prospects we have identified through our research as members of our Top 100 or Strategic 100 list.

So that's where we'll focus, on the social media activities that support the Contact Marketing mission. To assess the adequacy of social media as a Contact Marketing platform, you must consider the following three questions for each VIP on your list:

1. Does your target contact write articles, books, or a blog?
2. Is your target active in social media, and if so, which platforms?
3. Who do you have as common connections?

Armed with these three critical bits of information, social media can be a powerful ally in your Contact Marketing activities. Imagine, for example, if you were to discover that several of your Top 100 list members are active writers. Their articles are essentially invitations to have a conversation. They're showing you what they're interested in, what they think, and where they stand. It's the perfect entrée for striking up a conversation and, from there, a relationship.

Even as you're employing other Contact Campaign methods, combining them with smart social media usage makes a lot of sense. It helps you warm any cold-call situation and opens doors that otherwise may have remained closed. Remember, people buy from people they know and like. Social media gives you a head start and should always be part of your Contact Campaign strategy. Even the simple act of praising something a target VIP has said in a tweet, or favoriting, retweeting, liking, or sharing something they've already posted to Twitter or Facebook, can open the way to positive interactions.

There's really so much more to the linkage between Contact Marketing and social media, and there are far better people to offer strategies on this than I can. So rather than attempting to connect all of those dots in this short section, I refer you to Chapter 20, where I share the social media wisdom offered by the many experts and thought leaders interviewed for this book.

Category #8: Triggers

Estimated cost per contact: free

Author and blogger Craig Elias says he focuses on triggering events, or simply, "Triggers," a variation on the use of social media and Google Alerts, for his Contact Campaign strategy. And he has a solid argument for it.

Elias says he searches for people who've just taken on new jobs, because they're most open to change. "If they're spending a million or more dollars on something, most make their decisions within the first three months on the job," he says, adding, "Eighty percent of the time, the first person in the door gets to shape the problem, develop the solution, and win the business."

DiscoverOrg's Henry Schuck agrees, but widens the scope of target triggers to new funding. He says it's wise to recognize pain points but also to strike at the right time based on identifying triggers. Reaching out to a vice president of sales of a startup that has just received funding with a simple message of, "Congrats, but now how will you make your sales grow?" is enough to break through and win their business, notes Schuck.

Unlike other methods, triggers can't be made or launched by the Contact Marketer, but they can be a powerful determining factor in breaking through to prospects who become VIPs, based on their timing. Elias and Schuck both say determining when to connect is as important as strategizing what you'll send to break through.

Category# 9: Google Alerts

Estimated cost per contact: free

Google offers a wonderful, free service called Google Alerts. Are you using it? You should be. In case you're not familiar with it, Google Alerts allow you to set up an ongoing search for mentions of whatever you tell it to watch for. Once an Alert term is triggered, Google sends you an email detailing the mention. You should at least have alerts set up for your name and your company name; to do that, simply go to www.google.com/alerts.

Google Alerts, it turns out, is also a powerful tool for gaining the attention of your target VIPs. Best-selling author David Meerman Scott says they're almost foolproof connectors, and you don't even have to try to reach the target executive or get past their assistant. All you have to do is *mention* the person in a blog post and *they'll call you.*

Scott has plenty of examples of the tactic working brilliantly. "I once wrote a blog post that was critical of General Motors," he recalls, "and I ended up being invited to meet with their CEO for an in-person interview." In another instance, he wrote a review of recording star Amanda Palmer's new book, which resulted in direct contact and a tweet to her million-plus followers. He explains, "If a famous person has a book and you're the first to review it, they will see it and they will respond."

Scott says his *Marketing Lessons from the Grateful Dead* coauthor and HubSpot CEO Brian Halligan is always hearing from people trying to get a job. "Ninety-nine percent of them go the usual route, which doesn't break through in today's world," he explains, "but only a few have written blog posts explaining why they'd be worthy of a job." He says that not only shows the writer has marketing chops, but it breaks through directly to Halligan, because his Google Alerts feed directly to him. "What's different about this," he asserts, "is that people end up finding it and then finding you."

Author and blogger Mark Hunter agrees. He tells the story of a target company having just acquired a tech startup. "I posted a blog comment congratulating my target prospect," he says, "and added that integration is always a critical issue and I can help. It got me the call and the client."

Google Alerts are a "must do" for your Contact Campaign. They're simple, they're easy, and they're automatic. All you have to do is speak up online to start breaking through.

https://www.google.com/alerts; **free**

Category# 10: Mail

Estimated cost per contact: $1 to $35

Mail-based Contact Campaigns are at the core of what I do, so I have a great affection for this category. Remember, I started out creating campaigns for many of the world's biggest direct marketers, and even earned a nomination to the Direct Marketing Association's Hall of Fame for my work.

When you're engaged in mailings that reach millions, the strategic choices are quite different from what you'd use for a Contact Campaign. Because the list of recipients is minuscule, you can afford to add production values that would be out of the question on a large campaign. To put that in perspective, a mailing that goes to a million recipients must cost pennies apiece to break even. But a mailed Contact Campaign piece can easily cost even a few hundred dollars each and still make sense if it nets a few hundred thousand dollars' worth of business.

For me, this has been an invitation to go wild, to totally distort what a mailing is. If you think about it, the 18" × 24" BigBoards are really giant postcard mailings. Bending the usual parameters of mailed pieces can yield some pretty awesome results. In one campaign, I produced a folded letter that went into the envelope the long way. The envelope featured a colorful personalized strip cartoon (multiple panels, captioning done within the artwork in my own handwriting), which was then placed in a custom-designed, corrugated cardboard carrier. The carrier was made of fine, E-flute cardboard and included an exact-fit recess for the envelope and letter, creating a jewel-like presentation. The effect was stunning and very effective.

Another variation was the fold-over piece that formed an inner pouch for the letter and an attached gift card. When the piece was folded, a strip cartoon was visible on the upper flap, which then showed through a translucent vellum outer envelope. Completing the effect, I hand-addressed the outer envelopes below the cartoon showing through from inside. It was an impressive piece of mail no one could ignore. In fact, the recipients didn't ignore it at all; it produced a 7,500-fold return on the campaign based on sales.

Much of what is used as mailed Contact Campaigns takes the form of "dimensional mail," usually something delivered in a box. Author Chet Holmes gives us a great example with his "Trash Can" mailing.[3] Enclosed in the mailing box was a miniature metal trash can containing Holmes' wadded-up letter. The message started, "I knew you'd throw my letter away, so I thought I'd save you the trouble." As you might guess, a high percentage of recipients flattened out the letter, read it, and connected with Holmes.

Author Alexandra Watkins adds, "You've got to do something unexpected, something that makes people smile." She recalls the

Contact Campaign she sent to the chief marketing officer of Altec Lansing, consisting of a bright pink envelope, pink mints, and hand-picked stamps, which resulted in a hit. Postage stamps in particular can be a striking element of your campaign. I've used crops of the artwork of the cartoon inside to form a custom stamp, which gives it an amazingly coordinated appeal. Almost any custom stamp can be produced through Stamps.com.

J. Barrows Blog author John Barrows and *Nonstop Sales Boom* author Colleen Francis have found success adding gift cards and lottery tickets to their contact letters. Barrows used Dunkin' Donuts cards featuring his company's logo, along with a note asking for a meeting over coffee. Francis enclosed a lottery ticket in her Contact Campaign for a startup agricultural sales company. The accompanying copy theme was, "Don't take a chance on our offer, take a chance on the lottery instead." The copy went on to explain their chances of "winning" were far greater with her client, which closed not only a lot of meetings, but a 1,700-fold return based on resulting business.

Francis also emphasizes consistency in her mailed Contact Campaigns. She says 60 percent respond after the sixth touch, so in her sixth card she asks, "Do you really want me to go to the seventh card or will you talk to me now?" She says most salespeople give up before the sixth or seventh touch, which is a big mistake. When interviewed for this book, Bridget Gleason, Yesware vice president of sales, said that for her consulting practice, she sends quarterly postcards with odd, disarming themes and handwritten notes. As a result, on her second or third call, she gets through. Often the vice presidents of sales on the other end would tell her, "I know who you are, now I'm ready to talk."

Author John Doerr says when he has a list of 100 people and wants to produce a 100 percent connection, he sends a series of dimensional mailings, first containing single darts; then, finally, the dart board arrives with his message. Of course, his copy theme is aimed at hitting sales targets for his prospects, all of which produces a 30 to 40 percent response. "Still," he says, "the secret is the list, list, list!"

Author Dave Kahle and *Who The Hell Am I to Start a Business?* author Tara Truax focus on message and consistency, but their secret to breaking through is the mode of delivery. Both say pieces delivered in FedEx packs do best, because they look like important correspondence.

Kahle recounts a campaign he once received. "The FedEx guy walks into my office and says, 'Sign here,'" he explains, "so I stopped everything, opened the box, and found inside a 16-ounce bottle of Pepsi, a pack of microwave popcorn, and a yellow envelope." Inside the envelope was a note inviting him to relax and attend a twenty-minute webinar. "They'd done their research and invested in me," he says, "and because they were willing to spend $35 to talk to me, I made the appointment."

Other experts talk about the importance of handwritten notes as a way to break through and humanize yourself to your quarry. Magazine publisher John McDermott has a particularly clever take on the theme. He finds advertisements in magazines and newspapers, tears them out, and sticks them in an envelope along with a handwritten comment on a sticky note saying, "I saw your ad and a lightbulb went off in my head. If you're interested in what that was, give me a call." He says at least 40 percent call back and convert to relationships. When they call back, he tells them about a problem with the ad and how to fix it. "At that point," he says, "they ask, 'What do you do?' and I usually get their business."

Motivate People and *Objections! Objections! Objections!* author Gavin Ingham and *Score More Sales* blog author Lori Richardson have other uses for handwritten notes. Richardson likes to use custom cards saying, "Congratulations" and "Aspire, Shine" on the outside and a handwritten note inside, with her logo and business card. Usually, her notes are just a few well-chosen words, "Way to go!" when passing along her congratulations.

Ingham likes to pair his handwritten notes with cartoons, and in that way, he and I are a lot alike. We once produced an appointment-generation campaign for an insurance client, composed of a greeting card featuring an individually personalized cartoon on the outside and a handwritten note inside asking for the appointment. The outer envelope was also hand addressed. The campaign produced a 100 percent response against a list of 1,200 recipients.

Cards can also be quite useful for dislodging stalled sales situations. I often use a card with one of my cartoons showing an angry butterfly seated at a desk on the phone. If I were to send it to someone named Bob, the caption would read, *"Don't put me on hold, Bob. I only have a two-week lifespan."* Nine times out of ten, the target executive returns the call. I think this cartoon is particularly effective because it delivers the message, "Hey, we're wasting precious time—pick up the phone and call me," but it does it in an entirely disarming way.

CEO and blogger Matt Heinz and author Michael Krause say including executive assistants in your mailed Contact Campaign makes a lot of sense as well. Krause makes a habit of sending handwritten thank-you notes to whomever he meets, especially the receptionists and assistants along the way. "I sent one to this particular receptionist," he recalls. "Everyone was shocked, and she had it pinned dead center on her work desk." He feels strongly about including assistants, because as he points out, "CEOs often ask their admins how certain callers have treated them on the phone. It's important to them and it's important to the assistant."

Heinz says executive assistants never get mail and they should. "These people are not obstacles, they're allies," he says, "and they're keenly attuned to the CEO's interests and priorities." He advocates creating content for executive assistants along with their CEOs, based on making their bosses look good and improving their own career paths. "Think of the EA as your target as well," he says. "Care about what they care about; start there, and create value for them."

Mailed Contact Campaigns have produced some of the biggest results I have encountered thus far. One of the most extreme cases is the campaign I mentioned earlier that was produced by author and blogger Paul McCord. Before he became a top sales author, consultant, and speaker, McCord worked as a mortgage broker, and at one point, wanted to enlist the help of seventy local home builders as referral sources.

Drawing on previous experience in that industry, he devised a mailing consisting of a cardboard tube, a flow chart, and a simple note asking for a phone meeting. He knew builders were accustomed to receiving architectural plans in tubes, so they weren't likely to ignore his mail piece. And he knew they were used to following the progress of their projects on flow charts, so he also devised a way to express his value proposition as a flow chart.

The results were astounding. Of the seventy builders contacted, thirty became referral sources, and over the course of the following year, they generated over $1.1 million in mortgage fees. That came from a mail campaign that cost $175 all in, yielding a 628,571 percent ROI. If anyone doubts the value of Contact Marketing as a way to leverage a few dozen key contacts to quickly expand the scale of any enterprise, refer them to Paul McCord's example.

Stamps.com

No minimum order; you get all the services of the post office from your desktop, plus a 1¢ discount on postage over any stamps offered at the regular post office. PhotoStamps are what you'll want to create custom stamps.

http://www.stamps.com, http://photo.stamps.com;
$15.99 monthly service fee, $3.99 per sheet of stamps plus postage

Compendium

An array of inspirational greeting cards and other items for all occasions, including addressing any of your Top 100 list—including assistants—for your Contact Campaign.

http://www.live-inspired.com; **$2.95 and up**

CartoonLink

This is my company. CartoonLink offers membership-based monthly postcard campaigns featuring any of more than a thousand personalized cartoons. If you want your mail noticed, opened, and saved as a keepsake for months, this is the way to make that happen.

http://www.cartoonlink.com; **$500/month, membership required**

Points to Remember

✔ It's not necessary to spend anything to use Contact Marketing; thus, anyone can afford to use it.

✔ The telephone has been used in sales all along, but there are some specific techniques you can employ to reach senior executives.

✔ One technique is simply to ask for help finding the right person rather than pitching.

✔ Another critical element to reaching CEOs on the phone is timing.

✔ Persistence and a mixture of voice mails and email is often effective, as long it's about providing information rather than pitching.

✔ When you reach the CEO, be prepared with relevant information, or better still, "killer" questions that immediately engage the executive.

✔ Emails can also be quite effective at breaking through.

✔ My own trick is to plant a personalized cartoon at the top of the message, which often gets a lot of attention and encourages pass-along.

✔ Personalizing the cartoon with the target executive's name also ensures it will be passed along by the executive assistant.

✔ Timing is a useful consideration with email; senior executives are often most apt to respond to a message received early Saturday morning or early Sunday evening.

✔ Subject lines are vital to breaking through; make them personal, relevant, and fascinating, or focus on something that may be causing the executive to experience fear, uncertainty, or doubt.

✔ In email, it's often best to be extremely brief, perhaps as few as one or two lines.

✔ Social media has become a force in our lives and a critical element at any level of selling, especially in Contact Marketing.

✔ Social media can help you create a relationship with your Top 100 list members before you actually reach out to them in your Contact Campaign.

✔ Triggers tell you precisely when to connect with certain VIP prospects, based on events in their lives and resulting needs for solutions and help.

✔ Google Alerts provide an easy method for reaching top executives; the alerts cause the VIPs to call you.

✔ Mail-based Contact Campaigns can be extremely powerful, posting some of the biggest returns discovered during the research for this book.

✔ Cartoons—particularly personalized cartoons—work extremely well in mailed Contact Campaigns.

Dimensional mail, usually packaged in custom boxes, also grabs a lot of attention.

 Mailed pieces, due to their low cost, can be used effectively as multi-wave elements that project professional perseverance and break down a VIP's resistance to connect.

 Handwritten notes of all kinds are effective methods for humanizing yourself to your target contacts.

 Always think of ways to include executive assistants in your Contact Campaign mail plan.

"I'll be right there, just as soon as I finish this forecast."

CHAPTER 10

Media, Insight, Exposure, and Events

Switching gears again, let's examine a completely different tier of Contact Campaign categories, focusing on information, insight, and media. As you have read in earlier chapters, CEOs respond in their own self-interest and to any information that may give them a competitive advantage. One of their primary missions is to get their story out to their marketplace; helping them get there will help you get where you want to go, too. Let's take a look.

Category #11: Interviews and Media Presence

Estimated cost per contact: $0 to $1,000

Interviews are a tremendously effective method for gaining access to VIPs, and also for quickly fostering a warm relationship based on providing immediate value that is anything but a sales pitch. Interview requests can range from asking for advice to offering a valuable opportunity for the target executive to tell their story and share their thinking through meaningful media exposure.

American Marketing Association CEO Russ Klein says students often ask him during his college addresses how to connect with potential employers. His advice is to call the company and ask for an advice interview. "You start by contacting someone above your target, so there's a chance of producing a top-down referral from above," he says, "then you ask for fifteen minutes and explain that you don't want anything but advice." Klein says top executives rarely turn down a fresh graduate with a sincere request for advice, and at least one out of every ten interviews can result in a job. And he advises, "Never leave an advice interview without asking for the name of someone else who can give you advice."

> *Never leave an advice interview without asking for the name of someone else who can give you advice.*
> —RUSS KLEIN, CEO of AMA

Blogger Steve Meyer reminds us that checking first if the target executive has published an article or has been quoted recently in the press is a great way to connect. "The easiest way to reach me," he reiterates, "is to tell me you read something I wrote." Meyer says it's easy to find something the VIP has said with a simple Internet search, and it provides an immediate conversation starter, in addition to a valid reason for connecting.

The New Handshake coauthor and *Social Centered Selling* blog author Barb Giamanco favors acting as a connector between her target VIPs and the press or other authors. She watches for opportunities to make those connections simply by checking for releases of books, articles, and other interviews that relate in some way to her target executive's business, then offering an introduction to the author. If they bite, she has a reason to call her target and has something of great value to pass along.

Magazine publisher John McDermott amplifies Giamanco's point, saying, "Almost anyone can write and publish an article, and if it's written as a newsworthy piece, it can get picked up by various media outlets and promoted in social media." McDermott suggests turning the interview into a news event, and says he has never encountered resistance to the approach, either from the target's assistant or their PR handlers. "If you are able to get your article placed in the more esteemed media outlets," he says, "people become very excited to share their stories and, more to the point, engage with you."

But you don't have to be a member of the press or have deep editorial connections to offer real value through your interview requests. "If you don't have a show, start one," says Sales Lead Management Association president and founder James Obermayer. "Become your own media company." As part of his duties as president of the association, he hosts a weekly live web radio show that is then archived as a podcast. He says his show makes it easy to break through to virtually any VIP, and he finds their PR people are anxious to make the connection happen.

SalesGravy CEO Jeb Blount agrees. He finds that the technique of interviewing VIP prospects works consistently, but you must have a platform. "If I'm one of a hundred people trying to reach the target executive," he says, "saying I'd like to spend thirty minutes interviewing them for a book, white paper, or podcast always gets me through." He points to a recent Harvard study in which researchers found that blood rushes to people's brains when they talk about themselves. "It makes them feel important," he explains. "It makes them feel good." He reports that his interview requests produce a "roughly 100 percent penetration rate," and says he once landed a $250,000 consulting job simply because he'd interviewed a VP of human resources for his blog.

Of all the possible formats for self-generated media, podcasts seem to be ideal for the Contact Marketing mission. As author Tom Searcy points out, a podcast can be simply a recorded phone interview, which can then be transcribed and compiled into a "Best Practices" book.

For one of his clients, that was their strategy to establish a beach-head in a new market for their new construction division. "We con-tacted the biggest developers in the area, interviewed them, and published the transcripts as a book," Searcy explains, "and that got them hooked as clients." He points out that interviews leave the door open for callbacks to review any questions before publication. "It gives you a golden opportunity to send information on what you do."

Author Todd Schnick seems to have honed the podcast inter-view format into a Contact Marketing marvel. CEO of The Intrepid Group, Schnick recorded his first podcast in 2008, when he started interviewing recently laid-off executives who were embarking on unexpected consulting careers. "It was easy to connect with them," he recalls, "and it gave us some terrific content to offer our listeners." It wasn't long before he realized this would be his method for break-ing through to everyone he wanted to do business with.

Today, Schnick produces and hosts roughly a dozen regular pod-casts on a variety of subjects, making his company a virtual Contact factory for clients. And he's found that hosting a marathon of inter-views at trade shows can transform the scale of his clients' businesses almost overnight. "We re-engineer their show booth into a broadcast booth and invite sixty to seventy executives they want to connect with at the show," he says, "and it creates an immediate connection they can easily convert into client relationships."

Schnick says anyone can do this and advises, "If your goal is to reach business leaders, start a business show." He says there are many advan-tages to this Contact approach. "It's an easy ask; people are desperate to tell their stories," he says, adding, "The gatekeeper always wants to get the interview to happen." Best of all, the target executives will usually promote the podcast to their audiences, so your own audience grows with every podcast release.

Podcasts are such a good fit, I recommend that you start your own immediately. Requests for interviews are powerful Contact devices and the cost is negligible, even if you decide to add professional production values, even commercials. Being the host of your own podcast adds an important new factor to your VIP statement, and consider this: If you run your own commercial during the show, the most important set of ears is already tuned in. Those would be your target contact's ears. And you'll have their full attention.

> " *The target executives will usually promote the podcast to their audiences, so your own audience grows with every podcast release.* "

FreeConferenceCall

A free service, offering online meetings with up to twenty-five attendees, an iOS or Android app for on-the-go interviews, and that all-important easy-record feature to make podcasting easy . . . and did I mention it's all free?

http://www.freeconferencecall.com; **free**

Podbean

A one-stop shop for recording, editing, and publishing your podcasts—even hosting your own podcast site. Also includes a public-facing roundup of hosted podcasts, so you can share your content with a broader audience and even earn extra income from your content.

http://www.podbean.com; **$3 to $199/month**

OCTalkRadio

If you want a fully produced, professional-quality Internet radio show, OCTalkRadio's Paul Roberts offers a complete turnkey solution, including your own commercials and his reassuring voice and presence as engineer, producer, and "on-air" talent.

http://www.octalkradio.net; **$250/hr**

Category #12: Books and Articles

Estimated cost per contact: $1 to $150

If you're already an author, it's probably no surprise that a signed copy of your book can be a very useful tool for breaking through to CEOs, and it makes a substantial impression as part of your VIP statement. So you might think this category is only for published authors. I'm happy to tell you that is not the case.

Today, anyone can become an author in as little as a few hours. Or you can take a year to write and publish a solid book based on your experiences. A ten- or twenty-page e-book is a snap to put together and publish as a PDF, which you can attach to an email or offer from your site. Print-on-demand services such as CreateSpace and Lulu enable you to publish a beautifully produced book that you can sell on Amazon and other outlets. Blurb goes a bit further, enabling you to produce impressive hardbound books with photographic book jackets. And then there are the extensive marketplaces for e-books; Amazon's Kindle, Apple's iBooks, Barnes and Noble's Nook, and more. Becoming a published author has never been easier or more accessible.

The gold standard is still the traditional route of signing with an agent, who then markets your book to one of the publishing houses. What you lose in control of a self-published work you gain in terms of greatly enhanced credibility in the marketplace and quality of the end product. Having a major publishing brand, not to mention the might of their marketing, PR, and distribution channels, adds a great deal of weight to your VIP statement and market presence.

If you decide you want to use a book as part of your Contact Campaign strategy, the first choice you must make is whether to send your own or use someone else's. Obviously, there is far more leverage from using your own book, perhaps with your picture worked into the cover design. As author and columnist Dave Stein puts it, "Your book is the best business card you could ever have." Stein likes to make his book deliveries highly personal. "I like to go through the target contact's annual report to find a challenge I can help them overcome," he explains, "then add a sticky note to the cover, pointing them to a particular page, and write a note in the margins of the page." But, he points out, you can easily do the same thing with any book or even an article you or someone else has written.

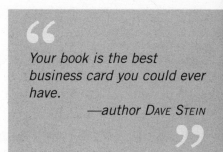

> *Your book is the best business card you could ever have.*
> —author DAVE STEIN

Most of the authors I interviewed echo Stein's sentiments regarding the use of their books as the ultimate calling card. Author Jill Konrath finds that her books not only prompt VIP executives to visit her site, but copies sold through bookstores also result in a lot of calls and letters asking for further discussion. Author Dave Kahle points out that you may not make money from the sales of your book, but it pays enormous dividends from the engagements that result from having a book on the market. "Whether you use it as a door-opener or someone finds it on the shelf at a bookstore," he says, "it makes a powerful impression of credibility and shows what you do."

Baseline Selling author and *Understanding the Sales Force* blog author Dave Kurlan says it goes a long way with CEOs he'd like to meet if he simply autographs his book, along with a quick handwritten note asking to talk. Author Dan McDade uses the occasion to send not only his book but also a $25 gift certificate and a coffee mug, with a note asking to have a cup of coffee together while talking on the phone. Alen Mayer, who wrote *Trigger Events* and *Selling Is Better Than Sex*, says VIPs often challenge him on the title of the latter, while he uses actual trigger events to make his bids for contact always relevant to their circumstances. "I try to be non-invasive," he explains. "I just want to see if there is an opportunity to help."

Author Alexandra Watkins turns the equation completely around and seeks out VIPs who also happen to be authors, using *their* books as her Contact Campaign. "I take a selfie in front of my pink refrigerator, which doubles as a bookshelf in my office," she says, "and then I send a note saying, 'I keep all of my coolest books in the pink fridge, and I'm glad to have yours included.'" She has reached *The New York Times* bestsellers Adam Grant, Sandy Carter, and *Shark Tank* cohost Barbara Corcoran that way, which netted high-profile tweets from all three about her own book.

Authors John Doerr and Andy Paul caution that sending a book—any book—without specific cause can be a mistake. Doerr says one of his clients sent 500 copies of his book, but didn't see a lot of response. "One of the recipients' assistants told him, 'Oh sure, we get about forty of these a week,'" explains Doerr, "which means you don't stand out." He says if you're not addressing specific concerns in your cover note, sending your book won't get you through. Paul says he uses social media before sending his book to ensure a higher level of engagement.

Still, author Colleen Francis says sending your own book is important, because if it resonates with the target executive, they want more of you. "Consultants worry that giving their books away for free discourages further sales or engagement," she says, "but nothing can replace you as a personality." She also insists that sending any book must be supplemented with a bookmark or sticky note explaining why it's relevant.

Francis also recommends sending articles with the same sticky notes explaining why the article has been sent. She tells the story of wanting to reach ad agency executives. "We sent copies of a *Fast Company* story on the shake-up among ad agencies," she says, "and at least 50 percent called me back."

ROI Selling author and *ROI4Sales* blog author Michael Nick says writing your own book can have other benefits, which bring VIPs to you. He reports having sold his company recently, and the buyers insisted on using his book as an ongoing contact device for the company as part of the deal. Since he makes royalties on each sale, the book added value to the transaction for both sides.

CreateSpace

A true miracle of the age of self-publishing, CreateSpace offers a complete, print-on-demand–based publishing platform for authors. And since it is a division of Amazon, it's already plugged into all of the print-based, bookselling platforms. The dashboard does a beautiful job of sales tracking, and the print-on-demand (softcover only) books are first-rate quality, looking like any other you'd find on any bookshelf.

http://www.createspace.com;
$2 and up per book if you buy them; otherwise, you *make* money

Blurb

Blurb is also a self-publishing platform, dedicated to producing high-quality hardcover books with fine, photographic paper jackets. Although the company caters to the "here's a book of my vacation photos" market, this is a great platform for producing one-of-a-kind books—even one-off custom magazines—that will help you impress and break through to your toughest VIP prospects.

http://www.blurb.com; **$2.49 and up**

iStockPhoto

If you're going to publish a book, it should reflect the level of professionalism you bring in your own business. iStockPhoto is one of many stock photo, illustration, and video sources that can supply the graphics you'll need to produce a gorgeous cover and a sparkling design inside. Google "stock photography" to find others.

http://istockphoto.com;
$11 per credit, most royalty-free licenses are 1 to 3 credits

Bowker

Every published book must have an ISBN (International Standard Book Number), and Bowker is the only official US ISBN agency. But they're so much more. Visit their sites to obtain your ISBN number and matching cover barcode, as well as help with cover design, self-publishing strategies, publicity, and more.

http://www.myidentifiers.com, www.selfpublishedauthor.com,
www.bowker.com; **$125 for a single ISBN, other prices vary by service**

Category #13: Video

Estimated cost per contact: $5 to $1,000

With the amazingly rapid pace of change in our lives, it's easy to forget that simple and inexpensive access to video has only been around for relatively few years. Even at that, it seemed to be the province of teens talking to their smartphone cameras, cute videos of kitties, and stupid human tricks. But I'm happy to report that video has become a prime tool for Contact Marketers as well.

I've mentioned it in Chapter 5, but the NoWait campaign serves as a truly inspiring example here, too. NoWait is an app designed to help restaurants and their patrons manage wait times for tables by turning diners' smartphones into "your table is ready" buzzer pucks. You check in at the podium and your request for a table is entered into the app, leaving you free to continue shopping, take a walk, or wait at the bar. What you don't have to do is wait in a crowded seating area for an hour.

NoWait's CEO tasked Luke Panza, the company's cofounder and vice president of marketing, with delivering an individually customized video to each of the thirty-five restaurant CEOs on their list. The twist was their method of delivery: Each video was distributed on a brand new iPad. Every unit arrived in the original Apple packaging, but with a few alterations. The tiny instructions booklet was replaced with a NoWait mini brochure, and the protective screen sheet was replaced with a sheet of instructions: Step 1, turn it on; Step 2, tap the NoWait video icon.

What awaited was a video, individually shot just for each target executive. It started with hidden lapel-cam footage, clearly showing the "interviewer's" point of view, walking up to one of their restaurants, then into the overcrowded waiting space within. When the interviewer finally reached the reservations desk, he was told it would be an hour-long wait. The interviewer continued, engaging in conversations around the room, asking how patrons felt about waiting so long for a table.

Then the video switched to a segment introducing the NoWait app, and explaining how it does away with annoyingly long waits. It was a beautiful delivery of the company's value proposition, using slick video production to present it in a fashion no sales rep could match in person. The video concluded with a segment showing the NoWait CEO speaking directly to the target executive, telling them how he loves eating at their restaurants, but hates having to wait an hour for a table. He then invites the target executive to connect with them and put the app to the test.

Panza says the campaign more than exceeded their expectations, with a 75 percent response, 38 percent in trial, and 17 percent of the largest restaurant chains in the country already clients. Panza also says that due to the long sales cycle involved, they expect to see the trial and close rates climb much higher over the coming year.

One of the more interesting aspects of the NoWait campaign was the marketers' experimentation with reaching various people in the organizations and reaching out to one versus a handful at the same company. They discovered that the CEOs and CFOs were not the right target, but the COOs were their sweet spot. "After all," Panza explains, "NoWait is an operational solution." They correctly identified the "CEO" of the problem, which became their recipe for explosive growth. Still, they found that it was effective to include the CEO on their contact lists, to ensure buy-in at the very top.

Author Tara Truax offers a fascinating variation on the practice of delivering personalized videos on an expensive tablet. "I send the iPad with a note saying I will pick it up at a certain date and time," she says, "and I ask for a few minutes of their time while I'm there." This is a brilliant tactic. You still get to deliver your personalized video message in an impressive form factor, but you also create a reason for stopping by and meeting the target executive. What are they going to say? You've reached out in an entirely clever and audacious way, and they're not going to steal your iPad. This is a powerful way to create an instant connection with the VIP.

But let's not get carried away. You don't have to spend hundreds of dollars apiece for an iPad to deliver your video. You can just as easily load it onto YouTube, Vimeo, or your own site. Better yet, embed it in an email to your targeted CEO. As author Gavin Ingham points out, "People love videos. A five-minute video will get you farther than a five-minute call will."

Even if you aren't comfortable on camera yourself, Find New Customers president Jeff Ogden and National Association of Sales Professionals CEO Rod Hairston have a few suggestions. Ogden's approach is to create a slide show presentation with a voiceover using SlideShare. Hairston's suggestion is to try the animated characters found on Live Spark to present your message. He says he used an animated rhinoceros character to sell a training program for Honeywell that helped the division grow by 15 percent.

Investor, social selling evangelist, and keynote speaker Jill Rowley points out that YouTube is the second most popular search engine, but it has no tracking ability. She became an investor in Vidyard because of the tracking technology it includes, allowing users to see view counts and how many times a video was viewed by a particular person. Another of her ventures, Switchmerge, allows users to personalize videos on the fly, as they're being viewed. "It merges video assets with CRM data," she says, "so the viewer sees a video that was truly made just for them. It's incredibly effective as an email embed."

> *People love videos. A five-minute video will get you farther than a five-minute call will.*
> *—author GAVIN INGHAM*

And finally, social selling strategist Julio Viskovich offers yet another use for video in your Contact Campaign. He uses the StoryQuest video platform to quickly record a fifteen- to thirty-second video summary of the call, which he embeds in a video after the first contact. "I often hear, 'Wow, I've never seen anything like this before,'" he says, "which reinforces the impression that I have really put some work into the reasoning behind my outreach."

Contact Marketing surely will find many more uses for video. I think this is one of the best ways to accomplish what we're all ultimately striving for in our campaigns: to humanize ourselves, to create an instant connection, and to quickly transform the contact into a highly profitable relationship.

SlideShare

A quick and easy platform for sharing videos, presentations, infographics, documents, and webinars from your website, blog, or social media outlets.

http://www.slideshare.net/; **free**

Vimeo

A high-end video hosting platform that supports ad-free high-def video.

http://vimeo.com; **$0 to $199/year**

Vidyard

Host videos, make them available for every platform, and track analytics in order to maximize conversions from views to clients. Unique calls to action are part of the package, with pop-up forms at the end of your video, so it includes a self-contained response.

http://www.vidyard.com; **call 800-530-3878 for pricing details**

Live Spark

AniMates are live, computer-generated characters that can interact with an audience in real time or can be recorded as your spokesperson in your videos.

http://live-spark.com; **$1,000 and up per project**

StoryQuest

Recently acquired by the SAVO Group, StoryQuest has become the company's Inspire Digital Postcard service. It provides a quick and easy platform for post-call follow-up and includes a host of other useful features for Contact Marketing campaigns.

http://www.storyquest.com; **$15/month per head, $5,000 to $10,000 for setup, depending on the size of your enterprise**

VideoHive

Stock footage, motion graphics, project files, and more; royalty-free video files from $2 and up; part of the Envato Marketplace, which includes royalty-free photos, code, graphics, audio, music, and other assets for video, print, and web that lend truly professional results to your videos and other projects.

http://videohive.net, http://market.envato.com; **$2 and up**

Category #14: Information and Insight

Estimated cost per contact: $0

If sending a book or article makes sense, why not engage in an ongoing campaign to provide information and insight as a way to break through? That's the thinking that sets this Contact Campaign category apart, because it involves a different kind of commitment to your VIP prospects.

Sales Heretic blog author Don Cooper says the real opportunity here is to create an ongoing resource campaign. His strategy is to provide resources that potential clients can pass along to their clients. The information not only has to be usable and free of cost, it also has to provide value or insight to your VIP list members. "Send them articles, podcasts, e-books, infographics, and PDFs," he explains. "Keeping it up means that critical relationship is building over time." Cooper believes you must earn a VIP prospect's attention, and providing information, value, and insight is a powerful way to break through, as long as you commit to making a consistent effort over time.

Author Linda Richardson points out that the Internet has changed the sales equation drastically, because buyers have already done most of their research before buying. So business expertise and insights are what prospects value now, not just product expertise. She says, "How is an insight like a refrigerator? When you open the door, the light goes on." Richardson sees insights as a critical part of what she calls "The New Selling."

But how do you come up with insights a CEO will want to hear? Richardson's approach is to ask questions whenever you get the chance, then focus squarely on the VIP's needs. "Offering an insight and not pitching," she says, "is what is going to perk them up, if it's on-target with their needs." Author Anthony Iannarino agrees. "CEOs are constantly watching what other people are doing, what are they looking at, and what books should they be reading," he explains. "If you can offer help with the strategic challenges they're facing, that's what they want." He emphasizes that you've got to have business acumen and do your research before you talk to them, which extends neatly to the strategy of providing a steady stream of information and insight. As Iannarino puts it, "CEOs want to see around corners, and the more you demonstrate you can help with that, the better."

> " Nobody wants to buy from the guy who thrusts his card in your hand looking to sell.
> —author BARB GIAMANCO "

Author Barb Giamanco amplifies the point further, saying, "The more you can give first and demonstrate you're not just someone who's trying to sell something, the more opportunities you'll receive." Giamanco also reminds us of the familiar mantra, that people buy from people they know, like, and trust. "Nobody wants to buy from the guy who thrusts his card in your hand looking to sell," she explains. "You want to be someone who people ask for their card."

There really are no shortcuts to becoming a trusted source of information and insights. It comes from making a commitment to searching out and digesting articles, social media feeds, and the like, from always watching for intelligence the VIP prospects on your list might appreciate.

A word of caution, though: If you're going to use this strategy, it becomes imperative to explore sources the CEOs on your list don't already monitor. Pulling stories from *The New York Times* and *The Wall Street Journal* may not surprise them much or provide much value. But events, webinars, and podcasts can be excellent sources of intelligence they might not commonly find. These can include direct contact with guest speakers after the event, which can generate a constant stream of information and insights your VIP prospects won't have and will find quite useful.

And here's an idea if you want to truly take it to an even greater level: compile your reports into a custom magazine, completely personalized to each CEO. Blurb (see the end of Category 12) makes that possible at an incredibly low price point of just $4.99. You can also use Blurb to deliver a custom-made book for each CEO for as little as $13.99 each.

Category #15: Events

Estimated cost per contact: $0 to $1,000

As Contact Campaigns, events can be incredibly powerful contact devices. You can approach them either as an attendee or host.

The easiest method is to make use of someone else's event. I recently attended the Dreamforce show in San Francisco, easily the biggest marketing trade show I have ever seen. There were more than a hundred thousand marketers and sales professionals in attendance; the show occupied every building in the Moscone Center campus and every hotel in the downtown area was sold out. Attendance was free and everybody I ever needed to connect with was already there, in that one location.

I was there for a few reasons. I already had clients in San Francisco to see. As one of the guest authors for the Salesforce blog, I had a private reception to attend. But really, I was there on the advice of keynote speaker and social selling evangelist Jill Rowley.

She says big shows like these are the perfect opportunity to execute what she calls a "Social Surround Strategy," in which she targets a handful of key people and connects with them on several social media platforms simultaneously. She then reaches out, making note of some of their key common contacts, and mentions she'd like to meet sometime after her speech at the show. Rowley says as Contact Marketers, if we're not attending the big shows in our own industries, we're missing our biggest opportunities to connect with our Top 100 and Strategic 100 list members.

Author Dave Stein says it's often useful to single out speakers for contact and plant yourself on the aisle toward the front to approach them after the presentation. "Don't bother them beforehand," he says, "and don't be the first person to shake their hand. Better to be the third or fourth, when they have time to talk." Sales Gravy's Jeb Blount posits, "Why not ask them to dinner? You'd be surprised at how many speakers have no dinner plans after their talks."

Ruhlin Group founder John Ruhlin takes it to the extreme. When he learned that one of his target VIPs was due to give a speech and that he was a Brooks Brothers fan, Ruhlin outfitted the man's hotel room with merchandise from the store. That evening, he called Ruhlin and said, "You have my full attention." *The Guerrilla Connector* author Richard Weiler talks about traveling to events relentlessly to make valuable connections happen. They don't have to be big ones to have a great effect. "I once flew to Philadelphia to attend one of my target VIP's local Meetup group," he recalls, "and he was immediately impressed." That single action landed Weiler a coveted spot on a national speaker's tour.

Author Jill Konrath says it's imperative to attend conferences, noting that one conference recently accounted for a quarter of her annual income. She says even if you don't have a big budget, you can make a big splash. When HubSpot first launched, they wanted to be involved in Dreamforce, but couldn't afford to be on the exhibit floor. So they did the next-best thing and rented a room to create their own event. "It worked," she says. "Look at them now."

Emotional Intelligence for Sales Success and *Sales Leadership* blog author Colleen Stanley says hosting your own event is a brilliant way to connect with VIPs on your contact list. Although Stanley has hosted a variety of events over the years, her favorite approach is to host monthly executive briefings. She says even if just a few show up, she closes business. "It's not the quantity," she says, "it's the quality."

Slammed! For the First Time Sales Manager author and *Your Sales Management Guru* blogger Ken Thoreson takes a similar approach within the IT world, but his focus is to move away from the technical side and have conversations with VPs of marketing and sales. "At the CIO level, they're highly analytical, they have a tremendous amount of pressure, and their average tenure is just eighteen months," he explains, "so it's critical in that environment to connect with multiple points of contact."

> **CEOs are usually hungry for an opportunity to connect with other CEOs and swap stories.**
> —*blogger STEVE MEYER*

Thoreson's favorite approach is to host expert summits of fewer than a dozen people with respected thought leaders. He often recruits CIOs to be those thought leaders, yielding a double advantage— invitations to exclusive expert summit events, and a chance to be a thought leader to their peers at other companies, producing more opportunities to connect. "In these events, it's important to be a member, not a vendor," he says. "Building trust is a huge factor."

Rapid Learning Institute CEO and blogger Steve Meyer advises staging your event early in the morning so that it won't interfere with their day, and making sure they know other C-level executives will be in attendance. "CEOs are usually hungry for an opportunity to connect with other CEOs and swap stories," he explains. "After all, they truly understand the value of networking." And as the host, Meyer gets to network more than anyone else in the room.

Events in any form can be tremendously effective Contact Campaign tools. They are a great way to immerse yourself in contact opportunities at the larger scale, and on the smaller scale, they offer Contact Marketers focused opportunities to connect with their VIP prospects personally and quickly.

POINTS TO REMEMBER

✔ Interviews are one of the quickest methods for breaking through to VIP prospects.

✔ Interviews must be coupled with real exposure, but there are many ways to make that happen, even if you're just starting out.

✔ Each time you interview an executive, they bring their audience to your broadcast or podcast, causing your own audience to grow with every installment.

✔ Some interviews can be done simply to get advice or to reach out to a VIP who has written an article, blog post, or book.

✔ Most chief executives have a duty to publicize their companies' stories, and their assistants and public relations operatives are only too happy to help make the connection happen.

✔ Producing a podcast can be as easy and inexpensive as recording a free conference call and loading it onto a $10-a-month podcast hosting service.

✔ Live podcasts at trade shows are a way of connecting with all or most of the VIPs in attendance.

✔ If you want a show-quality podcast, there are reasonably priced services available to put on a truly professional show, complete with commercials for you and your guest.

✔ Books and articles are also powerful devices for Contact Campaigns.

✔ If you are an author yourself, your book can become your best possible business card.

✔ You can also send books by others, but in all cases, include a note explaining why the book is relevant to your request for contact.

✔ If you are not an author, becoming one is exceptionally easy and accessible through various self-publishing platforms.

✔ A self-published book can look every bit as professional as any other you'd find on a bookshelf and can be produced in any quantity, from a single copy to thousands at a time, on demand.

✔ Having your book published professionally adds a tremendous measure of credibility to your name and can result in much greater impact in the marketplace.

✔ Your contact target's book can also serve as a Contact device, by reviewing, tweeting, or posting positive comments, or taking selfies while holding the book.

✔ Video provides perhaps some of the richest Contact Marketing opportunities of all.

✔ Videos can be delivered on physical devices, online, or as attachments to email, all to great effect.

✔ Many tools are available to personalize each video to its recipient.

✔   Video is a great way to humanize yourself to your VIP
     prospects.

✔   Sending a constant stream of information and insight
     produces trust and a deepening relationship over time, as
     long as it contains no pitching.

✔   Your sources for information should not include those
     the CEO already reads; look beyond *The Wall Street
     Journal* and *The New York Times* for items they haven't
     already seen.

✔   Don't just send information; include your comments to
     demonstrate your acumen and grasp of the CEO's current
     issues and concerns.

✔   Events can serve as powerful Contact Marketing devices.

✔   Use events hosted by others to make easy connections.

✔   Host your own events to produce deep connections with
     the participants.

*"You're kidding. That came out of
our marketing automation program?"*

CHAPTER 11

Over the Top

I saved the most entertaining categories for this final grouping. These are the rock stars in terms of entertainment value, but they are also too extreme to be considered the core of Contact Marketing. Still, they are great examples of audacity, creativity, and the kind of thinking that makes Contact Marketing so highly effective.

Category #16: Print and Billboard Media

Estimated cost per contact: $500 to $10,000

Some years ago, marketer Rick Bennett was approached by a client who wanted his startup to be the first on the market to offer a new web voice-portal platform. But to get to the next level, he needed to connect with one of the big players in the telecommunications sector. In other words, he needed to partner with someone like John Chambers, president and CEO of Cisco Systems; Bernie Ebbers, president and CEO of MCI WorldCom; or Ed Zander, president and COO of Sun Microsystems, for an infusion of cash and access to the enormous client bases each represented.

But how would they break through? Bennett's solution was to produce a contact letter addressed to all three target executives as a full-page ad and run it in *The Wall Street Journal*. Surely, he thought, John, Bernie, and Ed must be readers of *The Journal*, but even he hadn't expected what came next.

Yes, all three had seen the ad. But what surprised Bennett was how it had enlisted the help of nearly all of the target executives' colleagues and acquaintances, who were among the paper's 2.1 million readers that day—and how it sparked a feeding frenzy among their competitors. When the ad hit, John, Bernie, and Ed's phones lit up all day with calls from people they knew, asking if they'd seen it.

In the end, Oracle CEO Larry Ellison had also seen the ad, and swooped in to preempt the trio by making his own deal with Bennett's client, a transaction worth tens of millions of dollars. With that kind of money at stake, and considering who the target CEOs were, the strategy was entirely justified and the campaign an enormous success.

Bennett has had similar triumphs producing ads on foam core boards and delivering them by courier, rather than running them in the paper. He has used the tactic to precipitate other company acquisitions from big players, including a $500 million acquisition of one client's startup by Amazon. "The ad encapsulates the entire value proposition of the company," says Bennett, "so it is a very effective tool for getting the right people interested and motivated to move quickly."

Bennett says the same effect can be produced with carefully selected billboards. "For $7,000 a month, you can buy the billboard directly across the street from General Motors headquarters," he explains, "so if you want to reach anybody in the auto industry, that's the way to do it."

> "For $7,000 a month, you can buy the billboard directly across the street from General Motors headquarters . . . so if you want to reach anybody in the auto industry, that's the way to do it."
> —RICK BENNETT, marketer

We've all seen open letters in newspapers, calculated to generate a groundswell of response; Bennett has simply flipped the equation around, using it to elicit a response from a single, high-value contact target. His message is that traditional media doesn't have to be used in traditional ways. Bennett's work is a brilliant example of the kind of thinking that makes Contact Marketing such a bold, dynamic, and valuable tool for sellers, marketers, and business owners.

Category #17: Prepaid Disposable Phones

Estimated cost per contact: Under $30

This is a pretty simple premise. Buy a disposable phone, have it delivered to your target executive, and call the phone just as it's being delivered. Still, there are a few nuances you need to know.

Art Sobczak, author of the book and blog *Smart Calling*, recalls the story of a Contact Campaign involving a disposable phone purchased at Walmart. "They stuck it into a FedEx pack with a note saying, 'I'll call you at 10 A.M.,'" he says. "The secret was creating intrigue as to who's calling and why."

Just as important is knowing when the phone actually does arrive. Author Dave Kurlan recalls the story of a sales rep who sent a disposable phone to a CEO, parked outside his building, then dialed as it was being delivered. "It was actually ringing when the CEO got it," he says, "and so it naturally created intrigue."

Magazine publisher John McDermott admits he likes to use FedEx boxes that he delivers himself, with the disposable phone inside. "The boxes are free," he explains, "and I know precisely when they are delivered if I do it myself."

The key seems to be tightly controlling the timing of your call according to when the phone arrives. But others have reversed the equation, by preprogramming their own number into the phone, then delivering it with instructions to hit the speed dial to connect with the mysterious person who sent the phone.

These approaches are all based on using the phone itself as the Contact device, but I can also see a case for pairing them with other Contact tactics and using the phone as the response device. I have to wonder how it might have enhanced the impact of Dan Waldschmidt's swords (in Chapter 8) or NoWait's preloaded iPad video packages (in the previous chapter).

Category #18: Personal Interests

Estimated cost per contact: $0 to $100

Matt Heinz, CEO of Heinz Marketing, recalls a surprising story of how he had been contacted in a particularly clever way. The campaign came from a company in Texas that formulated a launch strategy around engagement with thought leaders, leading them to speak and blog about myDocket, a fledgling startup with an email-tracking app.

"What amazed me was how thoroughly they had done their homework," explains Heinz. "It's one of the best examples of Contact Marketing I've ever seen." The Contact Campaign piece that reached Heinz was an egg carton filled with plastic eggs and a note from myDocket CEO Jason Wesbecher saying, "Don't count your chickens before they hatch." Heinz was impressed because it compelled him to post about it in his blog, and he finds himself constantly mentioning the campaign. "The only way they could have known about my wife's and my passion for raising chickens is if they did their homework," he says, "and they did a great job of it."

Wesbecher says he sent personal Contact Campaign pieces to roughly two dozen sales luminaries, just to let them know about myDocket's offering. What was unique is that every one of the contact pieces was, well, unique. Each was based on personal interests they were able to find from each targeted thought leader's social media profiles. "We sent a pink Superman cape to Jill Rowley," he recalls, "and she has worn it onstage several times during speeches and given us plenty of very positive mentions, which is exactly what we'd hoped would happen."

Wesbecher says authenticity is key in this approach, along with a lot of research and playful creativity. "The idea is to create goodwill, not be boring, and make a friend," he says. Of the two dozen thought leaders on his contact list, he received calls from roughly 70 percent. The total cost of the campaign was less than a thousand dollars, but he says the exposure and positive mentions from key opinion leaders in his market has been priceless.

Skaled CEO Jake Dunlap recalls one of his favorite campaigns that involved researching the alma maters for each of ten targeted executives. "We found where they went to school and bought their sweatshirts," he explains, "and then we packaged each with a letter peppered with random facts about their schools and a request to meet." He reports that the Contact Campaign produced a high meeting rate with a healthy margin of sales conversions.

Author Dave Stein recalls the time he discovered that the CFO of one of his target companies was also a fellow pilot who kept his plane at the airport on nearby Nantucket island. He also discovered when the fellow most often flew in, then flew there himself. Eventually they met and struck up a conversation there on the tarmac, which led to introductions and a contract. Although this was not a Contact Campaign *per se*, he uses it to illustrate his point. "You must always be prepared with foreknowledge," he says, "in sales and certainly in Contact Marketing." That is particularly true when targeting personal interests in your campaign.

Sometimes taking the personal approach can help move a stalled contact situation along. Author Linda Richardson recalls the difficulty one her clients was having reaching a target executive at JPMorgan Chase. "The guy was always such a jerk," she recalls, "so my client did some digging and discovered he was a fan of the Watkins Glen car races. She bought a beautiful model Porsche and sent it to him." That, coupled with a personal note, enabled her to break through. Touching upon the target executive's personal interests changed his demeanor and eventually led to business.

Blogger Lori Richardson says, "It can be as easy as simply finding out which teams they follow, what their passions are, and then doing something creative, something that separates you from the rest." *CRM at the Speed of Light* author and CRM Hall of Fame member Paul Greenberg agrees: "We are all self-interested human beings," he says, "which is a good thing, not a bad thing." He says the best way to engage someone is to understand what they're interested in.

But what if press clippings, social media, and readily available information about a person's school or favorite team aren't enough? Author Orvel Ray Wilson suggests going deep undercover to get to the kind of information that motivates a given target executive. He tells the story of a sales rep who had been calling on an electronics manufacturer for months, getting nowhere. He was told, "We're happy with our vendor," and was hitting brick walls at every turn.

But the rep discovered that, on every sunny afternoon, there was always a cluster of the company's workers eating at the outdoor picnic tables just outside their building. So one day, he showed up with a stack of pizzas, asked if anyone wanted some, and struck up conversations. He asked about the defect rate of certain components and delivery times from their suppliers. Within thirty minutes, he had everything he needed to make his case. From there, he put it all in a letter and got the account. "Sometimes it helps to have friends in low places," Wilson says slyly.

Whether you decide to tailor your Contact Campaign pieces to each target executive's set of personal interests, or to take a more standardized approach, every contact effort should incorporate a deep understanding of who they are and what their interests and considerations are. It's a critical element of every Contact Marketing strategy and, as we've just seen, it can be a Contact Campaign all on its own.

Category #19: Investor Relations

Estimated cost per contact: How much do you want to invest?

It's up to you how much you'd want to invest in a given company, but as author Dave Stein points out, "Stockholders get special access to the C-suite and board members." He says buying even a little bit of stock entitles you to attend annual stockholders meetings, and all of the C-level executives will be there.

Stein advises, "Get there early; position yourself in the right place. Get fully up to speed on what they're experiencing and where they're planning to take the company." As the meeting comes to a close,

> "
> *Dave Stein notes that buying even a little bit of company stock entitles you to attend annual stockholders meetings, and all of the C-level executives will be there.*
> "

that's when Stein moves in with his own introduction and request for a meeting.

What's interesting about this approach is its simplicity. You invest a little and you become someone relevant and important to your target executive. If you don't like the results, you can always get your money back, plus or minus whatever change in value occurs in the stock.

Category #20: Over the Top

Estimated cost per contact: Impossible to determine

If one of the trademarks of a successful Contact Campaign is fearless adventurism, can it be taken too far? And does it make a good campaign? Many of the techniques and stories our experts have shared in the preceding sections could be termed over the top. I believe they worked because the level of audacity and creativity behind them tends to overcome the VIP's natural resistance to connecting with new people. They are always on guard, as are their assistants, but also watching for new and unexpected opportunities, insights, and market advantages.

So if you show a great amount of boldness in the way you reach out, it's natural to assume at least some of the targeted executives would see it as a positive demonstration of how you work and think, and how you approach problem solving. In that case, audacity, with clever and well-targeted thought behind the contact approach, is inherently valuable to the target VIPs.

There is a somewhat famous story about how Deutsch, Inc. CEO and CNBC host Donny Deutsch wanted to pitch a particular advertising account. His target was the head of the local Tri-State Pontiac Dealers Association and his approach was definitely over the top. For his Contact Campaign, Deutsch arranged to have a procession of car parts delivered to the target executive's home every thirty minutes.

Each part came with a note, turning the pieces into visual metaphors. With the rear fender came a note saying, "We'll cover your rear end." A headlight showed up with the message, "We'll light the way." It continued until the fellow relented and awarded Deutsch the account. That Contact Campaign alone doubled the agency's billings.[4]

Years later, Art Sobczak recalled hearing the story from Deutsch during an installment of his show on CNBC. "He was ready to send twenty-four packages in all," he says. "He wouldn't give up until he got the account. It would have gone on for twelve hours straight." What I find over the top about Deutsch's campaign was the relentlessness of the timing and, if true, the fact that it was all delivered to the target executive's home. But you can't argue with the results.

There's another reference to what the film *Forrest Gump* called "a certain fruit company" in this next story. Author Orvel Ray Wilson relates the tale of a software company representative who was anxious to sell an accounting package to the company. "The accounting team loved it," Wilson recalls, "but when they referred the poor fellow to Purchasing, he was told it wasn't in the budget." So the rep decided it was time to take it to the top.

The only trouble was, the CEO was also an international celebrity and *nearly* impossible to reach. The rep tried sending faxes, telegrams, and more, but nothing worked. Then he decided it was time to get outrageous. The next day, a delivery man showed up at the front desk with a wooden box containing a live homing pigeon, to be delivered to the CEO. Accompanying the caged pigeon was a note saying, "I've tried everything else to reach you, now I've resorted to this." The note went on to request that the CEO write the name of his favorite restaurant with a date and time on a tiny note, then place it in the capsule on the pigeon's leg and release it.

To the rep's surprise, the pigeon returned with the requested information, and the CEO showed up for the lunch. Not only that, he brought a signed letter of intent and the rep got the $250,000 sale. The cost of acquiring the contract? Lunch plus chicken feed, literally.

ROI was through the roof. But still, I think it's highly questionable to involve live animals in a Contact Campaign. What if the box had never been opened or tossed in the trash? What if the pigeon had died on the way there? That would have resulted in the delivery of a dead pigeon and possibly a warrant for the rep's arrest for animal cruelty. Still, he did get the business.

It might seem that I'm saying over-the-top Contact Campaigns are not okay, that they're not valid. That isn't the case. Actually, most of the campaigns described in this book could be described as over the top, but as you have just read, these hover just at the edge of going too far. When they don't run afoul of that line, they can be quite effective.

Ruhlin Group founder John Ruhlin shows us one example in his shirt campaign. I covered it in Chapter 8, where I described various Contact Campaign tactics based on giving gifts. It's just that Ruhlin's approach to giving gifts seems so over the top that I should mention it again here. The way he builds a grand element of theater in the method of giving the gift is ingenious. The fact that an actual clothier comes by to take measurements and show fabric samples to provide a custom shirt, before any attempt at contact is made, shows amazing boldness. And it works.

Axcelerate Worldwide CEO Rob Smith has a similarly outrageous approach to his Contact Campaigns. He was once tasked with helping a client's reps break through to ten technology CEOs, but he decided to flip the equation and make the focus of the campaign their assistants. The reps called each assistant and asked them to decide whether or not the package should be sent. They were asked further, if I send it, will you make sure the CEO gets it? Each assistant listened intently and gave their nod to proceed.

Smith then sent what he calls a "Smart Box," a custom, aluminum Zero Halliburton briefcase with a laptop computer inside, preloaded with a three-minute video. The package also included a cell phone. The cases arrived with a scratch-off card which, when scratched, revealed the combination to the locking mechanism of the case.

Each Smart Box cost $5,000, but the ten-piece campaign gener-
ated a 58 percent close rate and $24 million in sales within forty
days. Ruhlin's and Smith's Contact Campaigns were over the top
in terms of the individual attention and effort that went into each
instance of the campaign, but certainly do not cross the line of
going too far.

As I researched the material for this book, and particularly the tactics
and stories you've just read, I came across a number of instances
in which the tactics had drifted into the realm of being sales stunts
rather than Contact Campaigns. When is it a sales stunt rather than
a Contact Campaign?

I would say when the action taken is simply for show, or to cause
a grand interruption. And as I've already stated, a sales stunt is something that can easily reflect poorly on your brand. It might elicit feelings of awkwardness or perhaps anger for having been manipulated.
I can't deny that, more than occasionally,
they also work. I just don't see them as
being part of Contact Marketing.

Little Red Book of Selling author Jeffrey Gitomer is a master at doing these
well and making them work. In one case,
he sent his fifteen-year-old daughter
into a meeting with ad agency Young &
Rubicam to pitch a T-shirt campaign. It
worked; he got the business. But I won't
be advising that you send your kids to do your bidding. At least not
within the realm of Contact Marketing. I won't be recommending
that you trespass and block a VIP's parking space as part of your
Contact Campaign, either, because I think these stunts ultimately
deliver the wrong message.

> "All of this effort is directed
> at one goal: to build your
> network of VIP contacts. The
> more you have, the more
> introductions you'll receive,
> making your job easier."

In the end, all of this effort is directed at one goal: to build your network of VIP contacts. The more you have, the more introductions you'll receive, making your job easier. As one CEO puts it, "You earn your network over the course of your career." Still, having the tools described in the preceding chapters gives you the freedom to reach out and connect with virtually anyone at any time, with or without that golden introduction from a trusted source.

Points to Remember

✔   Over-the-top techniques are great for entertainment value and demonstrate the high level of boldness that often makes Contact Campaigns so successful and dynamic.

✔   Still, the over-the-top methods described in this chapter are not necessarily considered the core of what Contact Marketing is.

✔   Print media can be used to great effect in a Contact Campaign, but be prepared to spend a lot per contact.

✔   Contact letters run as full-page ads not only reach the intended target executive, but also can elicit reinforcing behavior from all of the VIP's contacts.

✔   Prepaid phones are a relatively inexpensive way to ensure a phone connection with a VIP prospect and can stir a lot of intrigue if delivered anonymously.

✔   Personal interests can be researched easily via social media and should always be part of the dossier you compile on any Top 100 list member before connecting.

✔   Personal interests can serve as Contact Campaigns all on their own.

✔   Becoming an investor in a target company can get your
     foot in the door with CEOs, and may end up making
     money if the stock goes up during the campaign.

✔   Over-the-top Contact Campaigns do work, but run the
     risk of backfiring more easily than other types.

✔   Sales stunts are definitely not part of Contact Campaigns;
     they're generally manipulative and reflect poorly on your
     brand.

SECTION III

YOUR CONTACT CAMPAIGN IN ACTION

"Click the 'Play' button?
That's your entire marketing strategy?"

CHAPTER 12

How a Contact Campaign
Works

Growing up in Massachusetts, I spent a lot of weekends with my family on our thirty-foot sloop, which was moored on the confluence of the West and East Branches of the Westport River, just to the north of the Rhode Island border. It was a beautiful place, one of those impossibly picturesque seaside New England villages surrounded by grassy sand dunes, where Horseneck Beach pointed the way across Buzzards Bay to the Elizabeth Islands and then on to Martha's Vineyard and

Nantucket. As beautiful as this place was, it could also be treacherous, and we learned to respect the ever-changing sea conditions.

One day, we made the hour-long drive to Westport, and just as we crossed the bridge over the river, we encountered a thick fog. My father pressed on, as he always did. As we parked at the yacht club and began offloading our gear, members of the club stopped by to consult with my father. *Are you going out in this? Shouldn't we wait it out? Why don't you hang out here with us, at the club?* He firmly waved it all off. We were headed out as quickly as possible.

As we progressed up the channel, the fog seemed to get thicker, but still my father pressed on. But as we cleared the mouth of the inlet, something truly amazing happened, something I will remember my whole life.

As soon as we passed the ends of the jetties marking the entrance to the harbor, the fog disappeared. Well, not exactly. It remained pressed over the marina and Westport River like a lid on a jar, but the rest of Buzzards Bay was completely clear. We had the whole place to ourselves, and it was a beautiful, sunny day as we cruised the islands.

Returning late that afternoon, as we reentered the harbor, the fog was still present, though thinning. As we made our way back through the channel, we could see many of our fellow club members with their boats beached on the sand, where they had laid out towels and blankets to "wait it out." They had spent their entire day hunkered down in the fog, never venturing beyond their self-imposed limits to see what lay beyond.

Contact Marketing is much the same. You'll be told some of the people you're trying to break through to are impossible to reach. You'll be told some of your goals are impossible to achieve. But you don't have to listen to any of that limiting, albeit well-intentioned misdirection. If someone tells you something is impossible, remember my sailing story and forge ahead. Find out for yourself and never "wait it out" under the fog of someone else's limitations. Your opportunities for growth and prosperity are endless and immediate. You just have to get started.

We've looked at an assortment of Contact Campaigns different people have tried, and I hope their creativity has inspired you. In this section, we will look at how to actually build your campaign once you have your Contact Marketing strategy in mind. I will walk you through some general tips and the steps to follow for a successful campaign. This chapter in particular sets up your initial approach and even includes some standard scripts you can follow or adapt as needed to articulate what you need to say.

Never Take "No" for an Answer

I don't mean "Never take 'no' for an answer" literally. If you reach out to an important contact and they reject your approach, I'm not suggesting you become a stalker. But you should take a thoughtful look at why they have resisted your contact request and determine if they should still be pursued, perhaps in a different way.

Reaching out to VIPs, particularly C-level executives and company owners, will be difficult and challenging. Some of what you'll encounter is their standard response to anyone trying to break through. They don't know you. You're asking for their time. They're already busy, already overcommitted. If they don't understand what you have to offer, it may take them a bit of time to come around.

Never taking "no" for an answer can take many forms. It could look like simple persistence. Or maybe a changed approach, sending articles of interest rather than relentlessly calling, if one approach or the other hasn't worked. Never taking "no" for an answer isn't about actually never taking "no" for an answer. It's about stepping into a new attitude, one that will allow you to press on when your inner voice tells you to stop because you're entering unfamiliar territory. Challenging yourself to break through, to stick with it, is every bit as important to your success as your actual campaign.

Famed real estate speaker Brian Buffini once decided he wanted Neil Armstrong, the first man to walk on the moon, to speak at an upcoming conference. So he sent a handwritten invitation. Nothing happened, so he sent another. When that failed to prompt a reply, he sent another. This process repeated until he finally received a note from Neil asking, "Are you going to continue to send me these notes?" Buffini wrote "Yup" across the top and returned Armstrong's note. And with that, Neil Armstrong, the first man on the moon and one of the world's most reclusive icons, agreed to deliver that keynote speech after all. It was such a coup that NASA later requested video footage of Armstrong's speech because it had so little of him in its archives.

If a given contact target's response really is a hard "no," don't let it discourage you. If they can't see the value in what you have to offer, go to their competitors. And once some of them become your clients, circle around and get in touch again, this time telling them they're missing out and falling behind. Contact is a fluid entity, constantly changing as conditions and events change. You will find that your determination is one of the most important elements of your Contact Campaign, so keep it fresh and alive. Believe in your mission and don't turn back. There are sunny skies and a beautiful blue ocean of possibilities waiting just beyond the fog and breakwater.

Steps, Flow Charts, and Scripts

You've already read about the various categories of Contact Campaigns in the previous section, so you know they don't all take the same path. Still, there are many common elements of a Contact Campaign, which we'll examine now.

When you're reaching out to a C-level executive, it is very likely you'll need to navigate a few obstacles to get there. If a company is set up traditionally, you'll start with the receptionist, who risks losing their job if they put the wrong people through to the CEO's office. They're often tough, but not always. After all, they need to direct the right calls through as well.

I find two approaches particularly useful. If I'm calling for the CEO, I'll ask the receptionist if the executive has an assistant I can speak with, and probably because I call with a confident tone and sound like I belong, I'm usually put through. It works whether I'm calling the famous CEO of a *Fortune* 500 company or if I'm trying to reach the owner of a smaller company.

The other approach is to use what I described in Chapter 9 in the "Phone" section. Start by telling the receptionist you're not sure who you should connect with and ask if you can explain what you're trying to do. They'll usually listen intently, as long as you don't take too long to explain yourself, and they'll refer you to someone. Once connected, repeat the same thing: "I'm trying to reach the person in charge of such and such. I was referred to you, but I'm not sure you're the right person. May I explain what I'm trying to do?"

This approach puts people in "help" mode and they almost always listen intently. Eventually, you will reach the right person, but stick to the script: "I've been referred to you, not sure if you're the right person, may I explain what I'm calling about?" By the time you're finished, you will have reached the right person, explained why you're calling, and the whole thing has taken place in a nonresistant mode.

In the context of a Contact Campaign, I am usually calling to follow up on a contact effort, so the next hurdle is to work with the target's executive assistant. Don't assume they're trying to act as a gatekeeper; work from the position that you have something worthwhile to bring to the executive's attention, and you're simply working with the assistant to help them help their executive.

This has to be done quickly, so you don't waste any of the assistant's time. My standard approach is to explain in just a few words why I'm calling, then ask if I can send an email to explain the reason for the call. This email component is critical, because it gives the assistant something they can easily pass along to explain why you called.

This is what a typical Contact Campaign looks like in flow chart form, with some simple scripts for dealing with receptionists and executive assistants on initial calls.

Contact Campaign Flow Chart

The Nature of Contact Campaigns

Contact campaigns involve highly individualized approaches to each target contact, and, people being people, you're likely to encounter a broad range of responses. In turn, you'll need to be ready to offer a set of responses as you move the contact along. But there are some commonalities, and the steps diagrammed below are likely to be a part of any contact campaign.

Receptionist

Goal: Get past this initial gatekeeper to CEO's executive assistant as soon as possible, with minimal explanation of your reason for calling

Call, speak with receptionist, ask for name of CEO's executive assistant, connect ASAP

Be ready to explain reason for your call, but avoid having to do this with the receptionist

Not Recommended

Using phone directory to reach CEO directly—it's premature, although that could come in handy later in the process, if you're having trouble breaking through

Executive Assistant

Goal: Get the executive assistant (also known as the EA) plugged in to your mission to reach the CEO, get their confirmed contact details, and make them your ally

Explain reason for call, alert EA that a package is to arrive and why

Be ready to send email explaining reason for requested contact

Send follow-up card immediately to thank EA for their help

Not Recommended

Being evasive in your answers, disrespecting the EA's authority, treating them like adversaries rather than the allies you need them to be

CEO

Goal: Get opportunity to speak on the phone or at least have your message presented, progress to a direct meeting or top-down referral to get the sale or strategic partnership you're seeking

Send Contact Campaign package, set time for initial call in letter

Call precisely at appointed time

Anti-pitch—get attention in first 5 seconds, finish in 30 or less

Wait—let CEO speak, listen

Answer questions, explore possible fit, determine next steps

Not Recommended

Whatever you do, don't waste a second of the CEO's time; know their company and anticipate their needs, and be ready to serve them with a well-conceived solution

Contact Campaign Scripts/Gatekeepers

> Your goal: Get through to the EA as quickly as possible, make them an ally, and recruit their help to get the contact campaign in the CEO's hands.

Receptionist

Goal: Get through to the executive assistant, give as little info as possible:

> Hello, does ((Mr./Ms. target name)) have an executive assistant I can speak with?

"Yes, hold on" ➡
Proceed to Executive Assistant section

> **Or, "Who's calling/What do you want?"** ➡
> I'm ((Title)) of ((Company) and I'm calling to alert ((Mr./Ms. target name))'s assistant that I will be sending a package. May I be connected?

"Okay, hold on" ➡
Proceed to Executive Assistant section

> **Or, "Can I say what this is in reference to?"** ➡
> Again, I'm ((Title)) of ((Company)) and I'm sending a package to ((Mr./Ms. target name)). I want to speak to his/her executive assistant to let them know it's coming and what it is. May I be connected now?

"Okay, hold on" ➡
Proceed to Executive Assistant section

> **Or, "I'm sorry, I can't put you through/I'll have to take a message"** ➡
> End the call, call back the next day, perhaps during receptionist's lunch break.
> ((Note: At this stage, avoid giving your name in case you don't get through and need to try this again at a later time. Also, keep in mind the receptionist only has the power to say "No" to your access, but lacks any authority to say "Yes" to your mission.))

Executive Assistant

Goal: Get her/his contact info, recruit his/her help setting up the contact, trigger sending Contact Campaign

> Hello, are you ((Mr./Ms. target name))'s executive assistant?
> ((Be sure to write down his/her name while introducing yourself))
> My name is _____. I'm ((Title)) of ((Company)) and I wanted to alert you that I will be sending ((Mr./Ms. target name)) a package. You can never be too careful these days, so I just didn't want it showing up unannounced and I wanted to make sure you knew what it was. Actually, it's a _____ for his/her office, and it's something I think he/she will really enjoy and find useful. In fact, I could also send you an email to confirm all of this, so you'll have the details. Would that be okay?

Contact Campaign Scripts/Gatekeepers continued . . .

"Yes, that's fine" ➡
Get correct spelling of assistant's name, email address, confirm delivery address, finish call

>**Or, "Wait, tell me more about what you want"** ➡
>Again, my name is _____, I'm ((Title)) of ((Company)) and I will be sending _____ to ((Mr./Ms. target name)). I'm doing this to introduce myself and from there, he/she can meet with me or refer me to someone else in the organization.

"Okay, that's fine" ➡
Get correct spelling of assistant's name, email address, confirm delivery address, finish call

>**Or, "He/she doesn't accept gifts/Let me connect you with someone else"** ➡
>Well, that's fine, but what I do concerns his/her overall strategy for the company. I'm happy to speak to anyone he/she recommends, but I always start with a conversation with the ((CEO/President/Owner)), simply because it involves the direction of the company.

"Okay, that's fine, go ahead and send it" ➡
Get correct spelling of assistant's name, email address, confirm delivery address, finish call

>**"I think you should contact _____ instead. I'll connect you now"** ➡
>((see Options 1 and 2 below))
>
>**OPTION 1**
>Okay, but can you please give me some assurance I'll be talking to the right person? I'll be discussing corporate strategy as it relates to ____. It will involve ____, ____, and ultimately, shareholder value and the net effect on your stock price or company valuation. Are you sure I shouldn't speak with ((Mr./Ms. target name)) instead?
>
>**OPTION 2**
>In that case, I'll withdraw. I am sure it will make sense to refer me to someone else in your organization at some point, but if I can't first address those strategic issues—issues that may mean millions of dollars worth of value and could change the direction of the company— with ((Mr./Ms. target name)), then I'll pass.

After the Call:
1. Enter assistant's name and contact information in tracking spreadsheet.
2. Note in Action Required section that contact piece should be triggered.
3. Make entries in Notes/Comments section to keep your team in sync as to progress of contact.

In most cases, you'll find the EA is eager to help—it's their job to keep unwanted callers out, but also to bring new opportunities to the CEO's attention.

What You'll Need to Create

As you've read in Section II, there are very simple types of Contact Campaigns that don't require the steps and materials others do. Some of the phone or email techniques obviously skip a few steps, as well as expense. In my experience, these work a lot of the time, and I include them in my strategy. But if I really need to break through and I want to make the best possible impression, it's time to use some of the more involved and powerful methods. These require several key elements.

The first of those is your contact letter. It must be succinct and powerful, and get to the point immediately. It should leave the reader with a clear understanding of who you are, why you want to get in touch, and how it will benefit them on a strategic level. It can't simply be based on the assumption that saving some money is enough; it has to be something significant that helps move their organization in the right direction.

Your contact letter is also for your benefit. It is a necessary exercise to get to the essence of your value statement, which is how you will open the initial conversation when you connect with your contact target.

You may want to include a second effort, something you send to a VIP prospect who hasn't yet responded. This could be a handwritten letter or an email. I often use greeting cards featuring various cartoons depicting their business success, often with fantastic results.

Cartoons are wonderful in this mission. A cartoon delivers its message in a delightfully disarming way, and it seems to allow you to say just about anything.

Whatever form it takes, your follow-up element should incorporate some way to compel the VIP to respond. It could be humor or it could touch upon a possible pain point. It should clearly explain how you can contribute without talking about your product or service, perhaps with a focus on how you're already helping the contact target's competitors. And it should always press for contact.

As mentioned earlier, you should also consider including a hold-back device in your campaign, which we will examine in more detail in Chapter 14. Hold-back devices are used to create leverage to make the requested meeting or phone conversation more likely to happen.

What You Can Expect

By definition, reaching out to VIPs is high-stakes business. As you begin, you're likely to find the experience intimidating, but stick with it. Like the sailing story at the beginning of this chapter, you're starting in the same fog everyone else is, the fog that prevents them from reaching out to people they perceive as being too important to possibly engage with them.

As you push your way through the process, it will become easier and easier. And then it will start to be *fun*. You'll become very comfortable dealing with the people you encounter on the phone, including the target contact's executive assistant. You'll see them as enablers rather than obstacles to your success.

The techniques I have shared with you in the previous section are designed to produce maximum impact. When I send my Contact Campaign and I hear about how excited the target was when it was received, *I get excited*. When they tell you your contact piece was one of the cleverest campaigns they've ever seen, you will experience the exhilaration my family and I felt when we cleared the fog and discovered the beautiful day awaiting us on the water. You'll be thrilled to see your ability to reach virtually anyone take form, as it reshapes your life's prospects.

Points to Remember

✔   The objective of Contact Marketing, of connecting with highly important and mostly unreachable people, is far from impossible.

✔ The saying "Never take 'no' for an answer" strongly applies to Contact Marketing.

✔ Reaching out to VIPs is daunting, but don't allow yourself to become intimidated; they're people just like the rest of us.

✔ If a CEO does tell you "no" is their final answer, go to their competitors.

✔ It's helpful to use a script when first approaching VIPs through your Contact Campaign.

✔ Scripts are an effective way of ensuring your message remains uniform across your sales team.

✔ Once you've chosen a Contact Campaign method, you'll need to create a contact letter and follow-up efforts, possibly including cards to thank executive assistants and prompt stalled contact efforts.

✔ Many of the most effective Contact Campaigns include a "hold-back device," designed to push the target contact to respond in the requested manner.

✔ Reaching out to CEOs will at first seem scary and difficult, but you will soon see it can actually be highly effective and a lot of fun.

*"How's this for our guarantee? 'If you're ever
dissatisfied, just let us know and we'll see what we can do.'"*

CHAPTER 13

Developing Your Contact Letter, Scripts, and Anti-Pitch

I have mentioned earlier in this book that I've often thought of Contact Campaigns as direct mail on steroids. My own campaigns, which use personalized cartoons, literally are adaptations of the countless record-breaking campaigns I've created for many of the world's biggest direct marketers.

Direct marketing campaigns seem to have fallen out of favor lately, as digital, search, social, and mobile marketing have taken over, but the lessons from this form of marketing are still quite valid. In fact, mailed campaigns have begun to take on a contrarian mantle. It's now novel, even exciting, to receive something tangible and well conceived.

At the height of my creative work for magazine publishers, I was paid as much as $25,000 to write a subscription campaign letter. It was a lot of money, but these letters were expected to work magic. They were always tested against the client's current "control"—their most effective campaign piece to date—to see if I could develop something new to beat it. Publishers are some of the most prolific testers in the world and their controls are nearly impossible to beat. If you tie a control, you just tied the record for their all-time most effective campaign.

It was a fiercely competitive environment in which to create. If you produced a piece that failed to set the new record, you were out. But if your creative pieces were setting new records, you were paid well. That's how it worked. So when I give advice on what your letter should say, I'm telling it from a perspective honed through hard-fought lessons learned over a twenty-year span, as someone who has produced countless record-breaking, control-busting campaigns.

Am I trying to impress you? Yes. I want to impress upon you the value of a well-written, powerful letter. When you write yours, or when you're giving direction to a copywriter to write it, do it as though your letter is worth that same $25,000 creative fee, regardless of the price actually paid. The stakes here are just as high.

What Your Letter Should Include and Say

The best letters—the ones that generate record results—always start with a point of agreement woven together with a hook that creates a desire to engage in the message. I've always had a big advantage in this, because my letters almost always start with a cartoon, just like the chapters in this book.

That may seem silly at first, but there is sound marketing reasoning behind it. Readership surveys have shown cartoons are almost always the best read and remembered part of publications, so they get more attention that just about anything you can put in print or on screen. If you think about it, the nature of humor is simply truth told with a twist. That's why, when we laugh at something, we often find ourselves saying, "That's so true!"

The cartoon acts as a device to grab the reader's attention, plant an immediate point of agreement, and produce deep engagement with my message. With or without a cartoon, that is what your letter must do to capture your target's interest. From there, your letter must lay out a quick, compelling, thoughtful, and informed statement of the issue you want to address.

Then comes your value statement. Keep it short and tightly focused on how it solves the target contact's problem. Don't get carried away with extraneous detail about your product or service. This is the same statement you will use eventually as you start your conversation with the prospect, and it should be confined to as few words as possible, without sacrificing the impact your solution can provide.

As I've stated elsewhere in this book, I strongly suggest you include a hold-back device, something of value related to your reason for getting in touch. This will be expressed in your first of two closing paragraphs, in which you explain what you see as the opportunity to be discussed, along with your promise to bring the hold-back device when you meet.

The closing paragraph should be a single sentence addressing the upcoming call or meeting. In *Selling to VITO*, Anthony Parinello advises setting a certain time and date for your call, noting that the target can have their assistant arrange a different time or they can call you directly at any time.

It's not a bad approach, but I find its execution problematic. If you're sending something physical, what if it doesn't arrive before the call date? And, although it is admirable in its drive to get the meeting to happen, I have found that setting the call date unilaterally comes across as presumptuous and is rarely honored.

Instead, I recommend asking the target to take the call. "Please take my call shortly," or "Please expect my call shortly," seems to work quite well and doesn't ensnare your campaign in logistical problems.

But we're still not done. What will appear in your signature block? If you're employed, you'll list your printed name, title, email address, and phone number. But are there other elements you can include, which form the basis of the VIP statement covered in Chapter 4? Do you hold other titles that may be relevant to the contact target? Is there a distinction you can include that will cause the recipient to feel excitement about your call?

Your signature file should be crafted carefully. Mine looks like this (shown here with underlines to indicate embedded links when used in email):

> Stu Heinecke
> President & Founder of <u>Contact</u> and <u>CartoonLink</u>
>
> Host of <u>Contact Marketing Radio</u>
> (live Thursdays 10 A.M. PST/1 P.M. EST, archived on <u>iTunes</u>)
>
> Author of <u>*How to Get a Meeting with Anyone*</u>,
> <u>*Drawing Attention,*</u> and <u>*Big Fat Beautiful Head*</u>
>
> *The Wall Street Journal* cartoonist
> DMA Hall of Fame-nominated <u>marketer</u>

Take a look at what I have here. I am the president and founder of my company, and host of Contact Marketing Radio, so there is some measure of importance expressed. That's reinforced with notation of my DMA Hall of Fame nomination, the fact that I am one of *The Wall Street Journal* cartoonists and that I am an author.

My own VIP statement is always evolving, but I can tell you this one already works quite well. Some of that has to do with *The Wall Street Journal* cartoonist and author statements, which cause a great deal of fascination and anticipation to get on the phone with me. It's up to you to produce a similar effect from your own VIP statement.

Direct marketers have long known that, in a typical letter, readers focus first on their own name and second on the postscript. They use that fact to their advantage by restating the offer in the "P.S." with a reminder of the expiration date. You should use it to restate the compelling reason why the meeting or phone call should take place. Do it in nine words or less.

When you write your letter, give special attention to the tone. The best letters always use conversational language to create an emotional connection with the reader. Leave out jargon and acronyms; don't produce something that reads as forced or overly formal. Let them know you have something of value to offer, something that will only be ignored at great cost and that you appreciate their openness to taking the meeting.

> " The best letters always use conversational language to create an emotional connection with the reader. "

Defining Your Process

Defining your process starts with a series of choices. Who is on your list? Are they primarily C-level executives? What is the issue you hope to solve for them? How difficult are they to reach? Do they have executive assistants? Which Contact Campaign method or methods are you planning to use?

Starting at the point where you've identified and researched your list members, you will need to assemble a flow chart. Include every step, so that others within your organization can duplicate your process with minimal instruction, or so they can step in and assist you at any point along the way.

As you saw in Chapter 12, my process starts with a call to the contact target's assistant. I have a script in mind, although I engage in free-flowing conversation. During this initial contact, I'll want to make sure I have confirmed the spelling of the executive's and their assistant's names, along with their email addresses. This serves two purposes. First, the assistant's address comes with permission to send emails, starting with a message I can copy and paste, to provide an explanation of my request for a meeting that can easily be forwarded.

Second, once I have the assistant's email, I can see how addresses are formed for all employees of the company. Firstname_Lastname@ company, FLastname@company, firstname.lastname@company, and even First@company are all commonly used email conjugations. Make a note of what that suggests the executive's email address may be.

Next, you'll include steps linked to producing, delivering, and tracking the Contact Campaign piece—be sure to make a note to send an email to the executive assistant when tracking information is available. Keeping the assistant in the loop tends to ensure their commitment to help you make contact with their executive.

Then comes the call to the CEO. Since you may not be starting with a set call date and time, be prepared to call a few times, perhaps over the span of a couple of weeks. Keep in mind, VIPs are busy people, are often out of the office, and their schedules are packed. It will take a bit of maneuvering to find mutual fits in your calendars.

Inevitably, you will find there will be some targets who don't respond. It is possible to connect with your targets at least fifty percent or more of the time, but be prepared to test different approaches before that happens. Meanwhile, you'll need to add a few follow-up steps to your process. These could take the form of greeting cards, letters, emails, or phone calls.

If a hold-back device is part of your campaign, it may need to show up twice in your process; once if the desired meeting takes place, and again if the target hasn't responded throughout the process. You may find that sending the held-back item produces the desired result after all, or you may decide to send another communication, asking what you should do with it. Should it be donated to a charity? If so, does the target have one in mind it should benefit? The goal, of course, is always to start engaging with the contact.

As you refine your process, keep your flow chart up to date. It will help keep you clearly on track, while ensuring your process is easily duplicated and multiplied by others in your organization.

Developing Your Scripts

Since this is part of documenting your process, you'll need at least three scripts, starting first at gaining entry with the receptionist. You can start with the scripts included in the previous chapter, but you really should develop your own to fit your particular campaign.

Scripts can be written out word for word, or arranged in outline form. I prefer the latter, because you have your talking points laid out on the page, but you're free to converse naturally. Use whichever feels best for you.

As you progress from receptionist to executive assistant, your script should include a quick explanation of who you are (your VIP statement tailored to the needs of the targeted executive) and why you're calling, as covered in Chapter 12. I think it makes sense to focus on the item you're sending to the executive, but be prepared to explain why you're sending it and what your ultimate goal is. This can be tricky. A truly determined assistant may cut you off, saying it won't be necessary to send the contact piece. I usually send it anyway, because we have no idea if the assistant has a firm grasp of the facts yet, and I don't want to argue it at that point. I would rather have the contact piece reach the target executive and let them decide for themselves whether there is reason to meet or not.

And finally, there is the million-dollar call itself to the VIP prospect. *A million-dollar phone call?* Absolutely, and we'll touch on this more in Chapter 16. You have to approach each contact with the attitude that each of these calls could be worth that much to you. So you'll want to be ready with a very special, very brief script. Remember to lead with a value statement that leaves the target asking, "How would you do that?" Or a question that has them saying "Yes, yes, yes!" in their heads. Do it in less than a dozen words. That's it. Have your "VIP statement" statement ready when they ask, "Who are you?" (covered in Chapter 4).

Developing Your "Anti-Pitch"

Developing opening lines is one thing; developing a pitch is another. And what I'm going to suggest to you is instead an "anti-pitch." Let me give you an example.

If I were to reach out to, say, Gail Goodman, CEO of Constant Contact, about my CartoonLink service, I would start with, *"I can double your members' email open rates. Is that of interest?"* But I would already have told her that in my contact piece, so I'd proceed with my anti-pitch.

I'd introduce myself: *"I'm Stu Heinecke, president of CartoonLink. I'm also one of* The Wall Street Journal *cartoonists and a hall of fame-nominated direct marketer. I have a device that has been doubling open rates for my clients, and I have a feeling that might be strategic for you to offer to your members. But I don't really know if that fits with your plans. Can you discuss that with me for a minute?"*

If she says yes, I would continue. *"From what I've been able to learn, you have 700,000 users of your email marketing platform. Constant Contact positions itself as an 'engagement marketing tool,' and you, yourself, have authored a book on engagement marketing. I'm thinking that, if you were able to offer my cartoon devices easily and affordably to your member base, it would increase their results, thereby increasing their engagement with your services. Does that make sense?"*

If she responds affirmatively, I'd ask her how she might see it fitting with their service. I'd ask what she might see as next steps and who I should connect with. I'd offer to send a copy of my book so she can understand the thinking behind the CartoonLink service. And I'd ask for her permission to correspond directly via email. And then I would end the call. As this new relationship begins, I want her to know that I respect her time. It's one of the most important things I can communicate to her.

I call this approach the Anti-Pitch because I'm not jumping down my prospect's throat, jamming in as many words as I can about my product before she cuts me off. I'm having a relaxed, exploratory conversation with her, and I'm giving her several opportunities to cut it off. But with each burst of information, I'm also telling her why I think there may be value for her. And I'm checking in constantly, to make sure she agrees with my thinking. If she doesn't, that's okay. She has given me some of her highly valuable time and I am grateful for the opportunity. It's either a fit or it isn't.

The one thing I am not doing is pitching. I'm collaborating and inviting her participation and scrutiny. I'm not trying to coerce her. I'm simply bringing something I think she may find interesting and strategically important to her attention. I haven't even mentioned my brand or any particular program yet.

Along the way, I have used my Contact Campaign to clear a path. I have a relationship with her assistant, I have demonstrated the effect I want to bring to their email marketing platform, and I have been very open about giving her an out. When you do that, the contact becomes intrigued. They start to trust you, because you have already shown a great deal of consideration. You're not pushing your way past a gatekeeper and onto the phone with the VIP. They wouldn't allow it, and even if you did get through, it wouldn't work.

You will need to craft your Anti-Pitch in the same way. Start with a brief statement that has them intrigued and asking, "How would you do that?" Then have an exploratory conversation, by saying "I have this solution that I think will work for your company/project/ etc., but I'm not sure if it is a fit after all. May I explain?"

The Anti-Pitch works in a way similar to the series-of-requests technique described in Chapter 12. As you explain your thinking and ask the contact if they agree and what they might see as next steps.

POINTS TO REMEMBER

✔ My own Contact Campaigns came from creating top-line campaigns for some of the biggest direct marketers in the world.

✔ The best contact letters start with a point of agreement woven together with a hook that creates a desire to engage with your message.

✔ I often use cartoons to engage readers quickly, as they are one of the most powerful engagement devices available.

✔ Humor is actually truth revealed with a twist; it gets readers saying, "That's so true!"

✔ Your Contact Campaign concept will drive the writing of the letter. Stick closely with the theme and focus on the value you will deliver to the contact target.

✔ Your letter must lay out a quick, compelling, thoughtful, and informed statement of the problem you want to help the CEO solve or address.

✔ The close of your letter should request that the recipient expect and take your call shortly.

✔ It's best not to dictate a specific date and time for your first call, as it can easily be ignored and leave your contact effort stalled.

✔   Your signature block should reflect your newly crafted VIP statement.

✔   Leave out jargon and acronyms from your letter copy. Write it from one human being to another, offering to bring something of value or significance to their attention.

✔   Don't turn your letter into a pitch. Focus solely on the value you want to bring to the CEO and why you're the best qualified source.

✔   Start with a script that you can modify on the go. Pass it along to others in your organization to standardize how they communicate with VIP prospects.

✔   Develop an "Anti-Pitch," a collaborative conversation to explore a possible fit for the CEO's company.

*"Just bring us something from
the dumpster out back. Surprise us."*

CHAPTER 14

Your Secret Weapon:
The Hold-Back Device

Throughout this book, I have said Contact Marketing is a fusion of sales and marketing that exists to support specific, direct, strategic sales contacts. Because Contact Marketing functions in this sales support role, it is easy to forget that it is also a true form of marketing, subject to the same disciplines applied to other forms of marketing.

When I was involved in mega-campaigns for publishers, there was a running discussion of "premiums," the free gifts offered to produce

191

a higher incidence of paid orders. Premiums often work well in that role, but they add expense to the campaign. When the measure of success hangs in the balance of a few pennies per piece either way, you can appreciate how sensitive these marketers were to adding the weight of any unnecessary expense to a campaign.

What worried the publishers even more was the requirement that, once they started offering premiums, they couldn't go back. They were stuck with the need to continually add that expense to their budgets. Even worse, it seemed once they used premiums in their offers, they had to continually raise the perceived value of the gifts, which then raised expenses further. It was a losing battle the publishers were anxious to avoid.

They also worried that their subscribers were becoming motivated more by the gift than the publications themselves. Their advertisers were catching on, too, demanding to know what percentage of the magazines' subscriptions were sold with premiums, and discounting the rates they were willing to pay to reach those readers.

As any good marketer knows, the solution is to test—to probe the possibilities and find out for certain what works, what doesn't, and why.

Hold-back devices are similar, in that they are items of value, offered in exchange for a desired response. In this case, we want our VIP quarry to agree to speak or meet with us. But there are important differences to consider in your campaign strategy.

The Contact Marketing mission focuses on a small group of target executives who have extremely high potential value to you or your company. So this isn't a situation in which a few pennies are going to throw the campaign into the loss column. What we really have is the opposite set of factors. We're working toward response rates of at least 20 to 50 percent and extremely high ROI numbers. If a $500 gift can tip the balance in your favor and you stand to gain a hundred-thousand-dollar sale, the expense will be insignificant in comparison to the gain.

Contact Marketers should not worry about the expense of a hold-back device, and in some cases, there is no added expense. The techniques in the "Half of a Gift" category in Chapter 8 rely upon splitting the campaign device in two; the remote-control model delivered with the promise of the controller when the meeting takes place, as an example. But in most cases, the hold-back device will be something of added value, rather than subtracted.

Why It's Needed and What It Does

Do you recall the example I gave in Chapter 1, about the Sandler Training test? I told you about using one of my cartoon BigBoards to break through to the president of the Sandler organization, a multi-national sales-training network. Then I recounted how the resulting campaign produced a 100 percent response and 8,000 percent ROI from the meetings it generated among five *Fortune* 1000 CEOs.

Along the way, I explained the brilliant hold-back device Sandler president Bruce Seidman suggested. The company uses copies of founder David Sandler's book, *You Can't Teach a Kid to Ride a Bike at a Seminar*, as introductory gifts to land new accounts. For the test, we devised a personalized cover that made the book look like it was about the target contact's own sales success story, complete with a byline by the CEO. *It became a book by the CEO about the transformation of their own company*. An image of the book was shown as part of the message on the BigBoard, along with a teaser, promising it would be presented to the CEO during the proposed meeting.

Since all five targeted CEOs ended up meeting with the Sandler franchisee, I have to assume the hold-back device had something to do with it. Certainly the cartoon piece did, too, as I expect they're still on display in each of the CEOs' offices all these years later.

Still, it is obvious the hold-back device performed well in its role. Many of us harbor the desire one day to write our own books, and the hold-back device gave recipients a chance to live out that fantasy.

It became a "must have" item, which is exactly what a hold-back device should be—something of personal importance or value to the target executive, something they can get only if they follow through with the requested meeting or phone conversation.

Developing Your Hook

Throughout your Contact Marketing strategy, you should be thinking about opening valuable relationships based on delivering unique and substantial value to your VIP prospects. That should be happening throughout your marketing, but it operates in overdrive here.

> *Many of us harbor the desire one day to write our own books, and the hold-back device gave recipients a chance to live out that fantasy. It became a "must have" item, which is exactly what a hold-back device should be—something of personal importance or value to the target executive, something they can get only if they follow through with the requested meeting or phone conversation.*

Put yourself in the prospect's place for a moment. You're busy. Maybe you're getting ready to travel or make a presentation to your board of directors. The phone rings constantly and, without your assistant's help, your email inbox would swell with thousands of messages from people you don't know, all of whom want a piece of your time and a chunk of your business. It's relentless and quickly becomes annoying background noise to which you are committed to filtering aggressively.

Your challenge, once again, is not just rising in importance to the target executive yourself, but aligning your mission to what is important to your prospect. We can assume they are all focused on achieving and exceeding their goals, on peering into the future to find new competitive advantages, and squeezing more efficiency from their operations.

That's a good place to start and, in some cases, may be enough to put your campaign on target. A good example of that in my own cartoon-based campaigns is using a cartoon that commemorates the recipient's success in business. I often use the cartoon shown at the top of the Introduction to this book in that role.

The cartoon shows several executives milling about in an art gallery, with two in the foreground admiring a painting of a positive trend on a sales graph, with the caption, *"That would look really good in ((Joe Sample's)) office."* Obviously, Joe Sample is a placeholder for the name of the recipient. That cartoon often causes my contact pieces to remain on display in CEOs' offices for years, which means my message and contact information also remain on display.

That's great, but what if it still isn't enough to get the target executive to commit time to your call or meeting?

Your hold-back device should be an extension of the initial theme and message, but should offer something of irresistible value. In the preceding example, I often include the promise of an autographed copy of *Big Fat Beautiful Head*, a book of my cartoons. The thought process behind it is, if the recipient liked the cartoon on the contact piece, they'll love getting an entire book of them, signed by *The Wall Street Journal* cartoonist himself as a reward for taking the meeting.

But your hold-back device shouldn't simply copy mine. To deliver value uniquely tied to you, your company, and your offering, you need to come up with something all your own. To offer true value, your campaign should focus on the recipient's needs, circumstances, and goals—but it should be suggestive of your value as a new confidant.

That requires an honest inventory of your company's unique assets. What is it you do that could be of value to the target VIP? If your company provides consulting services, is there a way you can produce an eye-popping report on the target executive's company? Most executives are hungry for honest intelligence that helps them see their company in relation to their competitors and the market ahead. And they would gladly welcome such a report.

If not a report, how about doing a bit of probing to identify the things the executive is talking about, and collecting a set of articles on the subject? Is there a book you feel best expresses the direction you'd like to take the target executive's company within your own offerings? Both of these make fine hold-back devices.

> *The hold-back device in your campaign should not become a bribe . . . Your challenge is to provide something they can't get elsewhere that helps them achieve their goals.*

The publishers I mentioned earlier can offer a cautionary tale about the kinds of things you might consider as your carrot. They often found that, the more valuable their premiums were, and the more independent they were from the magazines they were offering, the less the resulting sales would have to do with subscribers actually wanting the magazine. The audience was subscribing to get the *Sports Illustrated* football phone more than they were to get the actual magazine.

The lesson here is that the hold-back device in your campaign should not become a bribe, because that won't work with VIPs. They can afford the football phone if they really want one. Your challenge is to provide something they can't get elsewhere that helps them achieve their goals. More than anything else, it is to provide a compelling reason why the target executive needs to strike up a relationship with you and your company.

How It Supercharges Your Chances for Success

In any new business relationship, it's imperative that you always have more to offer. If you are the pursuer, you need to keep the process moving. In the early steps of your contact efforts with your VIP prospects, that need is magnified because they'd still rather ignore you at that point.

Hold-back devices can be thought of as that critical Step 2 of your contact process. If you've gotten an executive's attention with your initial contact effort, having a powerful second step ready to go enhances your success rate.

By the time you have delivered your hold-back device, you will have had three critical and positive points of contact: the initial campaign touch, the meeting or phone conversation, and the reward for having participated. You're already 90 percent there.

Of course, you still need to have a cogent case for your proposed sale or strategic alliance. But by the time you have delivered your hold-back device, you will have broken through the "I don't have time to talk with this person" wall. The target contact will have heard your Anti-Pitch and gotten to know you and your company, and you're now in a position to get some clarity on where the two of you go from there.

That's hugely significant progress toward changing the scale of your business. Moreover, if your Contact Campaign has done its job, the target contact not only knows you, they're starting to *like* you. They like the way you approach challenges, the way you think. And it's all tied initially to the quality of thinking behind your Contact Campaign. It just makes sense that a campaign that carries you through three critical steps of contact is going to be more effective than a campaign that only offers a single up-front touch.

Points to Remember

✔ Hold-back devices are a crucial third step in your Contact Campaign.

✔ They operate like marketing premiums, providing a critical push to get your VIP prospects to follow through on your request to meet or talk.

✔ Hold-back devices are something of unique value to the target executive that are relevant to their own lives and goals.

✔ Hold-back devices may be branded, but the less you focus on your brand and the more you focus on the target executive's current issues, the more valued the devices will be.

From *The Wall Street Journal*, permission Cartoon Features Syndicate
f 𝕏 in @byStuHeinecke ©CartoonLink, Inc.

"In that case, is there a better time to stop by?"

CHAPTER 15

The Critical Role of Executive Assistants

Executive assistants, administrative assistants, admins, secretaries, assistants, gatekeepers. Whatever you call them, if you're going to reach out to anyone of great importance, it's likely you're going to have to deal with them first.

Does the thought of an encounter with an EA cause your gut to tense? A study once determined that people were more afraid of public speaking than they were of dying. They must have left executive assistants off the survey, because for some reason, speaking with them seems to be one of the biggest fears of most salespeople.

When you raise the subject of executive assistants to most sales reps, the conversation often veers to frustration and how to circumvent them. But admins know when you're attempting an end run and they're more than ready for it. They're also tired of that whole approach, because it's so wasteful—*for them and for you.*

Given that executive assistants are such an integral part of the process of gaining contact with the people most important to you, isn't it time to take a fresh look at who these people are and how they can *help*, rather than prevent you from reaching your goals? Allow me to reintroduce you to the venerable executive assistant. It may just change your life.

So Much More Than Gatekeepers

Put yourself in their shoes for a moment. Let's say you're an executive assistant to a CEO. Unlike most of the people in the company, you report to the top. More than that, your results are on direct display to the CEO. If you screw up, the chief executive officer is directly affected, not to mention disaffected.

To say these people live in a pressure cooker is an understatement. They report to the same person the VPs do. It's a tough job, and only the most qualified people rise to these positions.

This may shock you, but I contend these are some of the sharpest people in their organizations. Rather than thinking of them as gatekeepers or glorified secretaries, you should think of executive assistants as stealth vice presidents. Their work receives as much visibility and scrutiny as any VP in the organization. And their decisions and actions either support or undermine their executive's effectiveness. *Executive assistants are themselves VIPs.* It shouldn't be surprising that, if you've been trying to circumvent, trick, or in some other way minimize the assistants you've been encountering, you won't be breaking through to the C-suite very often.

From now on, when you hear the title "Executive Assistant," think instead, "Vice President of Access." It will help you do your job and connect properly with these crucial members of your target contact's team. Think of them as top-level, critical advisors and influencers, and accommodate them accordingly in your Contact Campaign strategy.

Like any vice president, executive assistants are intimately aware of and involved with their executive's goals and strategies. They have a lot of duties, but perhaps their most important is encountering the many people who reach out to the CEO, and weeding through the stuff that has no relevance or should be handled by another member of their team.

If you speak to a CEO or company president in a casual moment, they're likely to emphasize how much they are in the "people business" and how critical it is to build a solid team they can depend upon. With that in mind, is it any wonder the best executive assistants are fierce defenders of their executive's time and resources? Can you see why, with the hundreds of calls and other modes of communication constantly fired in their direction, EAs must develop a high level of efficiency in their process of determining how each request for contact must be handled and who gets through?

You would do well to consider the executive assistants you encounter the most important person in the organization you're trying to reach. They are senior people in a critically sensitive role; in many ways, they are the people who actually get things done in their organizations. Yet for all of their importance, it's surprising to hear many of them say they're just doing their jobs and have no real authority. I respectfully disagree. They are the most important people you will ever encounter in your cultivation of critical contacts during your time in business.

Think of Them as Talent Scouts

Few people seem to realize that, as much as their role is to weed people out, executive assistants are equally tasked with letting the right people in. For that reason, you should think of them not as gatekeepers, but as talent scouts. Think about their unique role in the organization. Hundreds of people are trying to reach their executive, but most will waste their time with off-target pitches and personal agendas that have nothing to do with the goals at hand. But assistants are always watchful for the people, issues, ideas, perspectives, and opportunities that do fit their executive's goals, especially for the things the CEO would otherwise miss.

Think about that for a moment. The executive assistant, the person you may have been trying to circumvent all this time, is actually tasked with finding the rich opportunities that will otherwise go unnoticed. These people are not your enemies; they are your critical allies in the fulfillment of your goals. These are the people who can say to their CEO, "I think you should listen to what he has to say. He's a good guy." They are the people who can help you break through.

> *Executive assistants are the most important people you will ever encounter in your cultivation of critical contacts.*

The relationship that often exists between CEOs and their assistants is unique within the business world. When it's right, top executives respect and trust their assistants' judgment so deeply they often rely upon the EAs to make hundreds of decisions a day on their behalf. Do you see the pattern here? When you call in, the executive assistant is already making decisions on the CEO's behalf. *You're already in contact.*

So your job is not to circumvent, minimize, or trick the assistant. It is to help them find the markers in your call of something or someone worthy of their executive's consideration. This is critical:

You must go in with the belief that what you're bringing to the CEO is something of great value, deserving immediate attention. And you must be ready to express that quickly, because you're talking to a very busy, very important person.

Making the Executive Assistant Your Ally

Again, rethink your image of who the assistant is and what they're there to do. Yes, they will push the wrong people aside. But they're doing that so that they can invest time in the right people, perhaps *you*. They're ready to receive your bid for contact and engagement with the CEO. *You're on.*

The first thing you must do is to introduce the concept of *you*. And you do that with a single-sentence, power introduction that includes the VIP statement you formulated from your VIP makeover in Chapter 4. The goal is to spark their interest quickly, while establishing equal status with their executive.

Again, my VIP statement is: "Hi, my name is Stu Heinecke. I'm one of *The Wall Street Journal* cartoonists, a hall of fame–nominated marketer, and an author." Have I piqued the assistant's attention? Well, sort of, but not quite yet. What I have done is establish that I am someone with an intriguing background who is worth hearing, however briefly.

Next step is to quickly establish the value in my reason for connecting: "I have something I'd like to run by Ms. Smith that I think she will find both fascinating and useful in her present goal of expanding reach into the small business market." In this hypothetical statement of purpose, I am still being vague, but I'm showing that I value both the executive's and EA's time by already understanding one of their chief strategic goals. More importantly, I'm closer to establishing that I'm one of the people who should get through.

With just two statements, I've already established that I am someone of important and intriguing stature, who has taken the time to understand their business and current goals—and that I have something of value to the CEO to discuss. But I'm still not through.

I need to help the executive assistant further, by offering to put my reason for getting in touch in writing. So I ask, "May I send you an email to explain this further?" Most assistants will welcome this, because it gives them a chance to understand and even reread your introduction and reason for requesting a meeting.

More than that, you've made the assistant's job easier, because you have given them a ready explanation that can easily be forwarded—but with every step, you're also showing them how you work. You have the ability to focus on the needs of others and quickly get to the point. And you've shown great respect for the assistant's time. Can you see how, with just three quick statements, you've become a prospect for the talent scout on the other end of the line?

You've made things easier for the assistant, but you're also gaining important footholds. You're establishing an open door to the assistant, an important new relationship with a key person in the organization you want to engage. You now have their email address, so you're able to get through at any time, ask questions, and get their help navigating the waters ahead.

I've said it elsewhere in the book, but it bears repeating: By writing out your introduction and reasons for getting in touch, you also get to *control your message*. You don't have to worry about someone's incomplete and inaccurate paraphrasing, and you don't have to worry about the omission of key elements of your rationale for the proposed meeting.

Now you're well on your way. You've gotten the attention of the talent scout. Are you done yet? No!

Your Contact Campaign strategy should always include touch points with the executive assistants. They are VIPs, too, and are critical to your success. So you should be doing something to firmly cement that critical relationship. In my case, I always send a thank-you card, with my usual twist of a cartoon, personalized with the assistant's name. The cards always include a handwritten note inside, with my cartoonist's signature. That often seals the deal.

I realize not everybody is a *Wall Street Journal* cartoonist, so don't worry about sending one of your own cartoons—but even a simple handwritten note in a "Thank You" card can be quite meaningful and set the stage for much more to come.

My Own, Real-World Example

This has all been rather hypothetical, so let's take a run through one of my own Contact Campaigns. As you know from Chapter 7, I use BigBoards: giant foam core postcards featuring one of my personalized cartoons on one side and a message on the other from me to my contact target explaining why we should meet.

My Contact Campaign starts with a thorough understanding of who I want to connect with, what they'll gain from it, and why it is likely to meet their needs. That's my Top 100 list from Chapter 5, and my research on each of them is covered in Chapter 6. This is critical to making my campaign as effective as possible.

Part of my research for my Top 100 list is identifying who the executive assistants are. But I usually discover that when I first make the call. You know my VIP statement by now, but I'll repeat it here: "Hi, my name is Stu Heinecke. I'm one of *The Wall Street Journal* cartoonists, a hall of fame–nominated marketer, and author."

I quickly jump to my value statement, which you also know by now: "I'm sending a print of one of my cartoons about your boss, and while I want it to be a surprise to her, I don't want it to be a surprise to you. Of course, I'm sending it because I have something I want to discuss with Katherine [note the use of the CEO's first name] as well."

Next, it's time to create our connection. "May I send you an email to explain and include the tracking info for the cartoon print?" The answer is always, "Yes." Moreover, they're usually very excited to receive this print of a cartoon from a *Wall Street Journal* cartoonist about their boss. Remember, the executive assistant is always on watch for something extraordinary, something their boss might otherwise miss or something of great value to the executive or company. And I'm about to make the assistant look very good indeed.

Of course, sealing the deal is the card I send afterward, thanking the assistant for their help. I now have a champion, a critical contact who will serve as the quarterback for my Contact Campaign from inside the CEO's office. The effect continues when the BigBoard arrives, because the target executives are usually thrilled to receive it.

From the executive assistant's standpoint, we have done our jobs together. I have delivered unique value, and they have discovered it and brought it in to their executive. In the end, that's really what the assistants are there to do. It's not just about expelling the people who don't belong, even though to many, that may be the most visible part of what the assistants are doing. The most important part of their jobs is to discover *you* and the unique value you have to offer.

Points to Remember

- ✔ Executive assistants should not be thought of as gatekeepers, but as talent scouts.

- ✔ Most people think of assistants as those to circumvent, but doing so ultimately results in a defeat for you.

- ✔ In many ways, executive assistants are the most important connections you can make in an organization.

- ✔ EAs should be viewed as being on the same level as any other direct reports to the target executive.

✔ EAs are constantly on the lookout for the people, opportunities, ideas, and perspectives their boss will find useful and important in achieving their own goals.

✔ On the whole, CEOs deeply respect and trust the judgment of their assistants.

✔ Executive assistants have a lot more authority than anyone gives them credit for, including the EAs themselves.

✔ EAs should always be part of your Contact Campaign strategy. It cannot succeed without them.

✔ Your initial conversation with the target's executive assistant is critical; you must establish your equal business stature and value within the first two sentences you speak.

✔ Always offer to send a quick explanation of your reason for calling via email. It cements your access to the EA, makes it easy for them to pass it along to others, and allows you to tightly control your message.

✔ You should think of every EA as a potential ally and treat them as such.

"Okay, I've got you in our database and activated you in your sales automation and CRM programs. All that's left now is to have some sort of meeting."

CHAPTER 16

Making Contact

So far, we've examined the nature of CEOs and their executive assistants. We've expanded the definition of "CEO" to include anyone who is the "Center of Enterprise Opportunity," the key person in an organization you have targeted as a member of your Top 100 or Strategic 100 list. We've reviewed twenty categories of Contact Campaigns, all of which are powerful tools to help you break through to your best prospects for sales or strategic partnerships. You've had a VIP makeover and you are completely plugged into the goal of Contact Marketing, which is to produce a rapid expansion of scale in your business or career.

We have also examined the nature of Contact Marketing itself. A delightfully odd fusion of selling and marketing, Contact Marketing has been quietly producing results marketers have long considered impossible, including response rates as high as 100 percent and ROI in the hundreds of thousands of percent.

In the past, Contact Campaigns have been something marketers have produced from their own ingenuity and in nearly complete isolation from how others have approached the challenge of breaking through to their VIP prospects. This has been such an obscure practice that it hasn't even had a name until now. Of course, we're talking about Contact Marketing. You now have an unprecedented advantage, because you know what it is and how others have used it, and you have an abundant compilation of tactics to draw from for your own campaign.

Now it's time to pull it all together and start making the contacts that will change your life.

The Four Stages of Contact

Response rates, ROI, and expense-to-revenue figures tell you how your Contact Campaign performed once it is completed. But I find ranking each Contact during the campaign and tracking changes in those levels is critical to achieving optimal results. That is what the following "Four Stages of Contact" are for: to help you apply a standardized appraisal to each contact situation and take necessary actions to maximize the success of your campaign.

Stage 1: Indifferent

At the beginning level, your target contact is either unaware of you or your company, or may have a minimal awareness, but he or she is indifferent toward you or your brand. You're strangers. Or worse, the contact holds an inaccurate and unflattering picture of you or your company. External measures can help; your social media footprint, writings, and publicity can combine to change perceptions and make it more likely to make a meaningful connection with your target contact. The primary function of Contact Marketing is to help you push through this level of contact to the next stage.

Stage 2: Intrigued

At the second stage, something has piqued your target contact's interest to know more about you and what your company has to offer. This is typically when a contact will request more information or ask you to speak to others in their organization. It's a critical phase in your campaign, as it means you have genuinely moved the contact forward, perhaps toward the desired end result. But intrigue alone is not enough to make a sale or seal a partnership agreement. For that to happen, you must present a value proposition that the contact sees as a potential fit with his or her plans, and you must help them gain required consensus to move forward with a deal.

Stage 3: Committed

If you've reached the next level, you have pierced any initial resistance the contact has had toward meeting and dealing with you and your company, and you have provided a compelling case for moving forward immediately with a deal. The contact and their team have embraced your solution and placed their trust in you, your company, and your brand. This is also the stage at which most sales or partnerships take place.

Stage 4: Sponsor

When you've made it to the final stage, your contact has become a supporter, a fan. He or she believes wholeheartedly in you and your company and wants to share this satisfaction with friends and colleagues, who might also benefit from your services. Your name pops up in conversations, and the contact frequently cultivates referrals within and outside his organization.

The obvious next question is where do your contacts need to be on this scale in order to make a deal happen? The answer is not quite so obvious. Some deals can percolate quickly, rising during the first conversation from an initial contact to a commitment to do the deal, while others require more steps and time. Others may start at Stage 3 and then, surprisingly, stall.

Four Stages of Contact

	❶ Indifferent	❷ Intrigued	❸ Committed	❹ Sponsor
Stage				
Situation	Contact is unaware or indifferent, or may have misperceptions of you or your brand	Contact is interested, open to receiving more information or proposal	You have presented a compelling case and contact is committed to moving forward immediately	Contact is a client or partner and is a big fan of you and your brand
Required Action	Use methods to create awareness, change perceptions, use Contact Marketing to break through	Present value proposition that intensifies contact's interest and solves a specific and relevant need	Make sure all stakeholders have been addressed and included, guard against any sources of delay	Use Contact Marketing touches to cultivate engagement and knowledge of your activities and offerings
Outcome	Open new contact, generate conversation or meeting	Contact wants to move forward, has tools to create consensus	Transaction or partnership goes forward without resistance or delay	Your VIP clients become your biggest sources of business and growth

You can see in this chart that to initiate an imminent deal, most contacts must reach Stage 3, in which the contact is committed to you and your solution. Getting them to that level requires work and extra contact touches, which is why rankings should be part of your campaign tracking system. Every contact on the list showing a Stage 1 rank should be addressed with additional measures to push them along to the next level or, lacking any meaningful response, they should be removed from the list and replaced with a new prospect. Contacts at Stage 2 are hot prospects, but they require quick action to move them to the next level, to commit to your deal. These should receive a lot of your attention to discern what is needed to move the conversation along, who else needs to be involved, and which obstacles are yet to be cleared.

Contacts standing at Stage 3 should represent impending deals. If not, your critical mission is to discover what's standing in the way. This is often when deals can inexplicably stall as unknown factors come into play. Don't make the mistake of assuming that just because a contact has reached Stage 3, the deal is complete. You may find you will need to exert additional leverage here to see the deal through. "Oh, we just had another program come up as a higher priority" means your deal has just become stuck, just as dead as if it had been denied in the first place. Your job is to ensure it continues all the way through to launch and beyond.

Even in Stage 4, deals can go sideways. But this is also the magical level, where your contacts and opportunities should begin to multiply through referrals. If you find your deal stalling in this stage, something is fundamentally wrong and must be fixed quickly.

I experienced this recently with an important client in the insurance industry. In our initial test, the Contact Campaign produced a 96 percent response rate and 30,000 percent ROI, and my contact became a strong supporter. Still, the campaign stalled because the client hadn't secured budgetary commitments from the necessary stakeholders. A quick adjustment brought it all back into alignment, but it shows how even at the highest stage of contact and commitment, without constant vigilance and occasional adjustments, deals can simply dissolve.

If contacts are at Stage 4, does that mean they no longer should be part of your Contact Marketing program? Absolutely not. These are the people who have become critical to your success, because they're spreading the word about you and your services. So Contact Marketing then takes on a critical engagement mission: to keep these people in the fold, always discovering new things to talk about when they're talking about you.

> " Your personal brand is what people say about you when you're not there.
> —JEFF BEZOS, Amazon founder "

Amazon founder Jeff Bezos is known to say, "Your personal brand is what people say about you when you're not there." Contact Marketing efforts can directly affect what people, particularly your Stage 4 contacts, say about you. So doesn't it make sense to keep them constantly engaged with your message? Of course it does.

Returning all the way back to Stage 1, let's take a look at the mechanics of the calls you'll be making as you get your Contact Campaign rolling.

Initial Contact

This is it—it's showtime. You're on. You've done your homework, you already know a great deal about the target contact and how your opportunity fits with her objectives. You've already primed the conversation with your contact piece, which has piqued the CEO's curiosity and given a concise rationale for the meeting you're about to have. Be confident, be prepared, and be ready to see the scale of your enterprise change. At the same time, be respectful of the contact's time; get to the point quickly, and speak in terms of how you can help them achieve their goals. You're on your way.

Complications/What to Expect/Becoming a Phone Ninja

Some people walk into these situations with great ease, while others find it chokingly difficult. For those in the latter category, we need to talk about your phone skills and look at how you can be thrown off track.

When you make your initial call, you're already a target. You're asking to speak to the CEO or their executive assistant, which puts whoever you've just reached on the defensive. They know that if they put the wrong calls through, it could mean the end of their employment. Since they have had daily practice, eight hours a day, they're very good at deflecting your call. Your job is to stay on track.

The most common complication with your initial call to reach the CEO's executive assistant will be diverting you to someone you don't want to speak to. Unless you're offering something of strategic interest to human relations, a referral to that department is almost always a sign that the speaker on the other end of the line doesn't understand what you want to accomplish. *Never* accept a referral to HR; if they suggest that course of action, patiently re-explain what you want.

Remember, the executive assistant's job is to shed irrelevant calls quickly and protect the CEO's time—but also to find the hidden nuggets of opportunity their executive might otherwise miss. Your job is to make it through their potential obstacles. To do that, you must become a phone ninja. You need to be confident, have a balanced stance, and be ready to block and counterstrike with logic and relevance to the CEO's objectives.

Handling the Receptionist

If you encounter a live receptionist on your call, be courteous but focused. Avoid small talk; just state your request and be ready to tussle a bit. If they ask the nature of your call, volunteer the least amount of information necessary to get through. Don't try to convince them of the value of your call. Your objective is to reach the target's executive assistant. Get there as quickly as possible with the least amount of conversation possible.

Automated reception systems generally make your task of connecting with the CEO's assistant more difficult. Ideally, you'll be able to speak with a human receptionist, ask if the CEO has an executive assistant you can speak with, and be connected. But with a machine, you're usually left with a laundry list of departments and possible tasks to choose from to complete your call. Still, there are a few tactics you can use to break through.

When possible, push for the ideal—to reach an operator to get their expert referral to the target executive's assistant. Many companies employ both an automated system and a bank of operators. So the task becomes finding your way to that live receptionist. You can sometimes simply press "0" to reach an operator, or say the word "operator" into the phone. Other systems are set up so that you must listen to all of the options first, then press the appropriate key to reach the operator. On a few recent calls, I've had to press "4" or "9" to reach the operator; others state at the end of their options list that you can simply remain on the line or press "0" to reach the receptionist. Automated systems require patience and focus to find your way through.

The next level of difficulty comes from systems that provide a list of options with reaching an operator conspicuously absent. These often include a final option of leaving a message in the company's general mailbox. Don't leave one. It's the equivalent of tossing your message, and contact mission, into a deep, dark hole. If you find an option to reach a sales or customer service representative, these are often your next best choice. When you connect, I find it's best to apologize for connecting with them, but explain that there is no receptionist and you're trying to find the executive assistant to whomever you're trying to reach.

The final option is to dial into the target executive's direct line through the automated company directory. If you take this route, you have a choice to make. Some sales trainers would advise you to go directly into your pitch if you happen to reach the CEO, but I prefer to show restraint, and respect for their time and privacy. Thus, my approach is to explain that I'm trying to reach their executive assistant, so that I can make a proper introduction and explain my reason for reaching out. Surprisingly, this response often gets the CEO to ask directly what you're trying to accomplish, so be prepared to have that conversation straight away. If you end up leaving a voice mail, be courteous and explain that you're actually trying to reach their assistant. That will often result in a returned call from the EA.

The worst of the automated systems are those designed simply to repel outside calls. If you've ever tried to reach someone at Google or LinkedIn, you're familiar with this dismissive approach to even having phones. With these, you're essentially instructed to dial the person's extension or get lost. In that case, look for ways to connect via social media instead to get their direct dial number.

The Initial Call to the Executive Assistant

If you're on with the target executive's executive assistant, you're almost there. You're now in audition mode, so be sharp, focused, and ready to create what may become one of the most important connections you've ever made.

Not all executive assistants are alike. Some are relaxed and friendly, others are brusque and always in a hurry. Be alert to their style of interaction and be sure to match their speed, just as you do when you accelerate to smoothly enter highway traffic. If they're friendly, you can relax a bit in your communication pace. If not, move things along quickly. In either case, they will appreciate your perceptive approach to the call.

But always keep focusing on the target. The executive assistant needs to know two things from you right away: who are you and what value do you offer. So get to the point quickly, say "I'm so and so," launch into your VIP statement, then the reason for your call.

Executive assistants always want callers to be sincere and transparent. Be respectful, be sharp, be ready to respond to whatever the EA puts out. Help them do their job and they'll help you achieve your mission.

How to Make a Million-Dollar Phone Call

You need to be ready to have a million-dollar call at any time, so be prepared by developing a level of comfort with the idea of spending a few minutes with someone on the phone that can turn into a million dollars' worth of business.

You should also know precisely what it takes for any of your calls to amount to a million dollars' worth of business, and be ready to ask for it. If you don't know how to ask, or if you simply never get around to asking, how will you ever make significant breakthroughs?

Still, it's a daunting task. How can you ask anyone for a million dollars unless you're a professional sports hero, best-selling author, or an A-list movie star? It turns out, it's really not all that difficult. You just have to know *how* to ask.

More precisely, you have to have worked out ahead of time how that would piece together within your business model. If you work on the basis of a monthly retainer plus production of whatever you're offering, how much would you need to charge for the retainer, and how many units would you have to produce monthly to turn all of that into a million dollars' worth of business?

If you sell custom windows and you're approaching builders to use your product in their projects, how many homes, on average, would you need to turn that into a million dollars' worth of business? Then it becomes a simple matter of approaching the right builders who routinely build enough homes each year to easily hand you a contract worth a million dollars.

You might not find yourself selling that much each time you approach an important new prospect, but that's not the point. I want you to start thinking big, really big, because that is the true nature of Contact Marketing. To create explosive growth in the scale of your career or business, you need to know what to ask for.

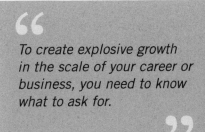

To create explosive growth in the scale of your career or business, you need to know what to ask for.

After all, you're using Contact Marketing to reach out to your highest-potential prospects, so you must approach the campaign ready to make much bigger sales and reap much bigger results than you're used to. Integrating the idea of making million-dollar phone calls routinely into your daily thinking should become a critical part of reaching your goals.

Of course, there's much more to your call with the CEO than knowing how to ask for a million dollars' worth of business. But you must start by believing you can achieve much bigger results than you ever have before.

POINTS TO REMEMBER

✔ There are four stages of contact: Indifferent, Intrigued, Committed, and Sponsor.

✔ Ranking each contact according to the four stages helps you measure the ongoing progress of your Contact Campaign.

✔ Each level of contact requires constant vigilance and immediate action to push them to the next level, initiate deals, and keep them on track.

✔ Stage 4 contacts may warrant the most attention in your Contact Campaign, because they can multiply your contacts and opportunities through referrals and constant evangelism.

✔ To make it all work, you must become a phone ninja, ready to take on any and all complications with intelligence, logic, and finesse.

✔ Your call starts with the receptionist—human or machine—and you must learn to quickly pass through this level of screening.

✔ Volunteer only the minimum amount of information necessary to get the receptionist's help and move on quickly to the next phase of your call.

✔ When faced with an automated reception system, sometimes the quickest way through is to dial "0."

✔ Always be ready to ask for a million dollars' worth of business—and know precisely how that can be achieved within your business model.

✔ Making million-dollar phone calls must become a routine part of your Contact Marketing mission to create explosive sales growth.

"I was thinking, you know, like,
one thing we could do is maybe sell more ..."

CHAPTER 17

Your Call to the CEO

In the previous chapters, we delved into the initial stages of making contact, including your initial encounters with the CEO's reception layer and that all-important audition with their talent scouts, the executive assistants. We also introduced the mind-set of making every call to a target CEO a million-dollar call.

It's a great start, but you'll need more than the intention of producing a million-dollar call when you speak with the CEO for the first time. In fact, if it is to be a million-dollar call, that will only come after a carefully laid-out plan of specific value and fit is explored, and only after your target is in agreement that there is sufficient value to proceed. Even then, the target's decision to press on can easily mean a yearlong cycle of testing and evaluation before you see the outcome you seek.

So let's take a closer look at what your first call or meeting should include and how you'll make your case.

What's Your Objective?

Before you fire, you've got to aim. So what is the objective of your outreach? Of course it's about extending the scale of your business or career, but how will your call extend the scale of your target executive's business? How is it relevant to their goals and how will it help the CEO achieve those goals more effectively or more quickly? The point of these questions is to remind you that you've got to show up with your homework done, and a clear idea of what you want to happen and how it will happen.

In Chapter 3, I explained how a CEOs is looking several years ahead, to plot the best possible course for their enterprises. They're hungry for information, but only if it's relevant to their particular circumstances—and only if it's a quick read, because of the demands on their time.

Everything you say on your call must fit into their framework. The best place to start is to clearly define your agenda. If you're seeking a meeting, what is its purpose and how will it benefit the CEO? (This is the key reason why they should take the meeting, so be ready with a strong case for it to occur.) Who should be present in the meeting? (The more people required, the less chance of it happening.) What is your honest estimate of how long it should take? (If you say it will take 10 minutes, stick to 10 minutes or less.) What do you want as the outcome? (Don't expect too much; a good plan of action is to propose a test and get the CEO's referral to the right people in their organization to make it happen.)

Maybe your call isn't about selling to the target executive's company, but striking up a strategic partnership. In that case, how will it work and how will it benefit the CEO's company? Answering the "What's in it for me?" question is crucial to any partnership. What level of investment is required for the CEO to take advantage of your offer? Every action the CEO takes must be framed in terms of ROI; be ready to help them see the value immediately. What is the CEO likely to see as a result of the partnership? (Show them how your proposed partnership might help them retain or gain customers, serve their clients better, improve their efficiency, etc.)

One of the easiest ways to make the most of your contact with a CEO is to set the objective of gaining their referral to the right person in their organization. Essentially, you're asking for their help, but in order to get it, you first need to explain the reason for your request. As stated earlier, a sales call puts people on the defensive; a request for help tends to lower their guard, making them far more open to considering the reason for your call.

> *Answering the "What's in it for me?" question is crucial to any partnership.*

Requests for referrals from CEOs can produce several key benefits. If the CEO has sat quietly, carefully considering your reason for the referral, you're gaining an opportunity to have them essentially put their stamp of approval on it. If they refer you to someone on their team, they're essentially saying, "This sounds interesting, I want you to check it out." In that case, the CEO is helping tremendously by introducing you to the "CEO" of the opportunity or problem you want to solve. If you succeed in getting your proposed sale or partnership to move forward, the CEO will remember thinking it was a good idea, lessening the chances of a veto just before you get their business. Most company operatives will have a tough time resisting the tug of a referral from their CEO. Your call becomes far more important when it carries the CEO's imprint.

Getting to the Point and Finding the Fit

Since one of your objectives for the call is to get the CEO to agree to your proposed agenda, I have found that it is far more effective to start with the suggestion to explore a possible fit, rather than asserting there is a fit. It's the essence of the Anti-Pitch in Chapter 13. Telling a CEO you already know there is a terrific fit with their goals is presumptuous and will only succeed in raising their guard.

Start instead with a well-crafted, quick explanation of what you're proposing, along with how it has worked for other clients. Continue with the statement that you're not sure if there is a fit, but you feel it's worth exploring. The target executive is far more likely to give it a thoughtful hearing. You may indeed find there isn't much reason for continuing, or you may both discover there are even better reasons than you'd imagined for you to team up. The more you make your call to the CEO informative and collaborative, the better your chances of a successful outcome.

Equally important, you must be quick to get to the point of your call. So what will that look like? You know the drill by now. You'll start by introducing yourself and making your single-sentence, twelve-words-or-fewer VIP statement. You'll move on to the reason for your call, which is why you think it fits specifically with one of the CEO's stated goals. Express it also in a dozen or fewer words, in a way that will leave the CEO wondering, "How will you do that?" Then you'll suggest a quick exploration and a course of action, which might be a test or a referral. Or the conversation may take an entirely unexpected direction, at the behest of the CEO.

Waste No Time

Always keep in mind that the CEO is on a different time scale than most. Show respect by calling when you say you will and keeping your side of the conversation brief but focused. Make it easy for the CEO to have the conversation and see the unique value you're trying to bring. Show them you understand their world by respecting the value of their time.

Actually, you won't be in charge of how long the call will take. The CEO will move it along briskly. A successful call will be surprisingly short; a failed call will be even shorter. Welcome to the CEO's world.

I want you to be prepared for the brief time scale you'll be working with at the CEO level. Your role in this will be to move your agenda along quickly. The CEO will let you know if they want to spend more time, so be ready to play by their rules.

Defining Next Steps

While the brevity of the phone call might be a surprise, never allow it to end without defining your next steps together. That won't make sense if the target executive tells you they aren't interested, but even there, you are free to ask if there is someone else in their organization with whom you can discuss the matter. At least then you might exit the call with a referral.

Assuming the tone of the call is positive, be ready to list the resulting action items and get a clear understanding of when you will either speak next with the CEO or hear from someone on their team. Get names, email addresses, and direct phone numbers. Make sure you exit with real next steps that will move the process along. You're on the phone with the CEO, and if you've had a positive outcome, make sure you get what you came for—a pathway to a breakthrough to expand your sales numbers or the scale of your business.

Like this chapter, your conversation with the target CEO will be brief but focused on the key points that will move things along, for you and for them. Never allow yourself to end these potentially life-changing conversations without a path leading everyone involved forward.

Points to Remember

✔ Any call to a CEO should be preceded by a few hours' research to understand their world, issues, and goals.

✔ When speaking with a CEO, you must have a clear objective for your call.

✔ If you're seeking a meeting, why is it beneficial to the CEO, whom should attend, and what will they gain?

✔ If you are proposing a strategic partnership, what's in it for them? What's involved?

✔ Requesting a referral is one of the most effective ways to get the CEO to listen to your reason for calling.

✔ Top-down referrals produce several advantages, which can be your shortcut to new deals.

✔ When speaking with the CEO, make sure you get to the point quickly. How it is relevant to their situation, and how will it provide unique value to their enterprise?

✔ Never tell the CEO you already know there is a fit between their needs and your solution; always ask to explore whether there is a fit or not.

✔ People will be more engaged in calls that are informative and collaborative, rather than pitch-oriented, which can greatly improve your chances for a successful outcome.

✔ When speaking with a CEO, appreciate the value of the time they're spending with you by not wasting it.

✔ You're not in charge of the brevity of your call; the CEO is.

✔ A successful call with a CEO will be surprisingly short; an unsuccessful one will be even shorter.

✔ Never exit a meeting with a CEO without a specific set of next steps to carry your initiative forward.

"So long, son. Send us a tweet sometime . . ."

CHAPTER 18

Now the Work Begins

By now, you have identified your Top 100 list, strategized and created your Contact Campaign, completed your VIP makeover, persuaded each executive assistant to put you through—and you've had your first conversations with your target CEOs, remembering that "CEO" is an acronym for whoever is the "Center of Enterprise Opportunity" for your outreach.

And *now* your work has just begun? Uh, well, yes.

You haven't created any breakthrough mega-sales or strategic partnerships yet, which is the reason you've made the investment in your Contact Campaign. This is not the time to sit back and relax, feeling like you've accomplished your mission. Not yet.

If you're running in a race and you've gone three out of the four laps, having passed all of your competitors along the way, have you won yet? Of course not. That can only occur once you've crossed the finish line. In your Contact Campaign, once you've made contact, you're almost there, but you haven't yet crossed that finish line. So let's get you there now.

Follow Through on Your System

You've probably noticed by now that, if you want to succeed at anything, consistency of effort is what gets you there. Experts have been telling us it often takes a minimum of six or more touch points before we ever break through to make a sale. At this point, you have only made your first, second, or third touch (including your hold-back device).

So it's time to get to work. As I have stated throughout this book, I always include the executive assistant in the campaign. When they have been helpful on the phone, particularly after the first contact, send them a card with a handwritten note of thanks inside. Once the initial meeting has taken place, thank them again for their help. The point is to start fostering a relationship and cementing your access to the CEO.

Even more critical is the nurturing of your new contact with the CEOs themselves. If you have exited the call with any sort of action items, anything you have committed to producing for them as a result of the call, make sure you follow through quickly and thoroughly. Make it your goal to exceed the CEO's expectations wherever you can. And be sure to thank them for taking the time to meet or speak with you.

If the result of the first call is the CEO's referral to someone else in the organization, in a sense, the process starts all over again. You're stepping in with a top-down referral, which is an enormous advantage, but it still requires effort to connect with this new person, including their executive assistant.

Nothing happens if the CEO doesn't follow through with the promised referral. So make sure it happens. You are your own advocate. Don't assume things are getting done. Make sure they're proceeding according to plan. It's all up to you to make it happen, so make it happen.

Your Critical Response

Please remember these words: *A deal delayed is a deal denied.* Keep that in mind as you push through your Contact Campaign process.

I am certainly guilty of having felt, once a very important new client or partner has said we'd do business together, that my job was complete, that it was time to celebrate. But a not-so-funny thing can easily happen at this stage. The deal can stall.

There's often no apparent reason for it and there's usually no immediate cause for alarm. So-and-so will be out the rest of the month, or they're committed to the project, but can't do anything until the start of the new fiscal year.

> *Make it your goal to exceed the CEO's expectations wherever you can.*

Maybe there is another, higher-priority project underway or a trade show in the next quarter that has your quarry's attention.

Whatever it is, these are potential deal killers. Even though it may not seem like it at the time, what's happening is your deal is being delayed. And once that starts, it may continue to be delayed indefinitely. The client or new partner may not mean to deny you this new deal, but if they never get around to it, it's as dead as if they'd simply said "no" in the first place.

So keeping your deals on track, doing whatever it takes to punch through delays and excuses, is your absolutely critical response to any new deal you set as a result of your Contact Campaign.

But how?

Often a delay is a disguised assessment by the other side that you don't have sufficient leverage in the deal. Your challenge, then, is to create new leverage quickly and apply it forcefully. If the new client has put other projects above yours on their list of priorities, it's time to examine the situation and find new leverage points.

One approach would be to see what their competitors might offer to have that same deal with you. Sometimes it's enough simply to ask, "If you're putting this on the back burner, would you mind if I approach XXX, your competitor?" It's important to treat your deal as highly strategic and valuable; if the new contact doesn't see it that way, perhaps the prospect of losing it if they don't act will help them see it differently.

A softer approach would be to continue to feed valuable, unbiased information to the CEO on a regular basis in support of the deal. Make sure they are constantly and fully aware of the opportunity at stake—and what they could lose if they continue to put the deal on hold.

In any case, you must always be on guard for delays and never validate them with inaction. It's up to you to make the deals that are most critical to your success not only happen, but happen as quickly as possible.

Addressing New Stakeholders

One potential source of delay could be obstacles created by unknown-to-you stakeholders. They may be raising concerns simply because they haven't been included in the discussion. So another part of your critical response should be to find out who all the stakeholders are and include them in your campaign as soon as possible.

The process of determining who they are is really pretty simple. It's a matter of picking up the phone and speaking to your new inside ally, the CEO's executive assistant. He or she will know who the additional stakeholders are and will have access to ask the CEO if there is any doubt.

Once you know who the stakeholders are, it's time for a new round of outreach, although these won't be nearly as challenging as the initial contact was. Often a simple phone call to their assistants, explaining that you're working with the CEO on a new initiative and you want to get their executive's input, is enough. Essentially, you're saying to all of the people who can delay or kill your deal, "I'm recognizing your importance and including you in the process."

Beyond that simple offer of recognition, you might come away with valuable insights that will actually make your deal stronger. Addressing additional stakeholders is simply a smarter way to do business; it ensures your deals go through with support from influencers who would otherwise remain hidden and potentially hazardous.

My favorite approach is to position these calls as interviews. Explain to each stakeholder you're doing this as a fact-finding step in your process, and that the results of the interviews will be rolled into a feasibility report to be presented to the CEO. This gives each subordinate a chance to have their contributions highlighted to the CEO, and with the recognition of their expressions of support or concern, they become invested in the same outcome you seek, which is to get the deal done.

Addressing stakeholders not only smooths the way; it makes your deal more important, because you now have everyone who matters on your side.

Completing the Job

The point of this chapter is to keep you focused on completing the job, on ensuring your deals become breakthroughs in your career or business. That's how you change the scale of your business.

Don't stop running your race in the third of four laps. Follow through on all promised action items. Make it your goal to exceed the CEO's expectations at every turn. Never allow your deals to be delayed. Include all necessary stakeholders and make sure they never get the chance to derail your deal.

It's your turn to break through to greater and greater levels of success. Make it happen!

Points to Remember

- ✔ You've come a long way with your Contact Campaign, but your first contact is just the beginning of the process that will lead to the breakthroughs you seek.

- ✔ Breakthroughs only come when you have finished the job, when your deal is completed and active.

- ✔ Once you have broken through, the consistency of your follow-up is critical.

- ✔ If a first contact with a CEO results in a referral, be sure to make the new connection quickly.

- ✔ If your deal is going to happen, it's up to you to make sure it goes all the way.

- ✔ Always remember, a deal delayed is a deal denied.

- ✔ Treat delays as a serious threat and act to overcome them quickly with additional leverage.

- ✔ Continue to "after-sell" your deal with constant information to the CEO in support of the opportunity.

- ✔ If delays continue, bring the opportunity to their competitors to reenergize the deal.

- ✔ One sure source of delay is unacknowledged stakeholders, so be sure to include them in your process.

- ✔ One way to bring all stakeholders into alignment is to arrange interviews with them to produce a feasibility report for the CEO.

"All those in favor of printing some more money say, 'Aye.'"

CHAPTER 19

Defining Success

Contact Marketing may be a newly identified form of marketing, but it's also an entirely new way of approaching the critical mission of becoming connected with the people who can make big things happen in your life. Becoming well-connected not only enhances your business results, it also transforms you into a VIP yourself. CEOs pride themselves on the personal networks they have built over the span of their careers, because they know the more connected they are with the right people, the better able they are to do their jobs, hit their goals, and move their companies forward.

Still, the immediate goal of Contact Marketing is to help you break through to your Top 100 or Strategic 100 lists, in order to create vast breakthroughs in your career or business. Success in that goal will present itself in many forms. In some cases, you will never meet the target CEO, but still get the referrals you need to make a deal happen. Or perhaps it leads to an introduction outside the organization, but doesn't lead to new business with the target company. You might find yourself in direct contact with a CEO, with no resulting business.

Are each of these outcomes failures or successes?

As with most things in life, the answer is complicated. Each of these scenarios may well lead to business—in fact, the first one already has—but perhaps in forms you may not have expected. In all three, there is at least some level of connection with the target contact, and that alone gives you the opportunity to expand your network. But only the first example resulted in direct business, while the other two may take some time before they produce results. It could even take a few years.

So how should you define success in your Contact Marketing campaign? Let's take a closer look.

Are the Executive Assistants Becoming Long-Term Contacts?

Executive assistants are often the first point of contact, and as I have addressed throughout this book, they are also your first measure of success. Remember, they are not gatekeepers—they're talent scouts. So how have the auditions been going?

Assistants are people, too, so they're fallible just like the rest of us. Some simply have surly personalities, or perhaps they are unhappy with their position. Maybe some hate their bosses, so they're not willing to seek any special advantage on their behalf.

But on the whole, executive assistants are usually some of the most clear-sighted people in the organization. They often wield tremendous power, even without the fancy titles or mega-salaries netted by their executive bosses. In some cases, they are essentially stealth vice presidents in the way they touch all areas of the organization; of all of the people in the executive suite, they're often the ones who get the most done.

What they say and how they react to your requests for contact is an important indication of your success as a Contact Marketer. So how have you fared so far in your campaign? Are the executive assistants becoming friendly parties and important long-term contacts? Or have they remained distant, or worse, have they closed the door on your contact efforts?

By taking this early measure, you can determine a couple of important factors. If the assistants are consistently thwarting your pushes for contact, they're giving you valuable feedback: "Rethink your approach." Figure out what you're missing. Are you breaking some sort of important protocol? Have you failed to present your reason for connecting as something of strategic importance to their bosses? Maybe all you're doing is pitching, which is perhaps the worst offense of all.

> My guess is that, nine times out of ten, assistants have curbed your advance because you've sounded like a salesperson looking to make a pitch.

If you find yourself in this situation, there is a simple solution: Just ask for their advice. Explain that you felt you were bringing something of strategic importance to their boss's attention and hadn't expected the assistant's reaction. Can they offer some feedback? My guess is that, nine times out of ten, they have curbed your advance because you've sounded like a salesperson looking to make a pitch. Always keep in mind that they want to let the right people through, so listen carefully as they describe what makes someone right for access.

Alternatively, if the executive assistants are mostly responding favorably, you have achieved your first level of success in your Contact Campaign. It's really something to celebrate, because impressing these tough judges is not easy. And it means you're heading in the right direction.

Your Response Rate

This is where Contact Marketing gets very exciting, because it is capable of producing shockingly powerful metrics. As stated earlier in this book, it is not uncommon for Contact Campaigns to produce response rates approaching 100 percent. If you are a marketer, you know results like that are considered impossible—but now you know that's not necessarily true if you're using Contact Marketing.

Still, we need to temper expectations, because I don't want you thinking that anything less than 100 percent is an unacceptable outcome. I have described campaigns in Section II that have been exceptionally effective with response rates in the 30 percent to 70 percent range. In the IT realm, we're seeing that even a 10 percent to 20 percent response can be a decent outcome, as these target contacts tend to be particularly standoffish—it seems like, if they had it their way, they wouldn't have to connect with anyone. So in some cases, breaking through at all can be a victory.

There is also the question of what constitutes a response. If, as a result of your outreach, a CEO indicates there is no opportunity with their company, is that a response? What if their assistant gives you the same answer, without consulting their executive?

Since the goal of a Contact Campaign is to get in touch with the target executive, I would say any direct contact as a result of your campaign is a response. It may not be the response you wanted, but it was an opportunity to present your case and you did make contact. At least you'll know that, after hearing what you have to say, that particular organization may not be the opportunity you thought it was. The CEO might even offer a bit of feedback as to why it failed to gather interest, in which case you have gained valuable insight you can use to steer subsequent efforts.

If that same negative answer came from the assistant with no input from the target CEO, I would not count that as a response, because the campaign did not produce direct contact.

So let's define what a response to a Contact Campaign is:

a)   any form of direct communication or contact with the targeted party, or

b)   a direct referral from the targeted party to someone in their organization who has authority over the issue or opportunity you're presenting, or

c)   any referral or introduction to a contact outside the target executive's company who is of value to the achievement of your goals for the campaign.

Using that scale, is your Contact Campaign producing the level of response you want? Can it be improved? Keep in mind, response rates are an important measure of your success, but they are not the whole story. What if you only get through to 10 percent, but each time it's worth millions of dollars? Isn't that an enormously successful campaign? Of course it is.

Your Return on Investment

I've described Contact Campaigns that have produced tremendously high response rates, and others that have scored returns on investment of more than 600,000 percent. My own Contact Campaign all those years ago, to the vice presidents and directors of circulation with the major magazine publishers, may have produced millions of percent ROI. After all, I spent $100 to put a personalized cartoon print and letter in the hands of about two dozen VIP contacts, and launched a business netting millions of dollars' worth of income as a result.

Response rates don't directly correspond to enormous returns on investment by themselves. What is significant is the combination of the right kinds of response in sufficient numbers, with a high average dollar amount per deal.

That's pretty simple. In the earlier example, if you "only" get a 10 percent response to your Contact Campaign, but each response amounts to a million-dollar sale, your ROI will be extremely high. Conversely, if you are getting through to everyone you target, but the average dollar value per contact is low, your ROI may be minuscule.

Taking these measurements will be extremely useful to your future success. In that 10 percent example, a high ROI despite a relatively low response rate indicates you have an enormous upside yet to come. Just figure out how to get that response rate higher. Boosting it to 20 percent would mean millions more in sales. In the latter example, the ROI indicates there's something off in the level of people you're targeting or perhaps in your revenue model. Can you target companies with bigger budgets to spend on what you sell? What can you do to increase your average sale amounts? Are you missing a more lucrative area of opportunity related to what you sell?

Actually, I must clarify that a true measure of return on investment is more complicated than the simple ratio of dollars spent on the campaign against the dollars generated by the campaign. A true accounting measure of ROI includes all expenses, including salaries, overhead, fixtures, interest, taxes, and more. A more accurate depiction would be income versus expense.

On that scale, the accepted industry standard for a lead-generation campaign would be a factor of ten or twenty against direct expenses. That would amount to a 1,000 to 2,000 percent rate. In Contact Marketing, you should be shooting for at least ten times those rates. If you're not hitting that mark, do some troubleshooting to figure out what adjustments may be necessary.

What Did You Accomplish?

Once again, the purpose of Contact Marketing is to get you in front of the people you have identified as most important to your goals. It doesn't stop there, though. Your reason for gaining access to those people is to produce exceptional growth in your business or career. And that shows up in the form of greater sales, greater influence, and a million-dollar Rolodex of contacts.

Did you connect with new contacts who can expand your network further through referrals? Have you opened new pathways to achieving other goals in your life? These things might not be obvious at first, but will come to light as you interact with the members of your network.

Take stock of your accomplishments. If you are using Contact Marketing, you should be finding yourself on a steep upward trajectory. If not, take a look at what your results are telling you, make the necessary adjustments, and prepare for the amazing breakthroughs that lie ahead.

What Were Your Breakthroughs?

I don't mean to say your only achievements should be greater connections in higher places, with nothing to show for them. I simply left the best for last. I expect you will become quite wealthy from the sales and partnerships you're about to produce. You may even embark on some wonderfully unexpected adventures in your life, perhaps along the lines of the way I met my wife (see Chapter 5). You may start a new cause or business that puts you in regular contact with your heroes. With Contact Marketing, there are no limits to the success you can bring to your life.

The dictionary defines the word "breakthrough" as "any significant or sudden advance." And that will be the ultimate test of the success of your Contact Campaign: Has it produced a sudden or significant advance in your life or business?

Points to Remember

✔ In the narrowest sense, the purpose of a Contact Campaign is simply to get you in front of the VIPs on your Top 100 list.

✔ The broader purpose of a Contact Campaign is help you achieve explosive growth in your career, business, and life.

✔ Measuring the success of your Contact Campaign involves some complexity and interpretation.

✔ Among the first results to evaluate is your success rate with executive assistants.

✔ Since EAs function as talent scouts for their bosses, their feedback is invaluable and should be sought out.

✔ If you are converting most of the assistants you connect with into long-term contacts, it's a good indication your approach is sound.

✔ Contact Campaigns typically produce response rates well beyond those experienced with other forms of direct response marketing.

✔ Although 100 percent response rates are possible, your campaign will likely produce a lot less yet still be highly successful and profitable.

✔ A Contact Campaign response is any direct connection, referral, or meaningful introduction to someone who can directly capitalize on the opportunity you're presenting.

✔ Response rates alone are not enough to evaluate the success of your Contact Campaign.

✔ ROI or income-versus-expense results provide direct feedback on the soundness of your campaign and revenue model.

✔ If your response rate is low, but your ROI is high, finding ways to improve response will pay enormous dividends.

✔ If your response rate is high, but your ROI is low, you're either shooting too low or asking too little for what you're selling.

✔ Part of what you should be accomplishing with your Contact Marketing is a far greater personal network of VIP contacts.

✔ The real breakthroughs should always be measured in terms of response rate, ROI, and the explosive growth of your business.

"You go on ahead, Fred. I'm going to hang out here in the elevator for a while and see if I can drum up some leads."

CHAPTER 20

Social Media's Expanding Role in Contact Campaigns

I have to admit, I'm one of those who've been slow to adopt social media. For a long time, I saw it as the equivalent of stepping into an elevator with a random group of people and expecting to have something meaningful occur in the thirty seconds it took to arrive at the top floor. It just didn't make sense.

Then I started using Facebook to connect with old friends from childhood, high school, and college. Nothing random about that. It makes every day, or any day I care to indulge, a virtual reunion. But has it ever amounted to anything useful for my business? No, not really. Still, I started to see how social media worked.

My next revelation came when, some years ago, I discovered one of my Top 100 list members had viewed my LinkedIn profile as part of their due diligence for a deal we were working. It was a shock and, because I hadn't expected to be evaluated on something seemingly so far removed from the core of my business, it was an urgent call to action. I updated and enhanced my profile the next day, and using the LinkedIn tools to automatically invite my previous contacts to connect, my "connections" count quickly rose above the magic 500 (any number of LinkedIn connections above 500 is shown as "500+," so it's important to top that number quickly).

> *Almost every sales thought leader I spoke with mentioned social media as a key ingredient for success in business, and as absolutely essential for successful selling.*

That was the day I came to realize how central social media had become to my life—to all of our lives. I had a similar reckoning as I conducted the interviews for this book. Almost every sales thought leader I spoke with mentioned social media as a key ingredient for success in business, and as absolutely essential for successful selling. Most of those experts are themselves authors of books talking about the social selling revolution, and how sales organizations either embrace social media or go extinct.

So I now share this stage with all of my gracious guest experts, who generously shared their thoughts on social media as it relates to selling, and especially Contact Marketing, for this book.

Social Media Is Critical for Breaking Through

Social selling evangelist Jill Rowley says, "To be interesting, you have to be interested in something other than yourself." She is firm in her belief that salespeople are going extinct, and they're being replaced by search engines and social media. "Evolve or go extinct," she advises, but how does this relate to the Contact Marketing mission? She says it's no longer proper to pitch and go for the close. It's now about asking for the honor of being included in your target contact's network and bringing their light into yours. "Relationships take time to cultivate," she says, "and that's the point of social selling, as well as Contact Marketing."

Nimble CEO Jon Ferrara has an interesting take on social media as a means of connecting with VIPs, since his company provides a popular social media app that helps make high-level connections quick and easy. "I build relationships with influencers with my core community based on authentic relationships and a 'pay it forward' mentality," he explains. "I always end the conversation with, 'How can I serve or help you?'"

Social sales evangelist and blogger Jim Keenan explains, "Social selling is a big part of my platform. I use it to broaden my reach, not to reach anyone in particular, but as a result, it makes it easy for me to reach anyone." It's an interesting point. The more active and connected you are in social media, the more you contribute to your own VIP statement, which is always a top consideration when breaking through to your VIP prospects.

Keenan points out that, in the past, the moguls became moguls because of reach. "The richest people in the world were in newspaper publishing," he says, "then reach moved to radio, then TV, and now, the average person can create reach [through social media]. The more reach you have, the more power you have."

HubSpot CMO and *The Sales Acceleration Formula* author Mark Roberge recalls a phone call he received from the vice president of sales of a *Fortune* 500 company. "He called me and said, 'We need your help, we need to meet.'" When the meeting took place, Roberge says, "they showed up with one of the best [PowerPoint] decks on the HubSpot model I'd ever seen. Naturally, they became a client." Roberge's point is clear: His reputation becomes his Contact Campaign. And that comes directly from his use of social media.

Keenan points out that you can't create reach immediately, that it comes over time and only if you're offering something people want. He asks, "What is it that you want to give to the world? You create reach by giving it in little drips and drabs. Do it every day and people will glom onto that."

Your Social Media Contact Strategy

"Whatever you start, you have to keep it going consistently," adds *GeekSpeak Guides* cohost Susan Finch. "It has to be based on real interaction, getting involved in communities and groups; otherwise it's a waste of time." That might sound like more of a commitment than you're willing to make, but Finch has an easy solution: "It can be as little as fifteen minutes a day," she says, "but if you don't have the time, get someone who can help."

Finch advocates making an appointment with yourself daily, to tend to your social media gardens. But which platforms are best? "That can't be answered," she says. "You've got to work with what you or your team knows or is willing to learn." One of the most common mistakes Finch sees marketers making is biting off too much by engaging in every social media platform out there. "Sometimes marketers think, 'Hey, we need to be on every channel or we aren't being effective,'" she explains. Finch's advice is to choose one or two platforms and make a firm commitment to stick with them.

Whichever platforms you choose, you'll still need to integrate them into your Contact Marketing strategy. While creating great reach is important for drawing others to you and enhancing your own VIP profile, if the goal is to connect with your Top 100, you should think in terms of addressing the following questions in your social media usage:

1. Does your contact target write articles, books, or a blog?

2. Is your target executive active in social media, and if so, which platforms?

3. Who do you have in common as connections?

Using these three questions as your guide, you'll be able to use social media to connect easier, faster, and deeper. But which platforms are right for you and your Contact Marketing strategy? Again, our experts weigh in . . .

LinkedIn

When author Anthony Iannarino describes the value of LinkedIn to his business, he puts it simply. "Some people want to know you first," he explains. "I won a million-dollar appointment from a LinkedIn connection."

Many talk about LinkedIn's unique ability to help users secure high-level introductions, and to show how you may be connected to virtually anyone (the Reachable platform helps this process even further; see Section IV, "Resources and Tools," at the end of this book). Author and blogger Barb Giamanco says, "When you can secure an introduction from a respected source outside the company, you get the meeting at least 50 percent of the time." She advises not only seeking introductions from common connections, but joining and becoming an active contributor to LinkedIn groups where your Top 100 are likely to be found.

Blogger Babette Ten Haken suggests reaching out using LinkedIn's InMail function. "They can check you out," she says, "so it has been very powerful." But author Linda Richardson cautions that using LinkedIn to secure introductions has its limitations. "If you try to get that introduction without the trusted source," she says, "you won't get through." Richardson also recommends combining alerts with your use of LinkedIn. "Every time something happens at one of my target companies," she explains, "I have a new opportunity to get in touch, with information and expertise they'll find valuable."

President emeritus of the Professional Sales Association Scott Plum says if you have 500 or more LinkedIn connections, there is a good chance you will find a common connection with virtually anyone on the platform. Plum's favorite approach is to ask one of his connectors to pass along an email he has written, rather than using InMail. "I ask my target, 'Will you take a call with me?'" he says, and adds, "In my email, I explain what I want to talk to them about, so they know I'm being respectful of their time." He finds the approach very effective for securing a quick ten-minute call.

Author and blogger Dave Stein takes it a step further. "The organization chart doesn't stop with the CEO," he reminds us. "I like to go above the CEO and find board members I know who know a member of their board. That makes it easy to get some time with the CEO." Stein, who also writes a regular column for *Sales & Marketing Management* magazine, advises taking time to discover all of your introduction sources and assets. "There's no excuse," he says. "LinkedIn makes it very easy."

Finch advises investing time to participate in LinkedIn groups, praising others' work publicly, referring people to articles, and more. But she warns, "Don't just share without commenting and giving a reason why you find a particular item interesting." Finch adds, "Don't use the canned 'I'd like to connect with you' message, either. People don't respond to that, so write your own."

I have found LinkedIn's automated feature to invite all of your contacts to become connections quite useful. It combines all of the people you've connected with through your emails, all of those listed in your address book, and any connections you have on Facebook and Twitter, and quickly converts them to LinkedIn connections. Your chances of finding common connections with your VIP prospects improves exponentially as your connections count increases. Even as a neophyte LinkedIn user, I can tell you it has already had a great effect on my own success as a Contact Marketer.

Twitter

If LinkedIn is the orderly business domain of social media, Twitter is the World Wide Wild West. Everyone from middle school kids to celebrities, despicable terrorists, protesters, pundits, junkies, renowned experts, and even the International Space Station astronauts and world leaders are there. And they're saying anything and everything.

In fact, it was Twitter that inspired the cartoon at the head of this chapter. It can seem utterly random, which it is, but it's also wonderfully involving of any subject, person, or mode of thinking you can imagine—which means it can be anything you want. You don't have to concern yourself with the latest distractions from television reality brats as they feed their insatiable craving for attention, or from the latest bout of self-destruction by yet another child actor. You choose your Twitter experience simply by whom you choose to follow and, more importantly, the subjects, issues, and interests you'll tweet about. That, in turn, attracts an entire audience devoted to your message, and suddenly, you'll have that all-important following.

But again, for our discussion of social media as a tool to support your Contact Marketing strategy, we must focus on the three basic questions in the "Your Social Media Contact Strategy" section above. And this is where it gets interesting. If your target executives' writings are public, Twitter is the perfect venue to give them wings. The authors will notice if their work is favorited or retweeted, and that's a very good first step toward gaining the attention of your VIP prospects. Those simple actions will quickly put you on their radar scope as a supporter.

But there's a whole lot more to it than that. Again, our experts weigh in.

Author Alexandra Watkins tells the story of a VIP contact she'd been trying to reach. "As soon as I tweeted, 'I'd love to get a copy of your book,'" she recalls, "I broke through." Blogger John Barrows counters, "It's not so much about what you tweet, but listening to what your Top 100 are tweeting, then reaching out through email, phone, or mail." From there, his approach incorporates a mix of touches, each with something different, useful, and fascinating, with good old professional persistence. "It will be appreciated if you bring different pieces of value each time," he says.

Blogger Don Cooper, who built a 68,000-member follower base starting in 2010, advises using retweets and hashtags (references to ongoing conversations already on Twitter, which broadens the reach of your tweets), but also publishing good content frequently and interacting with your network.

> " To author Jeffrey Gitomer, what matters most is finding ways to set yourself apart from everyone else in the channel, particularly your competitors. "

Social selling strategist Julio Viskovich says Twitter can give you an unfair advantage in your Contact Campaigns. "I was once trying to reach someone at Condé Nast," he recalls, "but wasn't breaking through after two months straight of calling. Then I drilled down in the guy's Twitter feed and discovered his interest in the Green Bay Packers. I mentioned [Packers quarterback] Aaron Rodgers in the subject line of my next email, and within fifteen minutes, he was on the phone."

Author Jeffrey Gitomer says social media offers all kinds of ways to break through to your target executives. But, he says, what matters most is finding ways to set yourself apart from everyone else in the channel, particularly your competitors. His favorite Contact Campaign trick on Twitter? Smiling, he says, "Have your whole staff post on your target's Twitter feed. Have them all tell him, 'C'mon Larry, meet with us.'"

Author Gavin Ingham says there's really no mystery to social selling: "People have separated social media and selling, and [are] saying selling has changed," he explains, "but social media is not separate from selling. They're the same thing."

GeekSpeak Guides' Susan Finch says she loves Twitter as a way to connect not only with a large following, but with Top 100 prospects. "I've made my quickest connections there," she says, "but you've got to be thoughtful about who you follow. You don't want to be following five million people and have twenty-five following you." To balance that count, and particularly to boost your number of followers, she advises posting images and using direct messages and hashtags to plug into ongoing conversations.

If at first you find the "Twitterverse" baffling, you're not alone. Just take another look at the cartoon at the top of this chapter and you'll know I've been right there with you. But even I, a late adopter of social media, have found Twitter to be surprisingly useful, even rewarding. You will, too, particularly in support of your Contact Campaigns.

Facebook

Facebook is another social media platform that I have been finding more and more useful, but I must say, not so much for my business. Many people seem to reserve their use of the platform for personal matters. I do—or did—as well.

It's not hard to see there is a booming business use of Facebook, but it seems to be almost exclusively a business-to-consumer focus. Companies, celebrities, bands, and others have Facebook pages that really have little to do with personal connections; it's where they post news and information about the organization, group, or person, but followers are kept at arm's length. They can "like" and "share" posted items, but don't expect to visit General Motors' Facebook page and strike up a conversation with the CEO. You won't reach Pamela Anderson (sorry, Borat!) or the surviving members of Led Zeppelin that way, either.

I have a Facebook account for my "Bystuheinecke" identity, where I post news and cartoons. I have always kept those separate from my personal account, but author Richard Weiler says that's a mistake. "There is a certain trigger that happens when you make a friend on Facebook," Weiler explains, "that becomes a fast-forward button to striking up deep personal relationships." He advocates inviting all of your business connections to become Facebook friends as well.

Weiler says we should think of his advice as a paradigm shift, to mix our business lives with our personal lives. He says that as soon as he made the shift, the opportunities started rolling in. "I've had all sorts of contacts come to me with surprise business," he says, "but the real surprise was how well they already felt they knew me." Following Weiler's advice certainly plays into the "people buy from people they know and like" aspect of selling and deal making—and, for that matter, Contact Marketing.

By now, you're familiar with blogger Matt Heinz's story of the egg carton Contact Campaign used to gain his attention. "I get stuff from people trying to connect with me all the time," he says, "but the level of detail they went to really impressed me." The secret ingredient for the campaign was Facebook, which clearly displayed Heinz's hobby of keeping chickens. Without Facebook, the campaign wouldn't have worked.

Google+ and Others

There are, of course, many other social media platforms, and for the purposes of Contact Marketing, the social mediascape gets a bit fractured from here. Marketers have been finding tremendous success with younger generations on Instagram and Reddit; Pinterest has been making great gains in user base as well.

But for purposes of supporting the Contact Marketing mission, Susan Finch says she's particularly impressed with Google+. She reports that the level of interaction seems to be just right for promoting her *GeekSpeak* show, and also for creating connections that turn into business. "Whereas LinkedIn is an audience of professionals working for others," she says, "Google+ opens the door to a lot more independents, small businesses, and entrepreneurs."

Whichever platform you choose, keep Finch's and my advice close at hand. Don't over-commit to more platforms than you can handle, and always keep those three basic questions—is your contact target an author, is he or she active in social media, and do you have common connections?—in mind as you formulate your usage of social media in support of your Contact Marketing strategy. Connecting with your Top 100 VIP prospects is the goal, not popularity—although as we've seen, that can help.

Points to Remember

✔ Social media has become a key ingredient in any Contact Marketing strategy.

✔ Social media and sales are no longer separate entities; they're part of a bigger whole called "Social Selling," or perhaps just "Selling."

✔ Some experts believe salespeople are being replaced by search engines and social media.

✔ As sellers, marketers, and businesspeople, we ignore social media at our peril.

✔ Social media has become the way we all can achieve valuable reach and exposure.

✔ The social media milieu is fueled by a "pay it forward" mentality, of being of service to people rather than pitching products and services.

✔ To be a successful user of social media, you must be interested in something more than yourself.

✔ Whatever social media strategy you use, you must be committed to keeping it going consistently.

✔ Only use the social media platforms you feel comfortable with and that you can commit to over the long term.

✔ Whichever platform you use in support of your Contact Campaign, be sure to determine where your Top 100

VIPs participate and whether you already have common connections.

✔ LinkedIn is where you can make important connections in the corporate world.

✔ When connecting with someone new on LinkedIn, don't use the canned "I'd like to connect with you" message—write your own based on whom you're addressing.

✔ Twitter gives you access to anyone and everyone—it's the World Wide Wild West, and it seems like the entire human population can be found there.

✔ Twitter can be distracting, but it provides powerful methods for connecting with people of all types, particularly your Top 100 list members.

✔ The actions of retweeting and favoriting your target executive's tweets puts you immediately on their radar screen.

✔ Use of hashtags allows your tweets to reach people who are following almost any given conversation or subject of interest.

✔ Facebook can help you gain a glimpse of a target executive's personal life and interests, which can be an invaluable insight for your Contact Campaign.

✔ Although commercial use of Facebook seems to be business-to-consumer biased, there may be value in connecting with target executives on your personal account; it gives them a chance to get to know and like you.

✔ Social media includes a large, fractured collection of other platforms and channels, which may not be as useful for your Contact Marketing efforts as the current big three: LinkedIn, Twitter, and Facebook.

"You're saying where do we go from here, when everybody else is saying, 'Where don't we go from here?'"

CHAPTER 21

Where Do We Go from Here?

Where do we go from here? It's really a two-part question. Where do *you* go, and where do we *all* go from here as Contact Marketers? To answer the first part, we'll examine the next steps that will allow you to expand your success, sales, and network. We'll look at how you can make Contact Marketing a regular part of your strategy, so that you continue to explore new opportunities and create sustained growth in your business and career.

To address the second question, I spoke with the leaders of the American Marketing Association (AMA), the Professional Sales

Association, the National Association of Sales Professionals, and Guerrilla Marketing International. They had some fascinating impressions to share about the Contact Marketing phenomenon, as well as some powerful advice for the future of the practice. Marketing and Sales have long been separate silos, and what excites us all is how Contact Marketing brings them together again.

Once you have completed the steps suggested in this book, you will have raised your own VIP profile, compiled a Top 100 list of VIP prospects, and instituted a Contact Campaign strategy. There are so many types of Contact Campaigns and such a wide range of cost options, you will surely have found one or a combination of tactics to create contact with nearly anyone you put in your crosshairs.

> *Marketing and Sales have long been separate silos, and what excites us all is how Contact Marketing brings them together again.*

This is going to be a lot of fun. While most salespeople dread the prospect of cold-calling anyone in the C-suite, you'll simply break through with ease. Your targeted VIPs will thank you for reaching out and congratulate you on your shrewdness and creativity. They will point to you as an example of how they want their own sales and marketing teams to perform.

Being able to connect with virtually anyone is a joy. It will make your life and career a lot more fun and fascinating. So now that you've gotten started, let's take a look at what's next.

Cross-Sells, Partnerships, and Referrals

Making a big sale is a thrill and very good for your business. But it's just the start of what can be a chain reaction of new opportunities. The reason for that should be obvious: Every VIP you connect with has hundreds of other connections who may be prime prospects for large sales, partnerships, and more.

The first place to look is within each VIP's organization. Are there other departments, divisions, subsidiaries, or sister companies that can use your products or services? Cross-selling is one of the easiest routes to more sales, because the company is already a customer and you've become one of their trusted vendors. It is also the least expensive method of generating more business because you're already known to the organization; you just have to plug into the full array of business opportunities there.

Strategic partnerships are another potent source of explosive growth. Some of your new VIP contacts will have vast sales channels they may want to open to your company, if you can demonstrate a strategic value for them. If you find a way to have your offering become part of theirs, you've found a golden opportunity to grow your own sales volume.

What about all of the opportunities your VIP contacts can open beyond their own organizations? Most C-level executives have built their networks over the span of their careers. They often have friendly relationships even with their competitors. Once you have delivered on your promise and they get to know, trust, and like you, your VIP contacts can become powerful advocates and open many more possibilities for new sales, partnerships, and more.

Many sales trainers say referrals are all you need to produce explosive sales growth. But as a Contact Marketer, you now have the same secret weapon I've had all these years. You can open new relationships at the very highest levels, and by starting at the top, you will quickly rise to that same stratospheric level.

Next Top 100 list

Once you start enjoying new success through myriad cross-selling, partnership, and referral opportunities, should you stop there? No! There's an interesting story I once heard about William Wrigley, Jr., founder of the Wrigley chewing gum empire. He was riding in a train with one of his junior executives, who was eager to impress with his business savvy.

"Sir, I have a plan that will save the company millions of dollars," he exclaimed.

"Oh, what's that?"

The young executive went on to explain that, if Mr. Wrigley cancelled all of his advertising, he could reap an enormous financial windfall from the savings.

"Young man," Wrigley asked, "how fast do you suppose we're traveling?"

He answered enthusiastically, "At least forty-five miles per hour!" Mind you, in the early 1900s, that was mighty fast.

Wrigley then asked, "How fast do you suppose we'd go if the engine was removed from the train?"

Obviously, the train would quickly lose momentum without the benefit of the engine's constant tug. Don't let that happen with your Contact Marketing efforts.

Once you have established a winning strategy, you should make it your highest priority to stick with it, to keep your momentum going. Your horizons can always expand further and you never know where that may lead. Thus, you should always consider your Top 100 list to be evolving. As you connect with VIP contacts on your list, new ones should take their place. As your company grows, as your strategic priorities evolve, so should your strategy for choosing who gets to be on your Top 100 list. Once you finish the 100, there should always be another 100 VIP prospects ready to go.

How Much Do You Want to Grow?

At some point, we all must face the question, "When is enough, enough?" It's particularly valid if there are limits to the scalability of your business, because every business has its limits. Or you may find that your time becomes too valuable to spend simply securing more business. Everyone has a point at which they don't want to press further, when they'd like to do more with their lives. And you should know where yours is.

But I would like to issue you this challenge: If you're satisfied with your current scale of business, what can you do to give back to the world?

I have not reached my limit, but I have created an exciting vehicle to help make the world a better place, again through the magic of cartoons. It is an organization called Cartoonists.org. Composed of a group of prominent cartoonists from around the world, the group has a mission to use cartoons to draw attention to and raise funds for various charitable causes. I don't know what those causes will be yet, because it's just getting started. But I'm excited about helping others, perhaps great numbers of people, through the lifting hand we'll be able to offer through our partner charities.

It's going to be fun and rewarding. And it will have nothing to do with selling more stuff, other than offering our artwork at auction to raise funds. I won't be involved to expand my business, which is precisely why I find it so intriguing.

I am also aware of the value I can bring, just being the kind of person who can break through to virtually anyone. It will be critically important as we reach out to involve others in our mission. I imagine there will be a lot of business tycoons who will find our ability to move their charities further along intriguing.

So when you consider the question of "When is enough, enough?" I hope you'll say, "Never." We can always shift our priorities, so that new missions come to the front and we continue to do what we've all done throughout our careers, which is being effective agents of change and building value. And if you do it right, Contact Marketing will always be an unfair advantage you can bring to the mission. Once you're a Contact Marketer, you remain one for life, because it's just so useful and fun.

The Value of Your Network

I mentioned it in an earlier chapter, but I'll repeat it here. One of the CEOs interviewed for this book told me, "You earn your network across the course of your career." You'll recall social sales evangelist and blogger Jim Keenan saying, "Reach is the greatest asset you have, even more valuable than your home." Nimble CEO Jon Ferrara figures your personal brand plus your professional network equals the net worth of your career. In each case, they could not be clearer in their advice: Your network of VIP contacts is one of the most valuable parts of your career. Obviously, you wouldn't have a career without your skills, education, or experience, but the web of important connections is what gives you great power.

Please make the most of this gift and be sure to share it with others. I will be continuing to share it, too, through my live, weekly Contact Marketing Radio show and iTunes podcast. You can find both by visiting www.ContactMarketing.agency or searching for "Contact Marketing Radio" on iTunes. I invite you to tune in, and if you have Contact Marketing success stories of your own, please share them with the rest of us. I can't wait to hear all about it.

The Future of Contact Marketing

Throughout the research for this book, I have been very fortunate to have spoken with many impressive thinkers who have known and lived the promise of Contact Marketing throughout their careers. I'm proud to have collected their voices into a single work to explain the marvel this form of marketing truly is.

I have also spoken to some of the key figures in the marketing and sales communities. While I was interested in their experiences, I also fielded valuable feedback as to where the Contact Marketing practice goes from here.

Just as our sales thought leaders expressed, these leaders' feedback was direct: We cannot allow Contact Marketing to decline into a mere collection of sales tricks and stunts. As CEO and author Rod Hairston puts it, "Tactics without psychology, congruency, and integrity are a big mistake. Otherwise it's just trickery."

American Marketing Association CEO Russ Klein reminds us, "Part of a VIP's identity is to be inaccessible; it's driven by ego." Hairston says, "Billionaires are not interested in helping you get going, they're interested in how they're going to get their next billion dollars. So you must always ask yourself, 'What do I bring to the table that will help them grow to the next level?'"

Does that mean Contact Marketing must become louder and more outlandish to break through? No. Klein says the AMA's agenda is to focus on the tension between best practices and next practices, and he advises Contact Marketers to do the same. "Best practices are great, but they create a certain safety and sameness," he explains. "But next practices involve a lot of risk, with the certainty that new breakthroughs will emerge." He maintains that it is through a balance of the two that Contact Marketing will thrive and grow.

Contact Marketing has always been about highly original thinking. It could be thought of as a subset of the Guerrilla Marketing principles taught by Jay Conrad Levinson for so many years, which is why I was so thrilled to be able to share his words in the foreword of this book. Sadly, Jay passed away before its completion, so I was not able to connect with him for a few final words. Thus, I connected instead with his daughter, Amy Levinson, who is now co-owner and CEO of the Guerrilla Marketing International organization, to get her perspective on the relationship between the two disciplines. "My father used to say, 'If it uses time, energy, and creativity, and doesn't rely on capital, and if it's successful,'" she says, "'then it's Guerrilla Marketing.'"

That the two disciplines are so closely aligned is a source of pride to me. Jay was one of the smartest, most creative, and alive human beings I have ever known. His tactics helped countless marketers and companies thrive in the face of overwhelming competition, often from much bigger companies. He was always focused on living by your wits and outsmarting the marketers who solved their challenges with loads of cash.

Here, we're simply using our wits to connect with the people who are most likely to help us break through to the next level and beyond, much like Jay did. For that, I am truly honored to be in his company. And to call myself a Contact Marketer. You should be, too.

Points to Remember

✔ As you make new VIP connections, they can be leveraged into many more opportunities through cross-selling, strategic partnerships, and referrals.

✔ Contact Marketing isn't just about changing the scale of your career or business; its use can extend beyond business to produce tremendous results in your personal life as well.

✔ Your professional network is perhaps the most valuable component of your career.

✔ Contact Marketing allows you to take a shortcut to build a powerful network of VIP contacts quicker.

✔ Strategic partnerships can add exponential growth to your business and should be a top priority within your Contact Marketing strategy.

✔ Your Top 100 list should constantly evolve, replacing contacted VIPs with new ones, and adding different types of VIPs based on your changing goals.

✔ In order to thrive, Contact Marketing must strike a balance between best practices and next practices.

"Things are going really well now,
so I'm seeing a therapist to work through it all."

BONUS CHAPTER

Channeling Your Inner Coach

Throughout this book, we've examined the explosive benefits of breaking through to VIP prospects, particularly CEOs and C-level executives. The point of this book is to empower you to enter their world easily and move among these difficult-to-reach people as one of them, as a VIP yourself. If you follow the advice within, you will greatly enhance your level of business and sales success.

But there's still one last issue to deal with: Calling on CEOs is not easy. If you haven't tried it before, you'll find these can be tense, pressure-filled exchanges. It may help to know that many seasoned sales professionals still sweat nervously when they're directed to call on the C-suite. We know the stakes are high and you will be tested immediately by the ranks of executive assistants out there. They're sharp people who need to parse their incoming calls into "accept" and "reject" categories quickly. If you're nervous or fearful, they'll sense it immediately and interpret that as reason enough to deny access.

Even when you do get through, you'll find CEOs can be an intensely intimidating presence. You'll have just a few seconds to say something that will grab their attention and stimulate their curiosity to hear more, and to hear it with an open mind. We already know their time is limited and valuable, and we know VIPs are expert at protecting it from unwanted distractions.

If it were easy, everybody would be doing this. But that is also your invitation to the greatness that lies ahead.

We All Have an Inner Coach

What you need, then, is a coach. You need someone who can help you get fired up, ready, and eager to meet the challenges ahead. But you also need someone with a clear head, who can see the opportunities you can't, someone who can direct you on a daily basis to set power priorities and slice through them like a ninja warrior.

Many important figures in the business world already work with coaches. It's likely many of the CEOs you'll connect with have coaches. So why shouldn't you?

One reason might be the expense. You wouldn't want to hire a cheap coach, as the results you could expect would be a waste of time. And the best ones, if they're available, will likely charge far more than you may want to spend.

What do these coaches have that you don't? They have a perspective that is different from your own. They see a forest where you see the bark on a single tree. They have a 30,000-foot view of your course on the ground.

But all that means is that they are not you. That's essentially it. Of course, they're smart people, but so are you. You're obviously motivated to blast your way to the top, or you wouldn't be reading this book.

So it might surprise you to learn that you are already all you need to succeed. You are already complete—you already know the answers to your toughest dilemmas. Now it's simply a matter of accessing them—through your inner coach.

In Psych 101, you learn about the various facets and inner workings of the mind. Our minds are incredibly powerful. Have you ever noticed, if you can't find a solution to a problem today, you'll often awaken with a clever idea the next morning? Our minds have been working on it overnight, while we get our rest—how amazing is that?

Even our identities are more complicated than they first appear. I'm me and you're you, right? Recalling those hours spent in the auditorium-sized classroom in Psych 101, I know that our identities are actually composed of an id, ego, and a superego. The three are distinctly

> *Our emotional intelligence is a powerful force in our lives; it's what processes our knowledge, observations, and perceptions into feelings. How we feel about things in our lives determines how we respond.*

separate. You're familiar with them all: Your id is your instinctual self, your ego is essentially your waking self, and your superego is that inner voice that scolds or praises you as you make your way through life.

Interconnected with those components of self, we all have an IQ, an Intelligence Quotient, and an EQ, an Emotional Quotient. Our emotional intelligence is a powerful force in our lives; it's what processes our knowledge, observations, and perceptions into feelings.

How we feel about things in our lives determines how we respond. It is such an effective mechanism, we're always playing catch-up, trying to figure out why we feel a certain way about circumstances in our lives.

What's useful about all of this is that there is a simple technique you can use to channel what amounts to your own, inner coach—a combination of superego, emotional intelligence, and innate problem-solving ability that can deliver all of the wisdom you'll ever need to constantly punch through to new levels of success.

If you can't come up with a solution to a given problem, your inner coach will help you find it. If you need a big-picture perspective to help guide you toward the achievement of your goals, it is ready to assist. If you feel discouraged, your inner coach will fire you up to burst onto the field like a champion every day.

The technique I'm about to teach you is not part of Contact Marketing, but it is a useful tool for motivating and guiding you through the challenges that lie ahead.

It's not something I invented. It's actually a simple form of self-hypnosis, something I call a "Psych." I do it most mornings, and as you can imagine, if I have just hypnotized myself to perform like a champion, that's what I do throughout the day. Not that I'm running through life like a robot, but I do push through the tasks at hand with a great deal more efficiency and with a focused sense of motivation. I'm having fun and I'm making significant headway.

The most amazing part of this process is that somehow, I get powerful, clear-sighted advice from myself about what's important, where to go, and what's possible. What more could you ask of any coach?

The "Psych" Process

Since this is a form of self-hypnosis, you'll need to start in a comfortable place, lying in a prone position. I usually do this when I first wake up, when some of my most creative thoughts seem to occur, in that dreamy state between sleep and full consciousness.

The basis of hypnosis is to achieve an induced state of profound relaxation. This is not sleep or some form of trance. It's simply achieving a deep level of tranquility and programming certain suggestions into your brain.

So you must be completely comfortable, on your back, arms at your sides, or hands just on your hips. There should be no forms of discomfort; if a blanket is tucked under your arm somewhere, pull it out and get fully situated.

The Psych process is pretty simple, but like anything, the more you practice, the better you'll perform. There is a preamble, a countdown, and then the Psych session itself. I'll first tell you what this process is, then I'll walk you through the actual experience, to help you see what I derive from it and what I hope to pass along to you.

The preamble is a lot like what you see in movies and television, in which the hypnotist waves a watch in the subject's face, saying, "You're getting sleepy, you're getting sleepy." Of course, movies often seem to get things wrong, or exaggerate or shorten them for effect. Here, the preamble is simply the process you will use to lead yourself to a complete state of relaxation, while orienting your thoughts to the task of self-direction toward success.

As you lay in complete comfort, you'll instruct yourself as follows:

"You are taking a walk down a flight of stairs that leads to a place of total relaxation. This is the place you go to thrive, to succeed, and to make your every dream come true. Now, with each step, with each count, you will be more relaxed than the one before. And here we go."

From there, you will count to twenty, with each number representing another step in that imaginary staircase. And, with each count, you instruct yourself to relax your body more deeply than the previous one, until you find yourself in a state of total relaxation, but full awareness. Upon reaching the twentieth step, you begin the Psych phase by releasing your mind to program a mode of thought, such as being excited about the possibilities in your life, or being laser-focused on a singular task. As you get more practiced, you'll find that the Psych phase will become a time of self-coaching and discovery of what amazing things you can accomplish that day.

And finally, when you feel it's time to release yourself, you recite this final direction:

"On the count of three, you will be wide awake, feeling great, and raring to go. And, one, two, three—GO!"

With that, you're finished and popping out of bed, ready to take on the day with great enthusiasm for what lies ahead.

Notice that I speak in second-person perspective during the preamble. You could say my superego is taking over and leading me through the Psych process, just like a hypnotist or coach would. That's important, because it is the start of giving control to the superego, so you can be coached.

Now, here's what it looks and sounds like when I do it.

I start with the preamble. *"You are taking a walk down a flight of stairs that leads to a place of total relaxation. This is the place you go to thrive . . ."* At that point, my body convulses with excitement. I run through the areas of business I want to see coming alive and how much per month I want each to produce. First, email marketing and marketing automation partnerships featuring my CartoonLink "cartoon device" system to give marketers an unfair advantage. Then my new Contact Marketing agency, "Contact," along with how many clients I'll have and what those engagements will produce. And finally, I focus on being a best-selling author.

Then I move on to the next part of the preamble with the piece, *"to succeed."* My body continues to writhe with excitement as I list the accomplishments I want in my professional life. "You're the best-selling author of *How to Get a Meeting with Anyone*, you're a *New Yorker* and *Wall Street Journal* cartoonist, a hall of fame marketing guru, and founder of Cartoonists.org." Every fiber of my being is screaming out, "Yeah!"

And finally, I get to the words, *"and to make your every dream come true."* Still convulsing with excitement, I scream two words in my head: *"San Juans!"* San Juans has become shorthand for San Juan Islands and the amazing lifestyle I foresee for my wife and myself there: to buy a large, waterfront property, with a main house and guest house/studio, a place of ultimate solitude and beauty, from which many adventures and great works will flow. That's my dream.

Then I finish the preamble. *"Now, with each step, with each count, you will be more relaxed than the one before. And here we go."* Now my physical state completely changes. My body knows what's coming, and as soon as I say the word *"Now,"* I'm already going into deep relaxation. I continue with the count, focusing on relaxing even more than I already am with each step, until I just can't move a muscle and all sense of tension is gone.

But when I hit twenty in the count, it all changes again as I begin the Psych. My body convulses anew, this time with my inner voice screaming, *"Oh my God, oh my God, look at what's happening! It's all coming true, look, look, look! Okay, let's look at today. You have these things coming up, but be sure to pay attention to this . . ."* And it goes on from there, a free-wheeling session of cheerleading and examination of what the most powerful things are that I can do that day. My inner voice, my superego, powered by my own emotional intelligence and innate problem-solving abilities, steps in as the voice of the coach and often points out things I don't even see. As a result, I run through my day in a supercharged state.

Finishing out the session, I command, *"Okay, now on the count of three, you will be wide awake, feeling great and raring to go. And, one, two, three—GO!"* And as soon as I hit the word *"GO!"* I pop out of bed with a terrific attitude, full of enthusiasm for what I'm doing, where I'm heading, and what I need to do today that will make an enormous difference in my life and move me closer to achieving my goals.

The Benefit of Working in a Supercharged State

If you use my Psych process, I expect it will morph, just as it did when I learned the basic self-hypnosis trick years ago from a book I once read. That original technique was confined simply to counting the stairs, then programming one thought over and over during the session. My version became much more elaborate to suit my needs. However you use it, propelling your way through each day with coached directives and a programmed sense of excitement and purpose can only help you reach your goals quicker and with greater results.

Your coworkers will surely notice you're operating on a higher plane than they most likely are. Your bosses will notice, too. If you are your own boss, you will notice an immediate change in your effectiveness, from the first day you use the Psych process.

In fact, everyone you come in contact with will notice your excited level of motivation and wonder how they can get some of that for themselves. It will draw people to you; it will cause them to like what they see in you. In other words, it will help you connect at the highest levels with ease. And isn't that the whole point of Contact Marketing?

POINTS TO REMEMBER

- ✔ It's intimidating to connect with CEOs and VIPs, so it is helpful to have an edge.

- ✔ Many top executives hone their edge by hiring a coach.

- ✔ We all have our own inner coach, waiting to be tapped.

- ✔ Your inner coach is a combination of your own emotional intelligence, superego, and innate problem-solving ability.

- ✔ Your inner coach can be activated at any time through a simple self-hypnosis technique, something I call a "Psych."

✔   While not part of Contact Marketing, the Psych technique can be very useful in helping you solve problems, directing yourself in the most effective ways, and instilling a winning sense of motivation on a daily basis.

✔   It consists of a simple set of steps: a preamble, countdown, and the coaching session itself.

✔   The more you practice, the more proficient you'll become, and the more success you'll derive from it.

✔   When you work in a supercharged state, people will notice, and it will draw attention and opportunities to you, which is the whole point of Contact Marketing.

SECTION IV

TOOLS & RESOURCES

Tools and Resources

As I researched for this book, I discovered many of the experts I interviewed also proved to be a tremendous resource for productivity tools. Some demonstrated the tools by using them as we connected; others expressed their enthusiasm for their favorite productivity enhancers.

In this section, I will share a collection of my favorites among those recommended by the experts. They range from simple time-saving calendar apps and social media multipliers to complex, algorithm-based platforms that help you become better connected and more. I am not affiliated with any of the providers behind these tools, nor am I making any representations as to their reliability or effectiveness, or the thoroughness of my understanding of what they offer, as that simply is not the mission of this book. I'm just passing along a list of tools that I think are pretty impressive and useful. I hope you will find them helpful as well.

Sales Intelligence

There were many strong suggestions for tools in this category. The Charlie app is one of my favorites in that it's free and helps you have more effective meetings by preparing an automated dossier for everyone on your calendar. It's fun to use and exciting when it works, but it has sometimes compiled a jumble of information from different people with the same name, producing embarrassing results in conversation. Spiderbook does something similar and can net useful information for meetings. LeadGenius can help you identify potential customers, and Sidekick by HubSpot gathers information about your contacts. My vote goes to **SalesLoft** as the top tool in this category. It can greatly streamline the building of your Top 100 or Strategic 100 lists, allowing you to gather VIPs and easily append all of their relevant contact and background data. It's a head start and the kind of unfair advantage I always want to see in my own Contact Campaigns.

http://www.salesloft.com;
start with a free account; fees go as high as $1,300 per month

Enhanced Email

You can do some wonderful and very creative things with email. I use my personalized cartoons constantly in my own emails, and my CartoonLink service enables Constant Contact users to be able to use my "cartoon device" in campaigns. It's great stuff and a lot of fun, but most importantly, the cartoons tend to significantly boost open rates, which is helpful when you want your campaign to be read. Vsnap provides a platform for quickly recording and embedding video messages in your emails, which is also quite engaging.

If you're ready to spend some serious cash, Switchmerge can produce completely personalized animated videos that plug into your CRM platform for a pretty special effect. But my favorite email enhancers focus instead on giving you metrics and intelligence on the performance of *each* email you send. ToutApp, Yesware, and myDocket are three such tools; each provides data on who has opened your emails, how long they spent with each page, and whether they downloaded attachments or forwarded it to colleagues. I'm voting for **Yesware** for this category, because I like the fact that you can get started for free, and I like the real-time mapping of response, which gives you a chance to shock recipients with your impeccable timing. (Them: "My gosh, that's amazing, I was just looking at your bio." You: "I know.")

http://www.yesware.com; **free to $40 per month per user**

Web/Blog

In this category, I heard a lot about some pretty commonly used tools. WordPress, as an example, was used by more than 24 percent of all of the websites using content management systems as of January 2015, according to W3Techs Web Technology Surveys.[5] So there would be little surprise if I brought it to your attention now as a great new productivity tool. But there were two suggestions that can add significantly to the effectiveness of your Web presence, including your blog if you have one.

For me, it's a tie for this category; **VisitorTrack by netFactor** (nominated by author Colleen Stanley) is an app that enables you to capture your site (or blog) visitors' names and more, all connected through Jigsaw, which then provides full contact information. Used in the right way, this can be of obvious benefit. **AddThis** (suggested by author Michael Nick), is a different sort of tool, in that it actively seeks social media shares and follows from your site. If your core purpose is to engage visitors, get them to spread the word, and become users, clients, and supporters, this is your tool. It even goes further, by helping to increase signups and registrations, and serving up top-trending content on your site to visitors. Best of all, it's free. Or you can spend a moderate amount for more functionality.

http://www.netfactor.com; **$300 to a few thousand per month**
http://www.addthis.com; **free to $99 per year**

Podcasts

Your recorded sessions can be simple phone conversations or complex, high-value productions that sound like professional radio broadcasts. Podbean is a wonderful tool for hosting and publishing a podcast, in part because they already have a built-in audience for your show. It's also priced so that no one could possibly say they don't have the funds in their budget. How low? Three dollars a month.

Still, if you're just getting started, nothing beats simple and free, and that's what **FreeConferenceCall.com** (recommended by author Tom Searcy) has to offer. There are no enhancements other than this one key feature: It's a free conference call platform that allows you to record your conversation with the press of a button. From there, the whole thing can be transcribed for print use. I mentioned podcasts in Chapter 11 as a way to break through to the VIPs on your Top 100 or Strategic 100 lists, using interviews as the door-opener. And FreeConferenceCall.com makes it about as simple as it could possibly be.

http://www.freeconferencecall.com; **free**

Phone

I have advised throughout this book that you must present yourself with full integrity and clarity, but now I'm going to break with that slightly. I don't want you to deceive anyone, but I also don't want your calls dismissed before you get to talk. It's a fine line. For this dilemma, I present something called **LocalPresence** (suggested by blogger Trish Bertuzzi), a service of InsideSales.com. The idea is simple; the developers believe a person is more likely to take a call if it comes from their own area code, and they have the numbers to support it. They claim to increase contact rates as much as 38 percent when switching out a toll-free area code and up to 25 percent when an out-of-area code is replaced with a local one, which is what LocalPresence does with your calls. And that might just make a critical difference in your Contact Campaigns.

http://www.insidesales.com; **$195 per month per user**

Social Media

Social media is a broad field, and once again, it will do no good to mention the obvious. Everybody I spoke with not only loves to use Twitter, LinkedIn, Facebook, Instagram, Google+, Pinterest, and more, but they also had amazing strategies for their use in sales situations, which you have already read in earlier chapters.

For this listing, I was looking for something more, something that makes your everyday use of these platforms all the more powerful. HootSuite does that in the form of real-time feeds to follow people and trends. SocialOomph helps put your social house in order by allowing you to schedule tweets, posts, and the like, as well as helping you pinpoint trends, people to follow, and more. Paper.li turns your social media activity into a beautiful, print-quality publication that you can share with your VIPs with pride.

But the tool I want to highlight here is **Nimble**. It provides a simple dashboard for climbing the social media rankings that seem to be on everyone's minds these days. Every morning, you receive a summary of who's just followed you, their Klout scores, and more. From there, it's pretty simple to network with the biggest extenders of your own reach.

http://www.nimble.com; **$15 per month per user**

Presentations

Our experts brought us two recommendations for presentation tools, **ClearSlide** (suggested by author Jill Konrath) and **SlideShare** (nominated by Find New Customers's Jeff Ogden). Although the protagonists from each company will surely argue their differences, I'm seeing them as essentially similar services. Both allow you to upload presentation content to the cloud, making it available in various popular formats like PowerPoint, PDF, and more, to all devices, including the smartphone in your pocket and the tablet in your case.

But there are differences after all. ClearSlide's platform is oriented to sales and marketing use, and engagement metrics. It can tell you where people spent their time while perusing your presentation. SlideShare provides something utterly unique in their platform—an enormous built-in audience for your content. Blogger and author David Meerman Scott used it to launch his latest best-seller, essentially putting the entire book into a SlideShare presentation.

http://www.clearslide.com, http://www.slideshare.net;
ClearSlide, $64 per user per month; SlideShare, free

Appointments

Have you ever noticed how long it takes to set up a simple appointment when you're making those arrangements via email? It quickly becomes a surprisingly detailed and drawn-out process. What day would you like to meet? Thursday. Okay, what time is good for you? 9 A.M. Is that East Coast or West Coast time? East Coast. Oh wait, I'm not available at six in the morning here in Seattle. Hang on, what about that following day, when are you available? Ten A.M. PST. Shall I send you an invitation? Please. Okay, who calls whom? What number do I dial?

It quickly spirals even further out of control if you're trying to coordinate more than two people. What's needed is a much simpler solution. Still, there are a few issues to work through. Is it just you or will a team be using the system? Are you willing to pay a little more to get full features, such as automatic reminders and integration with iCal or Outlook? Do you mind if your invitees see your entire calendar or just the availabilities you're willing to offer?

The tools in this category are changing rapidly. There are several that already make setting your own calendar a much simpler task. Assistant.to is a useful solution if you're using Google Calendars, offering a lot of functionality for just $39 per year. Calendly offers seamless Google+ integration and far more features if you pay $8 per month for the premium version. ScheduleOnce and TimeTrade integrate with different calendar platforms, offer scalability for enterprise users and individuals, and even coordinate between your desktop computer, tablet, and smartphone.

But there is one appointment-setting tool that stands out among the others: **x.ai**. This is a revolutionary application of artificial intelligence and what the developer calls "invisible software" to the task of setting confirmed appointments and keeping your schedule. To set it into action, you simply cc "Amy Ingram" (for "AI") on any email referencing a call or meeting you'd like to arrange with someone. Amy then takes over like a live, human assistant. The invitee receives correspondence from Amy, asking which of three time slots works best, then issuing a calendar invitation to confirm the appointment. Amy then adds it to your calendar. The artificial intelligence is so good, the other person can't tell they aren't working with an actual assistant, and I've seen Amy actually negotiate on my behalf when the target gives vague responses or leaves out crucial information. The future is here, and amazingly, it's free.

http://x.ai; **free or upgrade to professional or enterprise versions**

Crowdsourced Productivity

Productivity is such a broad area, and the three solutions offered here differ widely as well. MarcomCentral was suggested because of the way it streamlines marketing communications with an intelligent, enterprise-scale marketing asset-management system. If you have distributed users, along the lines of a real estate company with independent agents, this solution allows them to generate and order materials on demand, all while maintaining strict branding rules.

Upwork (formerly oDesk) pushes the boundaries of productivity in another direction, by enabling you to crowdsource various business projects—web and mobile development, creative work, accounting, marketing, sales customer service, and more—without committing major overhead. One of our experts cited Upwork because he found it to be an inexpensive ($4.50/hour) source for custom research.

Of the three productivity tools our experts suggested, **HourlyNerd** (suggested by blogger John Barrows) caught my attention. Here, you crowdsource outside consulting help, but it's all done by current graduate students at the top universities. Mark Cuban is an early investor, and their goal is nothing less than to disrupt the traditional consulting market.

http://www.hourlynerd.com; **$10 per hour and up**

Introductions

I've saved my favorite tool for last. It's **Reachable** (nominated by author Dave Kurlan), a service that integrates with your Twitter, LinkedIn, and Facebook accounts, and does something magical from there. Their algorithm analyzes who your contacts are and who they know, where they've lived and worked, and tells you who among your contacts can introduce you to anyone you may be seeking. For example, I wanted to reach Sir Richard Branson. So I connected my social feeds to Reachable and it directed me to several of my contacts who could make direct introductions. Amazing. And supremely helpful for any Contact Marketer.

Just consider the fact that, if you have 500 connections on LinkedIn, it's theoretically enough to get you introductions to as many as 125 million people, just by extending to second- and third-degree connections. Reachable sorts through them all, making virtually any VIP prospect a possible connection.

http://www.reachable.com; **$50 to $100 per person per month**

Acknowledgments

The need to write this book has been building inside me my whole career, ever since I discovered the amazing power of Contact Marketing to launch my fledgling business and quickly transform its fortunes. The more I came to know about Contact Marketing, the more I knew that someday, I would end up writing the book you hold in your hands.

Writing it has been an even greater pleasure than I had imagined, and a lot of the credit goes to the many people who contributed their genius and commentary to its pages. I feel like I've just been through an intensive graduate degree program in Contact Marketing. The whole thing has been a joyous voyage of discovery.

I have told you my story throughout the book, but returning to that beginning, when I first gave Contact Marketing a try, I had no idea it would resonate so soundly with so many smart, imaginative, creative, audacious marketers and thinkers.

Of course, the original inspiration for Contact Marketing must be credited to Jay Conrad Levinson, the brilliant soul who gave the world *Guerrilla Marketing*. He recognized how effective asymmetrical marketing warfare could be to create unfair advantages for individual marketers who were simply bolder, more clever, and daring than their much bigger rivals. That is precisely the sort of thinking that makes the Contact Marketing concepts discussed in this book so compelling and effective.

Jay's genius was legendary, but so was his kindness. He was always ready to help a friend, and he had many of them. I am proud to say he was my friend, as well as my mentor and the inspiration behind much of what I do in my business. So to have his words at the head of this book is an honor I cherish greatly. It's sad to know his foreword was probably the last of his writing, as he passed away not more than thirty days thereafter. So thank you, Jay, wherever you are, for your kind words and especially for the inspiration you have given to all of us.

As my own Contact Marketing story unfolded, there were several more key sources of inspiration. Chief among those was Rick Bennett, one of the most outrageous Contact Marketers I have ever known. With his contact-letter-as-full-page-ad-in-*The-Wall-Street-Journal* concept, he showed me there were endless approaches to Contact Marketing, and a deep well of inspiration for Contact Marketers to draw from.

The great bulk of material for the book came from my interviews with many of the most influential sales and marketing thought leaders of our day. Each is a true innovator, and without any intention of minimizing their contribution due to sheer numbers, I list them here in alphabetical order by first name for fairness: *Predictable Revenue* author Aaron Ross; *Selling Is Better than Sex*, *Trigger Events*, and *The Missing Piece to Sales Success* blog author Alen Mayer; *Hello, My Name Is Awesome* author Alexandra Watkins; *Amp Up Your Sales* and *The Sales Fix* blog author Andy Paul; *The Sales Blog* author and writer of the forewords for *Amp Up Your Sales* and *New Sales. Simplified.* Anthony Iannarino; *Smart Calling* author and *Art Sobczak's Smart Calling Blog* writer Art Sobczak; *Sales Aerobics for Engineers* blogger and *Do YOU Mean Business?* author and *Sales Aerobics for Engineers* blog author Babette Ten Haken.

I want to thank *The New Handshake* author and the *Social Centered Selling* blog author Barb Giamanco; *Sales4Startups* blog author Bennett Phillips; *EcSell Institute Sales Coaching Blog* author Bill Eckstrom; The Hacker Group founder Bob Hacker; Yesware, Inc. former vice president of sales Bridget Gleason; *Nonstop Sales Boom* and *The Sales Leader* blog author Colleen Francis; *Emotional Intelligence for Sales Success* and *Sales Leadership* blog author Colleen Stanley; *SHiFT!* coauthor and *Shift Selling* blog author Craig Elias; *The Truth About Leads* and the *ViewPoint* blog author Dan McDade; *EDGY Conversations* and *Dan Waldschmidt Blog* author Dan Waldschmidt; *Partners in EXCELLENCE* blog author Dave Brock; *How to Sell Anything to Anyone Anytime* author Dave Kahle; *Baseline Selling* and the *Understanding the Sales Force* blog author Dave Kurlan; *How Winners Sell* and *Dave Stein's Blog* author and *Sales & Marketing Management Magazine* columnist Dave Stein; Avidian vice president of sales David Archer; *The New Rules of Marketing & PR* and *WebInkNow* blog author David Meerman Scott; and *Sales Heretic Blog* author and Guerrilla Marketing trainer Don Cooper.

I am truly grateful to *Motivate People* and *Objections! Objections! Objections!* author Gavin Ingham; SymVolli blog author George Petri; DiscoverOrg cofounder and CEO Henry Schuck; Skaled CEO Jake Dunlap; myDocket CEO Jason Wesbecher; SalesGravy CEO Jeb Blount; Find New Customers president Jeff Ogden; *Little Red Book of Selling* author Jeffrey Gitomer; *SNAP Selling, Agile Selling* and *Selling to Big Companies* author Jill Konrath; keynote speaker and social selling evangelist Jill Rowley; social sales evangelist and *A Sales Guy Blog* author Jim Keenan; *SalesFromtheStreets* app producer and the *J.Barrows Blog* author John Barrows; *The Fundamentals of Business-to-Business Sales & Marketing* author John Coe; *Insight Selling* coauthor and co-president of the RAIN Group John Doerr; *Music Scene Magazine* publisher John McDermott; Ruhlin Group founder John Ruhlin; Nimble, LLC founder and CEO Jon Ferrara; and social selling strategist Julio Viskovich.

Thank you also to CEO coach and consultant Ken Edmundson; *Slammed! For the First Time Sales Manager* and *Sales Management Guru* blog author Ken Thoreson; SalesLoft CEO Kyle Porter; *Changing the Sales Conversation* author Linda Richardson; *Score More Sales* blog author Lori Richardson; NoWait cofounder and vice president of marketing Luke Panza; *High-Profit Selling* and *The Sales Hunter* blog author Mark Hunter; *The Sales Acceleration Formula* author and HubSpot CMO Mark Roberge; *Guerrilla Teleselling* and *Guerrilla Trade Show Marketing* coauthor Mark Smith; *Matt on Marketing* blog author and Heinz Marketing CEO Matt Heinz; *Smart Prospecting That Works Every Time!* author Michael Krause; *ROI Selling* and the *ROI4Sales* blog author Michael Nick; *Guerrilla Selling* coauthor and Guerrilla Marketing keynote speaker and trainer Orvel Ray Wilson; and *CRM at the Speed of Light* author and CRM Hall of Fame member Paul Greenberg.

My gratitude continues to *Creating a Million-Dollar-a-Year Sales Income* and the *Sales and Sales Management Blog* author Paul McCord; Buffini & Company special events coordinator Paul Thiboutot; *Mastering Major Account Selling* coauthor and *Sales Training Connection* blog author Richard Ruff; *The Guerrilla Connector* author Richard Weiler; Axcelerate Worldwide CEO Rob Smith; *Dirty Little Secrets: Why Buyers Can't Buy and Sellers Can't Sell and What You Can Do about It* author Sharon Drew Morgen; *Top Sales Dog* blog author Steve Meyer;

52 Sales Management Tips: The Sales Manager's Success Guide and the *Sales Management* blog author Steven Rosen; *Who the Hell Am I to Start a Business?* author Tara Truax; *SHiFT!* co-author and *The Pipeline* blog author Tibor Shanto; Intrepid Group CEO and *Live the Intrepid Life* author Todd Schnick; *Life after the Death of Selling* author and *Whale Hunting: How To Land Big Sales and Transform Your Company* coauthor Tom Searcy; sales blogger Tony Cole; and *Inside Sales Experts* blog author Trish Bertuzzi. I consider you all founding members of the Contact Marketing Hall of Fame, and I am honored to have your participation in the book.

In addition to thought leaders, I was fortunate to have the opportunity to interview several sales and marketing association leaders, who lent stories and expertise, but also their invaluable perspectives on the Contact Marketing practice. For that, I express tremendous gratitude to Russ Klein, CEO of the American Marketing Association; Rod Hairston, CEO of the National Association of Sales Professionals; Scott Plum, president emeritus of the Professional Sales Association; and James Obermayer, president of the Sales Lead Management Association. Thank you one and all for your contributions.

None of this would exist without the kindly obliging responses of the many VIPs, CEOs, C-level executives, and their often wonderfully helpful and astute executive assistants, who also inspired the writing of this book. Of special note, I wish to thank former president George H. W. Bush, former California governor Pete Wilson, former chairman of the Federal Reserve Ben Bernanke, American Express CEO Kenneth Chenault, executive vice president and chief strategy and business development officer of Williams-Sonoma Patrick Connelly, *Forbes* publisher Steve Forbes, and legendary radio personality and good friend Rick Dees. Your kindness showed me there is room for the rest of us to connect and work with the true VIPs of the world in profoundly meaningful ways.

One of the great surprises of this project was the opportunity to connect with several of the producers of the productivity tools mentioned in these pages. They were exceptionally helpful and supportive, including Laurent Ohana's help with his Reachable platform. Thanks also to the producers of SalesLoft, the Charlie app, DiscoverOrg, GeekTools, InsideView, ShiftSelling, Avention, LeadGenius, HubSpot, ToutApp,

Yesware, vSnap, myDocket, Switchmerge, VisitorTrack, AddThis, Freeconferencecall, LocalPresence, Nimble, Paper.li, SocialOomph, SoundGecko, ClearSlide, SlideShare, Assistant.to, Doodle, Schedule-Once, TimeTrade, Calendly, HourlyNerd, oDesk, MarcomCentral, x.ai, and the generous experts who suggested them.

No effort of this type happens without supporters, and there were many who made this book possible. Special thanks go to Gregg Wallick, Sandy Athenson, Bill Kent, Tim Johnson, Joe Exner, Rick Cunningham, Mark Pellicano, Mike Collins, Paul Mack, Kelly Steele, Alyce Peterson, Mariam Zadeh, Anne Marie O'Keefe, Jim Rice, Cherie Ware, Ron Braley, Mike Bell, Joe Lee, Brett Overman, Amy Grasseschi, Kimberly Jordan, Kathy Kmiotek, Tom French, David Rosuck, Jeffrey Krivis, Chris Smith, Matt Wheeler, Christine Simonini, Chris Guzikowski, Mark Fotohabadi, Al Williams, and Gary Ruff.

Of course, books don't happen without publishers and agents, either. For their expert guidance, patient assistance, and deep belief in my book, I offer my sincerest thanks to Matt Wagner, Glenn Yeffeth, Adrienne Lang, Leah Wilson, Debbie Harmsen, Jennifer Canzoneri, Sarah Dombrowsky, Monica Lowry, Jessika Rieck, Alicia Kania, and the entire crew at BenBella Books.

In my Contact Marketing and in my writing, I am fortunate to have the ability to sprinkle in some of the many cartoons I create. Some of the cartoons in this book appeared originally in *The Wall Street Journal*, and I would like to thank Charles Preston and Linda Wolf of Cartoon Features Syndicate for clearing their use here.

And finally, I come around to where I started and ended, this time to Jay Conrad Levinson's daughter and co-owner and CEO of Guerrilla Marketing International, Amy Levinson. Amy, you are a true friend. Thank you for your help with Jay's foreword, the thought leaders you connected me with, and the words of wisdom you offered on the future of Contact Marketing.

Notes

1. Anthony Parinello, *Selling to VITO, the Very Important Top Officer* (Avon, MA: Adams Media, 1994, 1999).

2. *The Wall Street Journal*, "Target Earnings Slide 46% After Data Breach," by Paul Ziobro, Feb. 26, 2014, http://www.wsj.com/articles/SB10001424052702304255604579406694182132568.

3. Chet Holmes, *The Ultimate Sales Machine* (New York: Penguin Group, 2007).

4. Steve Fishman, "Is He for Real?" *New York Magazine*, March 9, 2013, http://nymag.com/nymetro/news/people/features/n_8669.

5. http://w3techs.com/technologies/overview/content_management/all.

Index

About the Author

If ever there was someone destined to write a book like *How to Get a Meeting with Anyone*, Stu Heinecke is that person. A *Wall Street Journal* cartoonist, hall of fame–nominated marketer, and author, Heinecke discovered the magic of "Contact Marketing" early in his career, when he launched a Contact Campaign to just two dozen vice presidents and directors of circulation at the big Manhattan-based magazine publishers. That tiny $100 investment resulted in a 100 percent response rate, launched his enterprise, and brought in millions of dollars' worth of business.

The ability to connect with the people most important to realizing one's goals ultimately became an obsession. While Heinecke regularly employs his own cartoon-based contact methods, he became intensely interested in how others have solved this unique challenge. As a result, he has uncovered a highly unique form of marketing that until now has had no name, yet it produces response rates as high as 100 percent and ROI figures in the tens, even hundreds of thousands of percent. In *How to Get a Meeting with Anyone*, he not only gives Contact Marketing its name, but provides us with a definitive guide to what it is and how it works, and he has cataloged twenty categories of Contact Campaign types.

Heinecke is the host of Contact Marketing Radio; founder and president of "Contact," a Contact Marketing agency; and cofounder of Cartoonists.org, a coalition of famed cartoonists dedicated to raising funds for charity, while raising the profile of the cartooning art form. He lives on an island in the beautiful Pacific Northwest with his wife, Charlotte, and their dog, Bo.